Peter Charles Hoffer • William Stueck • Williamjames Hull Hoffer

Reading and Writing American History: An Introduction to the Historian's Craft

Volume 2

Fourth Edition

D0164934

Cover Art: *Classic Landscape*, by Charles Sheeler, 1931, courtesy of the National Gallery of Art, Washington, D.C.

Pearson Learning Solutions, 501 Boylston Street, Suite 900, Boston, MA 02116
A Pearson Education Company
www.pearsoned.com

Printed in the United States of America

1 2 3 4 5 6 7 8 9 10 V036 16 15 14 13 12 11

000200010270793725

BW/FC

PEARSON

ISBN 10: 1-256-41706-8
ISBN 13: 978-1-256-41706-4

Contents

3   THE HISTORIAN'S WORK: SECONDARY SOURCES
American Expansion During the 1890s   41

4   FINDING EVIDENCE: LIBRARY SKILLS
The Far West and the Metropolis, 1876–1920   53

5   THE "NEW HISTORY": BORROWING FROM THE SOCIAL SCIENCES
America in the Progressive and New Eras, 1890–1929   53

To the Teacher

If your institution has a history requirement, as ours does, most students in your survey course will be conscripts. The course is part of their core curriculum. The reason they *should* take history—the reason that it is required for a liberal arts education—is obvious to us, but students may find that reason distant and abstract. At the outset, we face the obstacle of persuading students of the relevance of the past.

Today's students are very present minded. This perspective may result from the general widening of opportunities for undergraduate education, or from the increasing pressure on young people to find a niche in the business or professional world before they leave college. Some universities have catered to those demands, allowing their professional schools to infiltrate undergraduate education and impose a dizzying load of pre-professional courses on students in the second and third years of undergraduate study. The ideal of a liberal-arts education, like the ideal of college as a sanctuary from the blooming, buzzing confusion of the workplace, has receded in the face of anxious careerism. Even if history courses offer a humanistic perspective on modern values, we cannot blind ourselves to the realities of college life. Students will leave our classrooms and step into a world whose distractions are so numerous and enticing that the past may not seem relevant

History courses compete for students' time and attention not only with extracurricular demands often hostile to scholarly inquiry but with many other courses in the undergraduate curriculum. In a sense, we sell history in a buyer's market. Our effectiveness as teachers can be measured by the extent to which we can persuade our students to give their history course at least the same time and effort they devote to other courses. One way to do this is to load the class with extra reading and outside assignments. If every instructor in every other course—all sellers in this market—adopted this stratagem, our increased demands would be effectively neutralized by the across-the-board escalation of the workload, in the manner of the "prisoner's dilemma."

There is another, better way to convince students that history is relevant: offer them the chance to become an apprentice historian—a *doer* rather than a consumer. If history is the vital connection between past and present, then training in the skills and methods of thinking about history is more than a legitimate way to attract students' attention; it is an integral part of the introductory course. Students who begin to *do* history will appreciate the study of history as no passive reader of textbooks can, no matter how hard he or she studies. We know from experience that, because there is so much to cover in American history surveys, little time remains to deal with basic questions of historical methods and skills. Mindful of this fact, in *Reading and Writing American History*, Fourth Edition, we combine a manual on historical methods, a set of exercises that help students to hone their skill in using those methods, and a reader in primary and secondary sources that runs parallel to the chronological progression of topics in the survey course. *Reading and Writing American History*, Fourth Edition, is also suitable for methods courses for the history major.

A Manual

The old proverb "The teacher opens the door, the student must walk through it" has guided our plan for the book. We bring students face to face with the basic questions that every history teacher and scholar confronts. We begin by explaining why history is such a vital field of study and how every culture's conception of history gives its members a sense of identity. We treat basic problems in the philosophy of history, including the difference between fact and opinion and the ways in which historians use historical evidence. We introduce primary and secondary sources, source criticism and classification, and explain how to find historical sources and specific facts.

Subsequent chapters cover a wide range of reading and writing skills, from how to use the library to how to construct an essay. We introduce varieties of historical analysis, including causation, change and continuity, reasoning by analogy, the role of the individual in history, and the use of numbers.

A Workbook

Every point we make is reinforced by exercises. Some can be performed on the spot. Others require a trip to the library. Some exercises are textual, and we provide the text. Others require students *to find* the text. We have included nontextual materials—maps, pictures, and graphs—so that students can *see* the past as well as read about it. The materials cover a wide range of subfields in American history.

The methods treated in each chapter build on lessons in previous chapters. Within chapters, each exercise rests on those that come before it. The first exercise is often a "think piece," requiring students to ponder a historical question; subsequent exercises entail more writing. Because we understand that grading so many written exercises would be no mean task, many exercises are designed for "self-grading" or for class discussion. Space is provided for out-of-class assignments. The pages are perforated so that you can require students to turn in their work, and they are three-hole-punched so that students can retain their work in one place. We encourage you to pick and choose among the exercises and assignments, personalizing the course.

A Reader

Most exercises include readings, which allow you to link training in methods and skills to the substance of your course. These selections include primary and secondary sources and mix traditional and current historical concerns. Students are thus exposed to both the classics of historical writing and the most recent contributions. Many selections serve as springboards for discussion as well as skills practice.

The reading selections in each chapter are keyed to the chronological progression of events in American history. This chronological progression not only allows you to couple instruction in skills and methods to your lectures and discussions but also make this book a supplement to your textbook or to other required readings. We have found in our own teaching that the best way to ensure learning is through repetition. The selections in *Reading and Writing American History*, Fourth Edition, afford you the opportunity to repeat lessons using a variety of relevant materials.

New to This Edition

When the first edition *of Reading and Writing American History* was published in 1994, we were confident that college and university administrators and teachers regarded American history as the centerpiece of a college education. In the years since then, the college survey course in American history has faced two stiff intellectual tests. The present edition of *Reading and Writing American History* is designed to respond to these challenges.

The first challenge grows out of an invitation college and university instructors have issued to themselves to incorporate the many different voices of Americans in the basic undergraduate curriculum. Most independent colleges and state university systems still require the study of history as part of the liberal arts core, but the survey course in American history is no longer an automatic choice for students or their teachers to fulfill this obligation. Multicultural programs and diversity requirements have created special courses that provide other options to students.

The authors *of Reading and Writing American History*, Fourth Edition, are committed to the idea that the survey in American history is *the* multicultural course, for there is no nation that compares with ours in its ethnic diversity. We are truly one people made up of many peoples. This edition attempts to capture and explore fully that diversity by adding additional readings, exercises, and discussion materials on Native Americans, African Americans, women, and changing patterns of migration. We have broadened the geographical scope of the volumes to include the peoples of the Southwest and the Caribbean.

The second trial that the American history survey course faces arises from the technology and information revolutions of our time. Many schools have introduced a computer literacy component to their basic undergraduate requirements. History may seem incompatible with such futuristic courses, but the fact is that historians have long used and valued the computer. Quantitative historians have relied on computer-driven software to calculate statistical associations and researchers have built computer databases from historical sources to study elections, population, and economic changes over time. More recently, many historical collections, archives, and libraries have gone online to make information available to users of the Internet and the World Wide Web. A number of history courses are now either entirely "online" (for example in "distance education") or rely on Web-based sets of documents. To meet the challenge of computer-aided instruction, we have added to this edition, up-to-date facts on word processing software and Web sites for historians, along with rigorous exercises on computer-assisted library searches and Internet research in historical sources. The result, we hope, is a work-text that combines the training in skills and ways of thinking that have long made history the "mother of all intellectual disciplines," with the most modern techniques and information sources for students of history.

Acknowledgments

The final version *of Reading and Writing American History*, Fourth Edition, was a collaborative endeavor. The authors have worked together at every stage of the project; Volume 1 is the work of Peter Hoffer, with some assistance from Williamjames Hull Hoffer, and Volume

2 is the work of William Stueck on all chapters except chapters 4, 11, 13, and 14, which are the work of Williamjames Hull Hoffer. Our colleagues provided incisive and helpful comments. For this edition, we are grateful to Edward Larson, Peter Moore, Nan McMurry, Diane Trap, and Michael Winship at the University of Georgia, N.E.H. Hull at Rutgers, Camden, and Daniel Mandell, at Truman State University, and Melinda Oblander and Brian Wood at Pearson Learning Solutions.

P.C.H.
W.W.S.
W.H.H.

To the Student

<hr/>

Think of a few of the monumental events of the past few years: the destruction of the World Trade Center in New York by Islamic terrorists; the resulting attack by the United States on the government of Afghanistan and the terrorist organization al Qaida; the U.S. war against Saddam Hussein's Iraq; the rise of social media like Facebook and Twitter; the Great Recession of 2008-2010; and the election of Barack Obama, the U.S.'s first African-American president.

What do all these events have in common? Several things, you might say. They all affected the relationship of the United States with the outside world. They all deeply impacted our lives in one way or another. They all took place during our lifetimes and reside in our memory. They all are part of history.

Perhaps the last fact did not occur to you. You may tend to think of history as the distant past rather than events of the last generation or even the last decade. In part, this may be because your previous history classes stopped long before the present. Although it is difficult to attain the perspective on recent events that we possess on more distant times, the fact remains that the former are very much a part of history. Thus when you enter a course entitled "The United States Since 1865," you have every right to expect it to extend all the way to the present. A major purpose of this volume is to demonstrate the connections between the distant past, the recent past, and the present, through frequent movements back and forth among them. It also will show you that many skills used to analyze the past apply to your present and future as well.

History often can appear to be a series of dry facts about the past It is true that dates, names, and events are essential components of history, but they alone do not constitute the discipline. Facts must be constructed through the accumulation of evidence. They also must be interpreted. Facts about the past, along with the methods used to construct and to understand them, make up the study of history.

These fourteen chapters examine many facts of American history since 1865, but, just as important, they introduce you to the methods that historians use to study the past. The exercises will require you to examine the works of historians and help you to grasp the discipline by exposing you to its products. In addition, because nothing facilitates the learning process better than practice, this book provides numerous opportunities to actually *do* history. Whether evaluating others' efforts or creating your own history, you will develop skills that should serve you well in a variety of endeavors outside the classroom. In the end, what you will take from this course will not be most of the facts. Instead, you should have a new perspective on the past and its relation to the present and the future. You also will have mastered a series of skills applicable to the workplace and beyond. These include basic abilities, such as comprehending a reading assignment and using the library computer catalog and the internet, as well as more complicated challenges, such as evaluating primary and secondary sources, writing essays, and interpreting numerical data. We hope that these skills will help you to derive greater satisfaction and a deeper knowledge of American history from your course.

This fourth edition of *Reading and Writing American History* is not intended to replace your textbook but to be used in conjunction with it or with the primary and secondary source anthologies your instructor has assigned for your course. The explanations, reading, and exercises in this worktext treat history as a way of knowing, a set of skills for making sense of the past. You may not be able to travel back in time or bring the dead to life, but you can use your intelligence and imagination to recreate those lost worlds in your own mind. *Reading and Writing American History*, Fourth Edition, was devised to give you the skill to navigate that journey into the past.

1: *What Is History, and Why Should We Study It?*

Reconstruction

History is the "universal discipline" because it deals with every aspect of human endeavor. Jonas Salk's discovery of a vaccine for polio, the election of John F. Kennedy as president, the child-rearing practices of the Quakers, and the introduction of the miniskirt all qualify as part of the human past and therefore as history.

If, in one sense, history is "everything that has happened in the past," in another sense it is far less than that (see Figure 1.1). Human beings have recorded only a tiny portion of what has happened to them. And only a small part of what was recorded has survived. Of the surviving materials, a significant amount is either inaccurate or misleading. In short, the past that we can know is far from complete. Partly to distinguish between the actual past and what we know of it, we sometimes define history as "the study of the past."

However incomplete our knowledge of it may be, the past is an important guide in understanding the present and anticipating the future. Stop for a moment and think about what you expected of this course when you first walked into class. Chances are, you based your judgment on one of two sources, and both were historical: your own experiences with history courses and accounts from fellow students who have already taken this course. You used die past—or testimony about it—to understand the present.

There are limitations to predicting the future from knowledge of the past. Perhaps your previous history teachers emphasized mastery of facts. To score well on examinations, you merely had to provide specific information, such as names of important figures and dates of key events. As a result, you may assume that memorization, the learning of one fact after another, is the primary task in studying history. This assumption will lead you astray in this course. Remembering facts is important, but if you devote all your attention to memorizing names and dates, you will have difficulty. This book emphasizes understanding processes and trends and developing a variety of skills in addition to memorizing facts.

History does *not* always repeat itself. Each event of the human past is unique. No two individuals teach a history course in exactly the same way. Sometimes instructors change their approach to a course from year to year. In short, using the past as a guide to the present and future can be tricky.

1

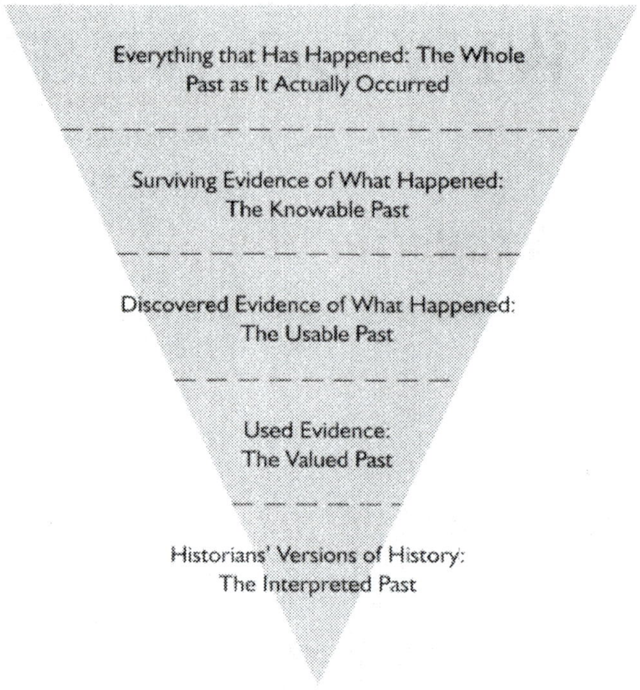

Everything that Has Happened: The Whole
Past as It Actually Occurred

Surviving Evidence of What Happened:
The Knowable Past

Discovered Evidence of What Happened:
The Usable Past

Used Evidence:
The Valued Past

Historians' Versions of History:
The Interpreted Past

FIGURE 1.1 *History as It Is; History as We Know It*

There is another way in which we use the past to guide us in the present: the past tells us who we are and gives us our identity. Without a sense of history, we would have difficulty understanding ourselves in relation to others. We could not grasp how and why our ethnic, racial, national, or religious groups distinguish themselves from others, or how and why particular generations—our own, our parents', our children's—perceive the world in different ways.

Just as personal histories are basic to individuals' identities, certain events and ideas from the past are fundamental to the way groups define themselves. Imagine our self-image as Americans without any awareness of the idea that human beings possess "certain inalienable rights," among them "life, liberty, and the pursuit of happiness." To be sure, our thoughts may not turn very often to our country's Declaration of Independence from Great Britain in 1776. Indeed, some of us may not have associated the idea mentioned above with that document. Yet many of the ideas stated in our Declaration of Independence have become so deeply ingrained in the identity of Americans as a group that, without the Declaration, we would have a wholly different conception of ourselves. This book seeks to refine your sense of identity as part of a pluralistic, vibrant society.

Reading and Writing American History also asks you to "do" history rather than just study it. This book encourages you to become an active, rather than a passive, learner. It aims both to familiarize you with the way historians think and to help you use that knowledge to enrich your own life. You should emerge from this course with a fuller grasp of how the past relates to your present and future, and with a capacity to apply this understanding to the world at large.

Chapter 1 introduces many of the skills you will be developing as you use this book. The chapter covers the Reconstruction era immediately following die Civil War. You will have the opportunity to compare Reconstruction to life in contemporary America and uncover patterns of change in the late nineteenth century. You also will learn to distinguish feet from opinion and to identify the various purposes of historical writing. Finally, you will be introduced to the history textbook, its nature and purposes, and how to use it. The exercises in this chapter open the gate to the study of history. By the end of this course, you will have gained a broad array of skills, from analyzing films and television programs to constructing essays based on historical sources and evaluations of quantitative data.

Past and Present

By taking us out of the present, the study of history alerts us to conditions other than those we encounter in our own lives. Studying a contemporary society other than our own might also serve this purpose. One advantage of going back in time, however, is that we can see how our society has changed, how what we face here and now in some ways differs from what our ancestors confronted in a bygone era. We tend to assume that current conditions—air pollution and inflation, for instance—are changeless phenomena, that they always have been with us and will be forever. Yet the study of the American past reveals that many of the conditions we live with today simply did not exist in earlier times. This fact suggests that our future, in turn, may not resemble the present. The study of the United States since 1865 can provide us with new perspectives on the present and new visions of the future. This section tests your skill in comparing past and present.

Exercise 1: Comparing Past and Present

The outcome of the Civil War ensured the Union's survival and slavery's destruction, but it left a host of other issues unresolved. In particular, the question of what the end of slavery would mean for African-Americans remained. Would they move rapidly toward equality with European-Americans, or would they remain relegated to a position of inferiority? Because the vast majority of African-Americans lived in the eleven states of the former southern Confederacy, the process of reintegrating them into the Union would go far in settling this question. This transition period saw an intense struggle, the outcome of which set the pattern of race relations in the United States well into the twentieth century. The following selections reflect some of the prevalent attitudes of the time and provide focal points for comparing a critical period of the past with our own times.

A The following excerpt is from a speech by Congressman Ignatius Donnelly (R, Minn.) in February 1866. Donnelly was speaking in support of a measure providing federal government funds for public schools for African-Americans in the South. **Read the selection and answer the questions that follow it.**

> . . . Having voted to give the negro liberty, I shall vote to give him all things essential to liberty.
> If degradation and oppression have, as it is alleged, unfitted him for freedom, surely continued degradation and oppression will not prepare him for it. If he is not to remain a brute you must give him that which will make him a man—opportunity. . . . If he is, as you say, not fit to vote, give him a chance; let him make himself an independent laborer like yourself; let him own his homestead; let the courts of justice be opened to him; and let his intellect, darkened by centuries of neglect, be illuminated by all the glorious lights of education.

If after all this he proves himself an unworthy savage and brutal wretch, condemn him, but not till then.[1]

1. What argument is Donnelly rebutting? _____

_____

2. What is the key point in his argument? _____

_____

3. What specific measures does Donnelly suggest the government should take to assist African-Americans? _____

_____

4. What noun does he use to refer to African-Americans?_____

_____

5. Why do you suppose that noun is no longer used to refer to African-Americans?_____

_____

_____

6. Today, some members of Congress argue in favor of "affirmative action" for African-Americans in the form of quotas in certain job categories and in the student bodies of institutions of higher learning. Does Donnelly advocate such action? Explain._____

_____

_____

B The next excerpt is from a speech in December 1866 by Senator George Henry Williams (R, Ore.). The issue addressed is woman suffrage, which was bound to arise in Congress during a period of intense debate on the rights of African-Americans. (Anytime politicians devote extensive attention to the rights of one group, other groups that feel aggrieved are likely to see an opportunity to air their discontents.) During the years immediately following the Civil War, a group of feminists petitioned Congress for an amendment to guarantee women the right to vote. Unlike African-American men, however, they did not enjoy early success. The arguments of Senator Williams prevailed. **Read the passage and answer the questions that follow**.

. . . it has been said that "the hand that rocks the cradle rules the world;" and there is truth as well as beauty in that expression. Women in this country by their elevated social position can exercise more influence upon public affairs than they could coerce by the use of the ballot. When God married our first parents in the garden . . . they were made "bone of one bone and flesh of one flesh;" and the whole theory of government and society proceeds upon the assumption that their interests are one, that their relations are so intimate and tender that whatever is for the benefit of the one is for the benefit of the other; whatever works to the injury of the one works to the injury of the other. I say . . . that the more identical and inseparable these interests and relations can be made, the better for all concerned; and the woman who undertakes to put her sex in an adversary position to man, who undertakes by the use of some independent political power to contend and fight against man, displays a spirit which would, if able, convert all the now harmonious elements of society into a state of war, and make every home a hell upon earth.[2]

1. What are Williams's two main points?

   a. _____

   _____

   b. _____

   _____

2. Why is woman suffrage no longer an issue in the United States? _____

   _____

3. With what issues do feminists preoccupy themselves today? _____

   _____

4. What differences between the 1860s and the present does the change in issues confronted suggest? _____

   _____

C The Civil War and Reconstruction left bitter memories in the South. The majority of European-Americans there accepted union only grudgingly, and they fought effectively in the aftermath of war to prevent African-Americans from achieving anything remotely resembling equality. In the following account, a European-American from Virginia, who had fought in General Robert E. Lee's Confederate army, expresses his attitude toward northerners and Reconstruction thirty years after its end. **Read the passage and answer the questions that follow.**

As a fit climax to, and exhibitory of, Yankee hatred, malice, revenge, and cruelty practiced during the war, the North bound the prostrate South on the rock of negro domination, while the vultures, "carpet-baggers" and "scalawags," preyed upon its vitals. The South . . . rose in its own might . . . and drove away the birds of prey, and her people are now free and independent, controlling their own state affairs without let or hindrance. . . . The South has always been the most chivalrous, conservative and Americanlike, holding more closely to the traditions, customs, and manners of the old days, where the high and unselfish principles of right, justice and honor, which go to make up the true gentleman and patriotic citizen, have always prevailed. The pure Anglo-Saxon blood still predominates in the South, as well as the spirit of the cavalier. Blood will tell.

The average Yankee has a very poor conception of what is right and honorable in his . . . intercourse with his fellow-man. . . . To drive a sharp bargain, to get money no matter how . . . and diffuse and enforce his own ideas and notions, seem to be the *summa summorum* [highest of the highest] of all his ends. . . .

. . . the South is coming to its own again. . . . The days of retribution will come when the evil deeds the North perpetrated in the South during and since the war, will be avenged, not in kind perhaps, but in some way.[3]

1. To this writer, how do northerners and southerners differ? _____

   _____

2. This writer's views were common to European-Americans in the South from the generation that fought in the Civil War. How do you think these views compare with those of European-Americans who reside in the South today? _____

   _____

3. What are the differences today between your generation and your grandparents' generation on issues concerning race?

_____

_____

4. How do you explain the differences? _____

_____

D The next two documents combine visual and written material. The first was drawn by Thomas Nast, the most famous political cartoonist of that era. Nast's cartoons in the magazine *Harper's Weekly* received widespread attention and often were credited with helping to bring to justice the notorious New York City boss William Marcy Tweed. Nast also used cartoons to express his views on Reconstruction. Initially, he showed great sympathy for the freed slaves, but by March 14, 1874, when the cartoon shown in Figure 1.2 appeared, his attitude had changed. The second document, a copy of a painting called *The Gulf Stream*, shown in Figure 1.3, is by Winslow Homer. Homer used watercolor and oils to depict Americans in natural settings. Many of his works made a social statement. Homer painted *The Gulf Stream* twice, first as a watercolor in 1884, seven years after Union troops left the South. He redid the work in oil in 1899 following a decade in which African-Americans in the South

FIGURE 1.2 *Thomas Nast Comments on Black Reconstruction Legislators*

FIGURE 1.3 *Winslow Homer's* The Gulf Stream
Courtesy of the Metropolitan Museum of Art.

increasingly suffered from lynching and from segregationist laws passed by state legislatures.
Examine these illustrations carefully, and then answer the questions that follow.

1. What are the differences between the physical and behavioral depiction of African-
Americans in Nast's cartoon and that of the African-American in Homer's painting?

_____

_____

2. What messages are the two artists trying to convey? _____

_____

_____

_____

3. Which depiction would be more likely to appear in a popular journal in the United
States today? Why? _____

_____

_____

Many Different Pasts

Unlike the history of some other nations, our history is not the story of a single group, its
members all speaking the same language, living in close proximity to each other, and practicing the same religion. Americans have hailed from many places and have represented
many cultures. We are a pluralistic society, even more so today than we were in 1865.

Pluralism, of course, offers many advantages. The wide range of popular pastimes we
enjoy, for example, results in part from the many cultures housed in our nation. (Think of
the various games available to us and their origins: bocce from Italy, soccer from England,

lacrosse from the Native Americans, Parcheesi from India, jai alai from Spain, and many more.) Yet pluralism also can lead to disagreement, misunderstanding, and conflict. The study of pluralism in our past can help you to exploit its virtues and survive its pitfalls in your own time and place.

Understanding pluralism in American history requires that you take an imaginative leap outside yourself. The world in which you have lived and the values you have derived from it have conditioned your vision of the past. Your immediate environment—your family, your friends, your church or temple, your community—has provided a network of impressions and beliefs. Because this network, or frame of reference, differs from that of members of past generations, a barrier separates you from them. Differing frames of reference have produced barriers between you and members of other cultures as well. By coaxing you to move outside your frame of reference, your American history survey course may persuade you to abandon some of your long-standing prejudices, or at least help you to understand people who do not behave the same as you do.

A first step in moving beyond your own frame of reference is to grasp the distinction between fact and opinion. Take a moment to reflect on selection C in Exercise 1. Think about whether most of the statements there are fact or opinion. A historical fact is a sound statement about what happened in the past, reached through the assembling of reliable pieces of historical evidence. Historical facts do not lie around ready-made like pebbles on a beach. They result from a laborious sifting through and piecing together of evidence, a process much like reassembling an ancient Greek vase from a mound of fragments.

But even documents that seem to be factual cannot speak to us. We assign meaning to their words, pictures, or images. To do so, we must use *historical consciousness*—that is, we must try to comprehend how people in the past thought and acted, and to imagine the conditions they faced. Every historical fact has behind it an exercise in historical consciousness, an effort by someone to move backward into another time and place.

Often opinion is not based on fact. At other times opinion goes well beyond fact in rendering a judgment. In either case, the writer's or speaker's own impressions and beliefs play a prominent role. Many of the views you hear expressed about the past represent opinion rather than fact simply because they do not rest solely on an attempt to relive the past. Opinion, in other words, may lack historical consciousness. It is sometimes difficult to distinguish fact from opinion, but you do it every day outside the classroom. Recall, for instance, the last time you heard a friend describe a mutual acquaintance. Chances are, the description contained a combination of fact and opinion, with an emphasis on the latter. Either in your own mind or out loud, you probably disagreed with or qualified parts of that description.

Exercise 2: Distinguishing Between Fact and Opinion

Separating fact from opinion is not always easy, as you will see in this exercise. Yet developing this skill is essential. Much of the historian's training and much of your course work demand the ability to make this distinction. Because historians try to do more than merely assemble facts, distinguishing them from opinions is essential to both reading and writing history.

Try your skill with the following passages on Reconstruction. **Circle the statements of opinion and underline statements of fact.** To get you started, we have circled a statement of opinion and underlined a statement of fact in selection A. We also provide an explanation of our choices. Do selection B on your own; use the same methods of identifying one statement of fact and one of opinion as we do in A.

A. What is perhaps most puzzling in the legend of reconstruction is the notion the white peo-ple of the South were treated with unprecedented brutality, that their conquerors . . . literally put them to the torture. . . . In fact, . . . <u>the great mass of ordinary</u>

<u>Southerners . . . were required simply to take an oath of allegiance to obtain pardon and to</u> <u>regain their right to vote and hold public office</u>. But what of the Confederate leaders . . . Were there mass arrests, indictments for treason or conspiracy, trials and convictions, executions or imprisonments? Nothing of the sort.[4]

Explanation: The author disagrees with the view that white southerners were "literally put . . . to the torture." In subsequent sentences he presents facts to make his case. However, one dictionary meaning of the word *torture* is "great mental suffering; agony."[5] Certainly the effort of Radical Republicans to move southern society in the direction of racial equality produced such suffering in many whites. Thus the author's judgment, though backed up by factual data, is hardly beyond dispute, because the data says nothing about mental suffering. Therefore, we have circled the first sentence as a statement of opinion. By contrast, the underlined sentence is readily documented as fact. The average white male southerner had only to take an oath of allegiance to the United States to regain his voting rights and the right to hold public office.

Try your hand at selection B; **circle a statement of opinion and underline a statement of fact.**

B. Politically, the Republicans had failed in their attempt to remake the South, but an effort is no less worthy for being in vain. They had hoped to make the race issue secondary to the economic one in the white voter's mind. They had no choice. Concentration on the race or wartime loyalty question would have doomed the Reconstruction coalition to minority status from the start. The strategy failed; . . . [but] for one brief moment, the Republicans shattered political patterns and opened up possibilities for men of all races and economic conditions. The moment passed, but the reconstructed states would not be the same again. The South transformed, though not in the way Republicans would have liked.[6]

Historians' Purposes

Historians pursue a variety of goals in practicing their craft. One objective, suggested at the outset of this chapter, is to teach lessons about the past that can be used in the present and future. Such lessons may have explicit moral content, as when an early biographer of George Washington concocted the story of young Washington and the cherry tree to demonstrate to American youth the importance of honesty. Historians sometimes direct their lessons toward influencing opinion on public policy issues. For example, many historians early in the twentieth century tried to dissuade readers from believing that the federal government should promote equality between the races. They claimed that people who held this belief during Reconstruction possessed questionable motives, such as the desire to advance the Republican party's fortunes by permitting African-Americans to vote. At other times, the historian simply attempts to entertain, to tell a story about the past that will capture and hold people's attention. Even in this day of television, VCRs, and movie theaters, many people continue to spend some of their leisure time reading historical articles and books.

Exercise 3: Identifying Historians' Purposes

Read the following selections and identify the historians' primary purpose. Alongside each passage, **write *teaching lessons or telling a story*.** Be prepared to explain your choice.

A The following selection is by a famous African-American, W. E. B. Du Bois, who was the first person of his race to earn a Ph.D. from Harvard University. Du Bois engaged in a variety of reform activities involving African-Americans. He also wrote some history. This selection is from his book on Reconstruction, which was published in 1935.

One is astonished in the study of history at the recurrence of the idea that evil must be forgotten, distorted, skimmed over. We must not remember that Daniel Webster got drunk but only remember that he was a splendid constitutional lawyer. We must forget that George Washington was a slave owner, or that Thomas Jefferson had mulatto children, or that Alexander Hamilton had Negro blood, and simply remember the things we regard as credible and inspiring. The difficulty, of course, with this philosophy is that history loses its value as an incentive and example; it paints perfect men and noble nations, but it does not tell the truth.[7]

B The following selection is from a biography of Andrew Johnson, who succeeded to the presidency after Abraham Lincoln's death on April 15, 1865.

Johnson had gone to bed early that night. Shortly after 10:15 he was awakened by a loud knock at the door. When he did not respond immediately, his fellow boarder at the Kirkwood House, former governor Leonard J. Farwell of Wisconsin, called in a loud voice, "Governor Johnson, if you are in this room I must see you." The vice president sprang out of bed. "Farwell, is that you?" he replied. "Yes, let me in," was the answer. The door opened, and Farwell, who had just come from Ford's Theater, excitedly told Johnson the news. The president had been shot. The vice president, stunned, grasped Farwell's hands, and the two men fell upon each other, holding on for mutual support. Soon there were guards outside to prevent any attempt to murder Johnson. Secretary of State Seward already lay seriously wounded in his home, and no one knew how widespread the assassination plot was.[8]

C The following excerpt is by David Donald, the Pulitzer Prize-winning biographer of Charles Sumner. Sumner was a U.S. senator from Massachusetts who, both before and after the Civil War, worked diligently to advance the cause of African-Americans. In 1856 his attacks on slave owners in the South led Congressman Preston Brooks of South Carolina to assault Sumner with a cane, nearly beating him to death. The act outraged many northerners, including the essayist and poet Ralph Waldo Emerson. Emerson is referred to at the end of the passage, which deals with Sumner's death in 1874.

Through the morning Sumner lingered in semi-conscious condition, while close friends like . . . [Judge George E.] Hoar visited his bedroom and many others paid their respects in the study. In constant attendance at his bedside were his secretary and . . . representatives of the [African-American community] . . . he had tried to befriend. "I am so tired," Sumner would complain from time to time. "I can't last much longer." Though his mind wandered, he fixed on two subjects. "My book," he kept muttering, referring to his *Works*, "my book is not finished . . ." Turning to his secretary, he said: "I should not regret this if my book were finished."

Even more insistent was the dying man's concern for his "bill.". . . When Hoar came to the bedside about ten o'clock in the morning, Sumner recognized him and managed to say: "You must take care of the civil-rights bill,—my bill, the civil-rights bill, don't let it fail." . . .

At about 2:00 P.M. on March 11, in great pain, Sumner begged for another injection of morphine, but when the doctors convinced him that it might be harmful, he appeared to grow more quiet and comfortable. . . . Half an hour later, however, he was seized by a violent spasm, followed by vomiting. Suddenly throwing himself back on the bed and gasping for air, he died.

Just before his death Sumner turned with complete lucidity to Hoar and said: "Judge, tell Emerson how much I love and revere him." Remembering Emerson's tribute to Sumner at the time of the Brooks assault, Hoar replied: "He said of you once, that he never knew so *white* a soul."[9]

Essential History: Your Textbook

We now turn from the nature of history to one of the most common instruments of a survey course: the textbook. A textbook is a synthesis—that is, it pulls together in compact form a huge amount of information covering a broad field of study. Textbooks encompassing large fields often have more than one author. Each author takes on the primary responsibility for the portion of the book that fits his or her area of specialization most closely.

Whereas American history textbooks may possess certain things in common—for example, they all address a wide range of topics in American history—they can vary a good deal in style, coverage, and interpretation. Some textbooks have numerous pictures, many of them in color, while others have only a few black-and-white images. Some are written for advanced students, others for beginners. Some emphasize political history; others favor social history—the everyday lives of ordinary people. Some textbooks offer a liberal interpretation of the American past, viewing change as necessary and good; others present a conservative interpretation, celebrating stability and continuity. If your instructor's key objective is to expose you to a wide range of opinions about the American past, his or her choice of textbook may present a variety of interpretations. If your instructor prefers to emphasize a particular subfield in American history—such as social history—in class, he or she may have chosen a book with a different emphasis, perhaps political history. Or your instructor may have chosen a book that reflects his or her own interpretative and topical preferences. Regardless of your instructor's choice, your textbook offers a blend of fact and opinion, and you should read it with that in mind. In other words, you should approach your textbook thoughtfully and critically, just as you would your daily newspaper or weekly news magazine.

Exercise 4: Reading Your Textbook

Whatever the particular characteristics of your textbook, it is likely to play an important role in your preparation for classes and tests. This exercise should help you to learn to use your text effectively.

The first step is to make use of chapter headings and introductions. Textbook authors use these devices to prepare readers for what lies ahead. **On the line below, write the chapter title of the first chapter your instructor has assigned.**

_____

_____

With that title clearly in mind, read the chapter introduction. In the space provided, summarize in your own words what you expect the chapter to cover. What is the main topic?

If it is Reconstruction, describe in a few words what you think Reconstruction means without using the word itself. What are the chronological boundaries of the chapter?

_____

_____

_____

_____

_____

Now read through the body of the chapter, writing down each subheading on a separate sheet of paper as you go along. Under each subheading, add the basic points made in that section. These points should be *not* simple facts alone (such as "Andrew Johnson succeeded Abraham Lincoln as president in April 1865") but rather conclusions that help give facts some meaning, plus a fact or two to illustrate each conclusion. (For example, you might note that Johnson differed from most Republicans in Congress during 1866. You could include the point that Johnson wanted the federal government to do less to assist the freed slaves than die Republicans wanted it to do. You also could list an illustration of the point, perhaps Johnson's opposition to funding for the Freedman's Bureau.) If you need a list of basic facts in chronological order, look through the chapter to see if it provides any chronologies or time lines. If it does not, then compile one of your own on a separate sheet of paper, but include only facts that seem essential for understanding the chapter title and subheadings.

When you finish reading the chapter, **write in the space provided the key points made in its conclusion**—for example, "Today Reconstruction generally is considered a failure, just as it was in the late nineteenth century, but in a different way." Do these concluding points follow logically from the material you wrote down from the chapter? If not, work through the chapter again to see whether you have missed something.

_____

_____

_____

_____

_____

If you follow this procedure for every textbook chapter, you will be taking a giant step forward in preparing for classes and examinations. Although your supplementary readings may not have all of the same learning aids as your textbook, they will have chapter tides, introductions, and conclusions. Even if the introductions and conclusions are not clearly designated, the first paragraphs and the last paragraphs usually summarize where the chapter is going and where it has been, respectively. Try to do two things as you read each assignment: (1) take notes, using tides and subheadings as guidelines, and (2) focus on key generalizations and the basic facts behind them, rather than on every detail. You may find these suggestions useful in understanding classroom lectures as well.

Tables, Charts, and Graphs

Most textbooks contain a variety of illustrations. In addition to breaking the monotony of text, these visual aids have substantive purposes. The final three exercises in this chapter are designed to sharpen your awareness of illustrations. Tables, charts, and graphs are common features of history textbooks, and learning how to use them will enhance both your reading comprehension and your understanding of the historian's craft.

One of the primary tasks of historians is to study change—when, why, and how it occurs, and its impact on human beings. In studying change within a group or a society, historians must collect evidence expressed in numbers. After collecting evidence, historians often *quantify* information, meaning that they use mathematics to measure trends in the data. They may do this by computing an average or a mean or merely by comparing numbers and searching for patterns. Historians sometimes display their results in visual form, such as in a table, a chart, or a graph.

Exercise 5: Reading Tables

This exercise contains a table, which is simply an orderly presentation of numbers. The table compares by age group the percentage of African-Americans and European-Americans in the Deep South who were unable to write. The percentage 78.9 for African-Americans in 1870 means that in that year nearly 79 out of every 100 African-Americans in the five states covered could not write. **Read through the table[10] carefully, and then complete the exercise.**

Percentage of Persons in the Deep South Unable to Write, by Age Group, 1870–1890

	1870	1880	1890
Age 10–14			
African-American	78.9	74.1	49.2
European-American	33.2	34.5	18.7
Age 15–20			
African-American	85.3	73.0	54.1
European-American	24.2	21.0	14.3
Age over 20			
African-American	90.4	82.3	75.5
European-American	19.8	17.9	17.1

One conclusion consistent with the figures provided in this table is that the rates of illiteracy between 1870 and 1890 differed substantially among African-Americans and European-Americans. Six more conclusions follow. **Circle the numbers of the conclusions that are consistent with the information in the table.**

1. Rates of illiteracy among African-Americans steadily declined in the Deep South from 1870 to 1890.

2. Rates of decline in illiteracy were most pronounced among African-American adults.

3. The size of the decline among African-Americans exceeded that among European-Americans.

4. Throughout the period, a larger percentage of European-Americans were illiterate than African-Americans.

5. European-American adults were less likely to be illiterate than European-American youths; the opposite was true for African-Americans.

6. The rate of change for European-American and African-American youth was greater between 1880 and 1890 than between 1870 and 1880.

Exercise 6: Reading Charts

The presidential election of 1876–1877 is one of the most controversial in our history. Normally, the Electoral College determines the outcome of such elections, with each state having a number of votes equal to its representation in Congress. But if no candidate achieves a majority of the votes in the Electoral College, the issue is resolved in Congress. In 1876–1877, the Republican and Democratic parties initially could not agree on who had won 20 of the 369 Electoral College votes. As a result, neither Republican candidate Rutherford B. Hayes nor Democratic candidate Samuel J. Tilden emerged with a majority. Congress established a special commission to determine whether Democrats or Republicans should fill the contested seats. The commission's ruling in favor of the Republicans gave Hayes a one-vote majority in the Electoral College.

Historians and political scientists often use charts to show voting patterns in particular elections. The chart, or political map, in Figure 1.4 shows the winning party in each state in

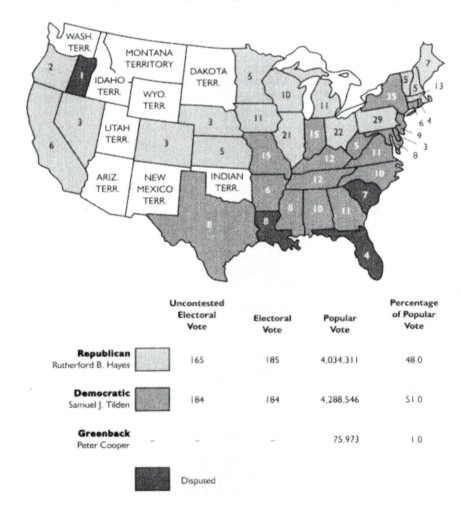

	Uncontested Electoral Vote	Electoral Vote	Popular Vote	Percentage of Popular Vote
Republican Rutherford B. Hayes	165	185	4,034,311	48.0
Democratic Samuel J. Tilden	184	184	4,288,546	51.0
Greenback Peter Cooper	—	—	75,973	1.0

Disputed

FIGURE 1.4 *The Disputed Election of 1876*

the election of 1876, except where the outcome was contested. If we were to place charts for several presidential elections side by side, you could use them to determine whether national politics had changed during the period covered. This exercise, however, asks you merely to pull information out of a single chart. Examine the chart closely and then respond to the questions that follow.

Questions on Figure 1.4

1. What do the numbers inside each state designate? (*Hint:* You may want to consult the U.S. Constitution at the end of your textbook to answer this question. Find Article II, Section 1, paragraph 2.) _____

_____

2. Why don't the unshaded areas have numbers in them? _____

_____

3. Would the numbers be the same for a political map of the election of 1996? Explain.

_____

_____

_____

_____

Exercise 7: Reading Graphs

You have read in your textbook about the tremendous devastation suffered by the South during the Civil War and about the difficult recovery in the war's immediate aftermath. The graph in this exercise (see Figure 1.5) shows developments in the South's economy from 1860 to the turn of the century. Like tables and charts, graphs provide visual displays of evidence. This graph shows changes in several economic indicators—that is, it measures change in aspects of the economy of a defined area over a particular period of time. It also addresses the question of whether change is primarily linear or cyclical. **Linear change** is indicated when a line on a graph always or nearly always moves in the same direction. **Cyclical change** is suggested when a line frequently changes direction. Three types of change are shown in Figure 1.6.

Examine the graph in Figure 1.5 carefully, and then complete the exercise. One conclusion derived from the graph is that substantial change occurred in the South's economy between 1860 and 1900. **Circle the numbers of the conclusions that follow from information in the graph.**

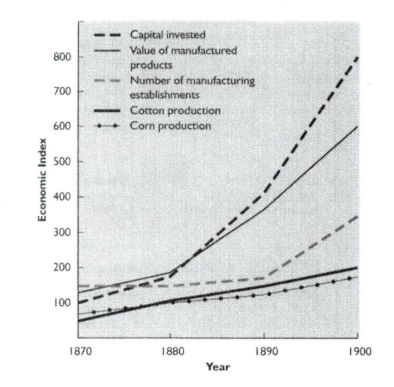

FIGURE 1.5 *The Economic Recovery of Former Confederate States, 1870–1900 (indexed at 1860 = 100)*

Source: *Twelfth Census of the United States, 1900: Agriculture*

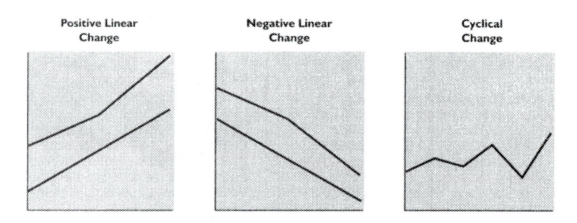

FIGURE 1.6 *Line Graphs Showing Three Kinds of Change*

1. Overall, change in the South's economy between 1870 and 1900 was basically cyclical.
2. Overall, change between 1860 and 1870 was basically linear. (*Hint:* To determine 1860 levels, carefully read the note below the graph.)
3. Of the *categories of production* represented, manufacturing showed the greatest increase between 1870 and 1900.

4. There is a correlation (mutual or reciprocal relation) between capital invested and the value of manufactured products.

5. Overall, the rate of increase in the number of manufacturing establishments was higher than the rate of increase for corn production.

This chapter has introduced you to history as a discipline—its nature, its uses, and some of the skills it requires. As your course proceeds, you will find yourself confronting many tasks, some drawing on familiar skills and others calling for new ones. Whether new or familiar, these abilities will serve you well in the world beyond this classroom. If you are asked to write an essay or to analyze a film in this course, you may be tempted to say to your teacher, "But this is a history course, not an English course;" or "This is a history course, not a film course." Keep in mind that the educated person possesses the capacity to integrate knowledge—that is, to apply it outside the context in which it was originally acquired. In the midst of constructing a coherent, grammatical narrative in Chapter 6 or contemplating the symbolism in the movie *Working Girl* in Chapter 9, remember that nowhere in your educational experience will you be expected to apply knowledge and skills from as wide a variety of subjects as in a course on the "universal discipline"—history.

We now turn to the exciting world of primary sources—documents that, as relics of a past age, are crucial to our understanding of times and places other than our own.

Notes

[1] *Congressional Globe*, 39th Cong., 1st sess., February 1, 1866, 589.

[2] Ibid., 39th Cong., 2nd sess., December 11, 1866, 56.

[3] W. H. Morgan, *Personal Reminiscences of the War of 1861–5* (Lynchburg, Va.: J. P. Bell and Co., n.d.), 272, 278–80.

[4] Kenneth M. Stampp, *The Era of Reconstruction, 1865–1877* (New York: Knopf, 1965), 9–10.

[5] Funk & Wagnalls, *New Comprehensive International Dictionary of the English Language*, Deluxe Reference Edition (Newark, N.J.: Publishers International Press, 1982), 1326.

[6] Mark W. Summers, *Railroads, Reconstruction, and the Gospel of Prosperity* (Princeton: Princeton University Press, 1984), 300–301.

[7] W. E. B. Du Bois, *Black Reconstruction in America* (New York: Russell and Russell, 1935), 722.

[8] Hans L. Trefousse, *Andrew Johnson* (New York: Norton, 1989), 193.

[9] David Donald, *Charles Sumner and the Rights of Man* (New York- Knopf, 1970), 586–587.

[10] Roger Ransom and Richard Sutch, *One Kind of Freedom* (Cambridge: Cambridge University Press, 1978), 30.

2: *Evidence of the Past: Reading and Looking at Primary Sources*

Late-Nineteenth-Century America

In the 1950s television series "Dragnet," Sergeant Joe Friday always asked witnesses to give him "just the facts, please." He never got facts alone, however. What he got was different versions of the same event. On some points all witnesses may have agreed, but rarely did they concur on everything. Through careful investigation, Sergeant Friday attempted to separate the reliable evidence from the unreliable, and in so doing he pieced together an accurate version of the event. Historians work in much the same way, although their evidence tends to be written rather than oral.

The Variety of Primary Sources

Historians call the materials they use to determine the facts **primary sources.** By definition, primary sources are materials created during the period being studied. Newspapers and magazines are prominent among published primary sources, as are transcripts of legislative or court proceedings and presidential press conferences. Unpublished primary sources include private letters and diaries, among other things. Sometimes the private papers of prominent people get published, although normally not until many years after they were written. For example, both Harry S. Truman and Dwight D. Eisenhower kept diaries while they served as president, and in the 1980s substantial portions of these writings appeared in print Woodrow Wilson did not keep a diary, but he wrote many letters during his years as a professor and college president and later as a politician. The bulk of these have been published over the last thirty years. The vast majority of surviving letters and diaries, however, remain unpublished, stored in people's attics or cellars or in manuscript collections in research libraries.

Primary sources also include a wide variety of unwritten materials. Pictures, paintings, maps, buildings, and automobiles all qualify as primary sources. So do airplanes and space capsules like the ones on display at the Air and Space Museum in Washington, D.C.

Historians of the recent past often interview people who participated in events, just as detectives question people who experienced, witnessed, or might have committed crimes. Even though many oral histories are made years after the event in question, they qualify as primary sources as long as the testimony is given by a person actually involved in that event. Thus spoken memoirs also belong in the category of primary sources.

The following exercises seek to develop your skills in identifying primary sources and evaluating their authenticity, reliability, and meaning. By the time you have completed this chapter, you will have worked with a variety of such sources, from traditional written materials to pictures and drawings.

Exercise 1: Identifying Primary Sources

The years after the Civil War and into the 1880s saw the "long drive" reach its height in the Southwest and plains states. During this drive, ranchers moved cattle from Texas, New Mexico, and Arizona to the Great Plains, from western Kansas northward, where the animals were loaded on trains and transported to slaughterhouses in Kansas City or Chicago. Two accounts of the long drive follow. The third selection describes the transition from the long drive to a more modern system of raising and marketing cattle.

Read the passages and write in the margin whether or not they are primary sources. If you are uncertain, say so. Be prepared to explain your answers.

A. Another offspring of the railroads and the Civil War was the cowboy of the Old West. The late 1860s saw . . . Texas crammed with 5,000,000 head of cattle raised under . . . conditions of open range, fancy roping and short shrift for the rustler. Their owners, eagerly seeking markets . . . , began to drive them northward to shipping points on the new railroad for loading into cars for the Kansas City and Chicago stockyards . . . The traditional population of the country into which the Kansas Pacific and. . . . the Union Pacific were pushing consisted of thousands of Indians living off millions of buffalo. Now Uncle Sam was herding the Indians into reservations and appallingly efficient professional buffalo hunters . . . were wiping out the great lumbering beasts. This left the grass and water of western Kansas free for cattlemen, and it was soon learned that . . . cattle could winter well enough on the Great Plains unsheltered . . . Gradually the cattle country . . . spread into Wyoming and northward beyond the Canadian line.[1]

B. The [ranch] boss informed us that we were to take another herd of cattle north, away up in the northwestern part of Nebraska . . . This announcement was met with exclamations of approval from the boys . . . It did not take us long to round up the herd and the second day from the time we received the order we were off. . . . It was now late in the season and we had to hurry in order to get through in good weather, therefore we put the cattle to the limit of their traveling powers. . . . Our route lay over the old Hays and Elsworth trail, one of the best known cattle trails in the west, then by way of Olga [Oglala], Nebraska, at that time a very small and also a very tough place. It was a rendezvous of the tough element and the bad men of the cow country. There were a large number of cowboys there from the surrounding ranges and the place looked very enticing to our tired and thirsty crowd, but we had our herd to look after and deliver so we could not stop, but pushed on north crossing the Platte river, then up the trail that led by the Hole in the Wall country, near which place we went into camp. Then as now this Hole in the Wall country was the refuge of the train robbers, cattle thieves and bandits of the western country, and when we arrived the place was unusually full of them, and it was not long before trouble was brewing between our men and the natives which culminated in one of our men shooting and killing one of the bad men of the hole. We broke camp at once and proceeded on our journey north. We arrived at the ranch where our herd were to be delivered without further incident.[2]

C. In the old days when the Chisholm Trail was new, it was the custom of some trail bosses to point the wagon pole at the North Star in the evening so that in the morning they had only to glance at it to know which direction to take. Those days were gone; after crossing Red River, a child could have found its way to Abilene without going astray.

Soon after the season of 1871 got into full swing, so many herds were moving toward Kansas that it was often difficult to keep them from treading on one another's heels. By midsummer overgrazing made it necessary to detour from the trail for a mile or two to find grass. . .

As they moved into Dickinson County the drovers were harassed by fences and the organized resistance of the farmers. Still another herd law had been enacted, and this one had teeth in it. In some places the old brush fences had been replaced by a new invention . . . named, appropriately, barbed wire. It was cheap and it was deadly enough to turn back any critter. . . . The Texans . . . couldn't have surmised that in a few years it would be adopted by cattlemen north and south, and in time become the great safeguard for the orderly functioning of the livestock industry.[3]

You may have concluded from Exercise 1 that it is easier to determine what is a primary source than what is not. Sources written in the first person or in the present tense usually qualify as primary. Yet most memoirs (primary) and works by historians (secondary) are written in the past tense; newspaper articles (primary) and works by historians (secondary) generally use the third person. Although it is a good guess that sources written in both the past tense and the third person are secondary in nature, we frequently must do more than read a brief passage from them to tell for sure. The preface or introduction to a book often provides key information by revealing something about the author and the circumstances under which the document was written.

Survival of Primary Sources

Now let us consider the survival of primary sources. We saw in Chapter 1 that only a small portion of human events are ever recorded. Those that are documented often disappear from memory through the destruction of primary sources. War, fire, rain, insects, and rodents are among the great ravagers of historical evidence. So are humans. Just as we do today, people for centuries have been cleaning out their homes and places of business, discarding old newspapers, magazines, pamphlets, advertisements, and personal letters, many of which would have interested future historians. Thus only a tiny portion of what humans have created ultimately survives.

Are there common characteristics of the materials that survive? Or are survival rates merely a matter of chance? Not surprisingly, wealth and official position have a decided effect on the survival rate of evidence. What the government, its agents, and the wealthiest portion of a people leave behind has a much better chance of surviving the ravages of history than a poorer persons things. Letters and diaries are the products of people who can read and write and have some reason to put pen to paper. Until very recently, most poor people were illiterate. They were thus unlikely to leave behind letters or diaries. They did leave evidence of their lives, but this information must be carefully deciphered. Historians interested in social history—the lives of ordinary people—often have turned to anthropologists' and archeologists' methods to literally dig up evidence of how poor people lived. Historians working from the mid-nineteenth century on can make use of photographs, but pictures of ordinary people are far less plentiful than those of the rich and famous.

Despite the loss of so much information about the lives of ordinary people, historians still can piece together evidence of their experiences. This process is called history "from the bottom up" because these people were often on the bottom rung of society. Of course, most of the documents and other primary sources that have survived come from official sources and allow us to see government and society "from the top down."

The following exercises ask you to think about the survival prospects of various types of primary sources and to distinguish between public and private documents.

Exercise 2: Survival Prospects

Next to each item in the following list **write** an *S* if you think the item would be likely to survive for 100 years. If you think the item would not survive, write *NS*.

_____ diary of President McKinley

_____ southern sharecropper's home

_____ financial records of Andrew Carnegie's steel company

_____ mansion of the Vanderbilt family

_____ home of one of the workers in the Carnegie steel mill

_____ dress suit of a poor Italian immigrant

Exercise 3: Private and Public Documents

Examine each of the following documents. In the space provided, **write *private*** for those written by people acting as private individuals—that is, by people outside government or by people in government but acting outside their official capacity. **Write *public*** for documents that represent attempts to explain or make policy, and **write *unclear*** for those that do not quite fit either category.

A The following is a transcription of a handwritten letter.

My Dear Mrs. Felton:

I feel very grateful for your kind words of sympathy for me in my sorrow. Only those who have trodden the same path can understand what it is.

When I see you I want to tell you all about my little darling; her beautiful little life & her even beautiful death. She was <u>so lovely</u>—such an idol with all. But I cannot write about her the tears blind me so.

How is dear little Howard? I hope he will be hearty & well when I see him.

I was so sorry not to know when you were in Atlanta. Present me kindly to the Dr. and believe me

Your affectionate friend
Fanny Gordon[4]

Kirkwood
August 27th/77.

_____

B The following is from President Grover Cleveland's message to Congress of December 1885.

The fact that our revenues are in excess of the actual needs of an economical administration of the government justifies a reduction in the amount exacted from the people for its support. Our government is . . . never better administered, and its true spirit is never better observed, than when the people's taxation for its support is scrupulously limited to the actual necessity of expenditure, and distributed according to a just and equitable plan.

The proposition with which we have to deal is the reduction of the revenue received by the government, and indirectly paid by the people from customs duties. The question of free trade is not involved, nor is there now any occasion for the general discussion of the wisdom or expediency of a protective system.

Justice and fairness dictate that . . . the industries and interests which have been encouraged by such laws, and in which our citizens have large investments, should not be ruthlessly injured or destroyed. We should also . . . protect the interests of American labor . . . ; its stability and proper remuneration furnish the most justifiable pretext for a protective policy. . . .

I think the reduction should be made in the revenue derived from a tax upon the imported necessaries of life.

We thus directly lessen the cost of living in every family of the land, and release to the people in every humble home a larger measure of the rewards of frugal industry.[5]

────────

C The following document is a letter from Carl Schurz, the secretary of the interior, to a Republican ally, George William Curtis, dated December 29, 1879.

I intended to answer your last note some time ago but the current business of the Department would not let me do so.

It seems to me that it is time for the opponents of General Grant's nomination [by the Republican party for president] to act. The "boom business" has been so much overdone that the public mind is open for a reaction. . . . All that is necessary is that those who are earnestly opposed to the third term should openly say so. You strike the nail on the head in saying that the real danger consists in "the habituation of the popular mind to personal government." But I think you are not right in your apprehension that the people have no clear appreciation of that danger. It is just this appreciation, together with their remembrance of the corruptions and abuses of the Grant regime, that makes the Germans so unanimous in their opposition to the third term. I see this cropping out everywhere. Without the German Republican vote several of the Northwestern States, such as Wisconsin, Illinois and Ohio, cannot be carried. . . Now let it be known that the Independent Republican element in New York is of the same mind . . . and the back of the Grant movement will be broken. . .

I write to you with entire **frankness**. . . . I hope you will communicate with me, of course, in entire confidence.[6]

────────

Authenticity and Reliability

Exercise 3 was relatively uncomplicated. The texts themselves offered important clues as to their nature. Yet evaluating a primary source can be challenging. The first tasks are to determine its authenticity and reliability. Only after completing that step can we move on to assess its meaning.

Imagine that you have in your hands something that purports to be a primary source. You want to determine its genuineness. Is it what it claims to be? There are famous forgeries that still haunt historians. Not so long ago one of the most respected English historians authenticated Adolf Hitler's "diaries," which allegedly suggested that Hitler never intended to commit genocide. When the forger was revealed, this historian issued a qualified apology. The fact is that any historian can make a mistake.

The first clues to authenticity are physical. Is the document or artifact old enough to originate in the period from which it supposedly came? Was it found in an appropriate place? Does it use language or was it the product of tools from long ago? Is the handwriting genuine? One good way to authenticate a primary source is to compare it with similar sources that have already been authenticated. The problem with this method, though, is that the most interesting discoveries often contradict or add to existing sources.

Another good way to prove the legitimacy of a primary source is to find references to it in other well-established sources. It then fills a gap in our evidence. Of course, such gaps are often invitations to forgers. For example, a missing reply to a letter begs for a forgery. Entire sets of documents can be forged. Between 1861 and 1869, the Frenchman Vrain-Denis Lucas sold more than 27,000 forged letters, many of them supposedly written by famous scientists such as Galileo, Pascal, and Descartes. Two of the letters tried to show that the Frenchman Pascal, not the Englishman Newton, had discovered the law of gravity!

The issue of authenticity does not arise with the bulk of primary sources used by historians. Many documents, especially official ones, go into a specific collection soon after being created. For suspect documents, archivists frequently run standard checks before making them available to scholars. So despite an occasional notorious case, few historians, especially those who study recent American history, spend much of their time authenticating documents.

A far more common problem for historians of nineteenth- and twentieth-century America is the reliability of evidence in primary sources. Just because a source is authentic does not mean that it is reliable. After all, the authors of genuine primary sources may have been in a poor position to witness the events they describe. Their powers of observation may have been weak, or they may have possessed an ulterior motive for describing events as they did. Before relying on these sources as evidence, therefore, it is wise to ask a series of questions even of authenticated primary sources. These questions include the following: Was the author of the source well situated to see the event described? Was the author well acquainted with any or all of the people described? What was the character of the author—was he or she a truth teller or a fabricator of stories? Did the author have a personal interest in the event described? Is the language used in portraying the event calm and balanced or emotional and polemical? Was the source created immediately, within a short span of time, or after many years?

As you can see, determining the reliability of primary sources is often complex. It is a task, nonetheless, that is commonly performed by people outside the history profession, although they usually don't think of their evidence as primary sources. Recall the testimony of Professor Anita Hill and Judge Clarence Thomas before the Senate Judiciary Committee during the fall of 1991. Hill accused Thomas of sexual harassment during the time she worked for him several years earlier. Thomas adamantly denied her story. The senators on the committee had to decide which person to believe in order to determine how to vote on Thomas's nomination to the Supreme Court. Millions of Americans who watched the dramatic proceedings on television made judgments as well, even though they had no direct say regarding Thomas's fate. This is merely one case in which people confronted the task of evaluating evidence about the past as a means of reaching a conclusion in the present. Most of us engage in the same kind of activity on a regular basis in the normal course of our lives.

Exercise 4: Evaluating the Reliability of Primary Sources

The population grew rapidly in late-nineteenth-century America. Between 1860 and 1900, the number of people in the United States increased from 31.5 million to more than 76 million. During that time, over 13 million people came from other countries to live in America. As a result of this phenomenal growth, the center of population moved steadily westward, and cities expanded dramatically. Whereas in 1860 census takers classified only 16.1 percent of the population as urban, by the turn of the century they placed more than twice that percentage in this category. New York City grew more than threefold, Chicago more than tenfold. The increased crowding in cities and the growing diversity of their populations after 1880, as well as increasing disparities in wealth, created many problems, which in turn often led to conflict.

The two primary sources that follow are accounts by popular newspapers of an incident that resulted from friction between business and labor in Chicago. Known as the Haymarket Square incident, this event occurred on the evening of May 4, 1886. It grew out of a struggle by organized labor for the eight-hour workday. On the previous day, striking laborers and police had clashed near a McCormick Harvester plant in the city, leaving one laborer dead and several on both sides injured. To protest alleged police brutality, radicals in the labor movement called a mass meeting for the next night at Haymarket Square. As a result of a police effort to break up the meeting, eight policemen died, and dozens of civilians were killed or wounded. In the event's aftermath, conservative forces launched a nationwide campaign against labor organizers and socialists who sought to alter the structure of economic and political power in America. Chicago authorities arrested eight radicals for allegedly planning or provoking the incident. A jury convicted all eight, and seven received death sentences. Of the seven, four were hanged in November 1887, a fifth committed suicide the day before his scheduled execution, and the governor of Illinois commuted to life imprisonment the sentences of the other two. In 1893 a reform governor, John Peter Altgeld, pardoned the three remaining prisoners, declaring that they were innocent of the crimes for which they had been convicted.

Carefully read the following newspaper accounts of the actual incident and answer the questions that follow. (The map provided in Figure 2.1 of the Haymarket neighborhood may help you to visualize the event.)

A From the *Chicago Tribune*, May 5, 1886, p. 1:

A HELLISH DEED.

A DYNAMITE BOMB THROWN INTO A CROWD OF POLICEMEN. . . .

A dynamite bomb thrown into a squad of policemen sent to disperse a mob at the corner of Desplaines and Randolph streets last night exploded with terrific force, killing and injuring nearly fifty men. . . .

An Incendiary Speech

The following circular was distributed yesterday afternoon:

ATTENTION, WORKINGMEN!
GREAT MASS-MEETING
Tonight, at 7:30 o'clock,
At the
HAYMARKET, RANDOLPH STREET, BETWEEN
DES PLAINES AND HALSTED.

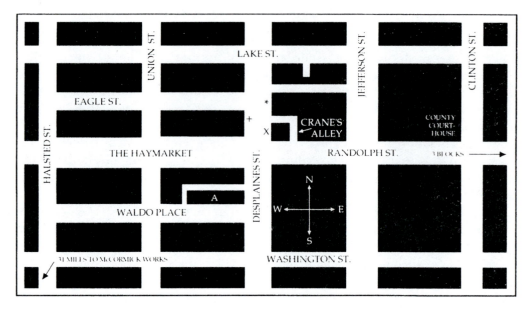

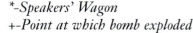

A-*Desplains Street Police Station*   *-*Speakers' Wagon*
X-*Point from which bomb was thrown*   +-*Point at which bomb exploded*

FIGURE 2.1 *Map of Haymarket Neighborhood*

Good speakers will be present to denounce the latest atrocious act of the police—the shooting of our fellow-workmen yesterday afternoon.

THE EXECUTIVE COMMITTEE.

In response to this about 1,500 people gathered, but a shower dispersed all but 600. Several speeches had been made of a more or less rabid character when Sam Fielden, the Socialist, put in an appearance.

"The Socialists," he said, "are not going to declare war; but I tell you war has been declared upon us; and I ask you to get hold of anything that will help to resist the onslaught of the enemy and the usurper. The skirmish-lines have met People have been shot. Men, women, and children have not been spared by the ruthless minions of private capital. It had no mercy. So ought you. You are called upon to defend yourselves, your lives, your future. What matters it whether you kill yourselves with work to get a little relief or die on the battlefield resisting the enemy? (Applause.) What is the difference? Any animal, however loathsome, will resist when stepped upon. Are men less than snails or worms? I have some resistance in me. I know that you have too. You have been robbed. You will be starved into a worse condition."

At this point those on the outskirts of the crowd whispered "Police," and many of them hastened to the corner of Randolph street. Six or eight companies of police, commanded by Inspector Bonfield, marched rapidly past the corner. Fielden saw them coming and stopped talking. When at the edge of the crowd Inspector Bonfield said in a loud voice: "In the name of the law I command you to disperse." The reply was a bomb, which exploded as soon as it struck. The first company of police answered with a volley right into the crowd, who scattered in all directions. . . .

What Another Reporter Saw.

Fielden was apparently about winding up his address when a dark line was seen to form north of Randolph street and in front of the Desplaines Street Station. For some time no attention was paid to it, but it gradually moved north. . . . As the line approached a cry arose in the crowd: "The police! The police!" and the south end of the crowd began to divide towards the sidewalk and walk south to Randolph street. But the wagon in front of the Crane Bros. Manufacturing Company was not vacated by the speaker and the other "leaders." Fielden continued speaking, raising his voice more and more as the police approached. . . . The police, marching slowly, were in a line with the east and west alley when something like a miniature rocket suddenly rose out of the crowd on the east sidewalk, in a line with the police. It . . . fell right in the middle of the street and among the marching police. . . . The bomb lay on the ground a few seconds, then a loud explosion occurred, and the crowd took to their heels, scattering in all directions. Immediately after the explosion the police pulled their revolvers and fired on the crowd. An incessant fire was kept up for nearly two minutes. . . .

Questions to Consider

1. Does the headline of the article suggest any point of view? If so, what? _____
_____
_____

2. Is the word *mob*, used in the first paragraph, a neutral word, or does it suggest a bias? How about *rabid* later on? _____
_____

3. Does the article merely describe Sam Fielden's speech, or does it purport to quote it? Does your answer suggest that the reporter was present at the incident? _____
_____
_____

4. How does the description of events under the heading "What Another Reporter Saw" compare with the description before it? Is it more or less biased, or about the same? Are there any factual discrepancies? _____
_____

5. Does the fact that the newspaper published both of the reports suggest anything about its point of view and reliability? _____
_____
_____

B From the *New York Times*, May 5, 1886, p. 1:

ANARCHY'S RED HAND

RIOTING AND BLOODSHED IN THE

STREETS OF CHICAGO

POLICE MOWED DOWN WITH DYNAMITE

STRIKERS KILLED WITH VOLLEYS FROM REVOLVERS. . . .

Chicago, May 4.—The villainous [sic] teachings of the Anarchists bore bloody fruit in Chicago tonight, and before daylight at least a dozen stalwart men will have laid down their lives as a tribute to the doctrine of Herr Johann Most [an anarchist leader]. There had been skirmishes all day between the police and various sections of the mob, which had no head and no organization. In every instance the police won. In the afternoon a hand-bill, printed in German and English, called upon "workingmen" to meet at Des Plaines and Randolph streets this evening. "Good speakers," it was promised, "will be present to denounce the latest atrocious act of the police—the shooting of our fellow-workmen yesterday afternoon."

In response to this invitation 1,400 men, including those most active in the Anarchist riots of the past 48 hours, gathered at the point designated. At Des Plaines street, Randolph street, which runs east and west, widens out, and is known as the Old Haymarket. . . . It was just off the northeastern corner of the plaza and around the corner into Des Plaines street, 100 feet north of Randolph, that the crowd gathered. A light rainstorm came up and about 800 people went away. The 600 who remained listened to speeches from the lips of August Spies . . . and A. H. Parsons, an Anarchist with a negro wife. The speeches were rather mild in tone, but when Sam Fielden, another Anarchist leader, mounted the wagon from which the orators spoke, the crowd pressed nearer, knowing that something different was coming.

They were not disappointed. Fielden spoke for 20 minutes, growing wilder and more violent as he proceeded. Police Inspector Bonfield had heard the early part of the speech, and, walking down the street to the Des Plaines street police station, not 300 feet south of where Fielden stood, called out a reserve of 60 policemen and started them up the street toward the crowd. The men were formed into lines stretching from curb to curb. The Inspector hurried on ahead, and, forcing his way through the crowd, reached a point close to the wagon. Fielden had just uttered an incendiary sentence, when Bonfield cried:

I command you in the name of the law to desist, and you," turning to the crowd, "to disperse.

Just as he began to speak[,] . . . from a little group of men standing at the entrance to an alley opening on Des Plaines street, opposite where Fielden was speaking, some thing rose up into the air, carrying with it a slender tail of fire, squarely in front of the advancing line of policemen. It struck and sputtered mildly for a moment. Then, as they were so close to it that the nearest man could have stepped upon the thing, it exploded with terrible effect.

The men in the center of the line went down with shrieks and groans, dying together. Then from the Anarchists on every side, a deadly fire was poured in on the stricken lines of police, and more men fell to the ground. . . The police answered the fire of the rioters with deadly effect. In two minutes the ground was strewn with wounded men. Then the shots straggled, and all was quiet and the police were the masters of the situation.

Questions to Consider

1. How does the headline of article B compare with that of article A? _____

_____

2. What does use of the word *villainous* in the first sentence suggest about the point of view of the article? _____

_____

3. Why do you think the article mentions that one of the speakers had "a negro wife"?

_____

_____

4. How do articles A and B compare in their coverage of Fielden's speech? _____

_____

_____

5. Is there any point on which article B provides more detail than article A? _____

_____

_____

6. How do the two articles differ on who first fired guns? _____

_____

7. Now it is time for you to evaluate the reliability of these articles. Using your answers to the preceding questions, as well as the reliability questions provided on page 24, evaluate the accounts. (Some of the reliability questions will be more useful than others.) Identify at least three points of similarity in the articles and three points on which they differ.

Similarities:

a. _____

_____

b. _____

_____

c. _____

_____

Differences:

a. _____

_____

b. _____

_____

c. _____

_____

8. If you had to provide an account of the Haymarket Square incident on the basis of one of the two articles alone, which one would you choose? _____

Why? _____

_____

_____

_____

9. What additional evidence would you seek if you were a historian writing an article on the incident? What kind of useful evidence would you expect might have survived?

_____

_____

_____

10. Explain how these documents take you out of the present. What sets them apart from articles on the front page of today's major newspapers? _____

_____

_____

_____

_____

The Interpretation of Primary Sources

Evaluating primary sources involves more than just questioning their authenticity and reliability. It also requires you to judge their meaning. In interpreting the past, historians think extensively about what the available primary sources mean. What are the authors of the sources trying to say? What was the meaning of their choice of particular words or phrases? How important was their message to others of their time? Why was their message important or unimportant? Did it help to shape opinion, official or otherwise, or did it merely reflect it? If the sources are nontextual—pictures, paintings, or drawings—what do they say about the society of the time? For example, does the clothing worn by people in a picture reflect the prevailing style of a particular time and place or class? If so, what does it suggest about economic and social conditions? These are only a few of the questions historians ask once they have confirmed the authenticity and reliability of their sources.

The remaining six exercises ask you to analyze drawings as well as written materials. They will expand your understanding of changes that were taking place in late-nineteenth-century America, especially in relation to gender, and perhaps help you comprehend changes that have occurred since the late nineteenth century.

Exercise 5: Women and Economic Change

Industrialization ushered in rapid changes in late-nineteenth-century America. Advances in technology made possible major savings in the human labor required to produce most finished goods, from processed food to machinery. This development led to reductions in the average workweek among laborers in manufacturing from sixty-six hours in 1860 to sixty in 1890 and forty-seven in 1920. Labor-saving devices also appeared in the home, cutting sharply the time required to carry out many household tasks. One result was more time available to Americans, especially in the growing and increasingly prosperous middle class, for nonproductive activities such as leisure and education. Another result was to give women a wider range of activities outside the home.

The passage below is from *Women and Economics*, a book published in 1898. Its author, Charlotte Perkins Gilman (1860–1935), wrote extensively about women and their inferior position to men in American society. Here she discusses the impact of economic change on women's status. Read the passage and answer the questions that follow. Keep in mind that Exercise 10, the final exercise in this chapter, asks you to write a paragraph about middle-class women in late-nineteenth-century America based on this document and the documents in Exercises 6, 7, 8, and 9. You will find the exercises helpful as you ponder linkages among the documents.

The change in education is in large part a cause of this . . . slow emergence of the long-subverted human female to full racial [sic] equality . . ., and progressively a consequence. Day by day the bars go down. More and more the field lies open for the mind of women to glean all it can, and it has responded most eagerly. Not only our pupils, but our teachers, are mainly women. And the clearness and strength of the brain of the woman prove continually the injustice of the clamorous contempt long poured upon what was scornfully called "the female mind." . . .

No sociological change equal in importance to this clearly marked improvement of an entire sex has ever taken place in one century. Under it all . . . goes . . . the one great change, that of the economic relation. . . . Just as the development of machinery constantly lowers the importance of mere brute strength of body and raises that of mental power and skill, so the pressure of industrial conditions demands an ever-higher specialization, and tends to break up that relic of the patriarchal age,—the family as an economic unit.

Women have been led under pressure of necessity into a most reluctant entrance upon fields of economic activity. The sluggish and greedy disposition bred of long ages of dependence has by no means welcomed the change. Most women still work only as they "have to," until they can marry and "be supported." Men, too, liking the power that goes with money, and the poor quality of gratitude and affection bought with it, resent and oppose the change; but all this disturbs very little the course of social progress.

A truer spirit is the increasing desire of young girls to be independent, to have a career of their own, at least for a while, and the growing objection of countless wives to the pitiful asking for money, to the beggary of their position. . . .

For a while the introduction of machinery which took away from the home so many industries deprived women of any importance as an economic factor; but presently she arose, and followed her lost wheel and loom to their new place, the mill. To-day there is hardly an industry in the land in which some women are not found. . . .

Consider, too, the altered family relation which attends this movement. Entirely aside from the strained relation in marriage, the other branches of family life feel the strange new forces, and respond to them. "When I was a girl," sighs the gray-haired mother, "we sisters all sat and sewed while mother read to us. Now every one of my daughters has a different club!" . . . We invariably object to changed conditions in those departments of life where we have established ethical values. For all the daughters to sew while the mother read aloud to them was esteemed right; and, therefore, the radiating diffusion of daughters among clubs is esteemed wrong,—a danger to home life. . . .

The growing individualization of democratic life brings inevitable change to our daughters. . . . Girls do not all like to sew. . . . Now to sit sewing together, instead of being a harmonizing process, would generate different degrees of restlessness, of distaste, of irritation. . . . As the race become more specialized, more differentiated, the simple lines of relation in family life draw with less force, and the more complex lines of relation in social life draw with more force; and this is a perfectly natural and desirable process for women as well as for men.[7]

1. What, according to Gilman, had happened to the status of women in the United States over the past century? _____

_____

2. Why did the change occur? _____

_____

_____

_____

3. Identify one specific manifestation of the change in the workplace. _____

_____

_____

_____

4. How did men react to the change and why? _____

_____

_____

_____

5. How did mothers react to the change and why? _____

_____

6. What does Gilman mean by the "growing individualization of democratic life"? _____

_____

_____

7. How did the change influence family life? _____

_____

_____

_____

_____

Exercise 6: Mothers and Daughters in an Era of Change

The passage below was written by Jane Addams (1860–1935), founder of the Chicago welfare settlement Hull House in 1889. In it she speaks to some of the emotional costs to women of changes that were occurring in the late nineteenth century, especially among the increasing number of women raised in prosperous middle-class families. The daughter of a successful merchant in Rockford, Illinois, Addams was the first woman in her family to graduate from college. Unlike the vast majority of women of her background, she never married. After nearly a decade of uncertainty and anxiety she decided on the course that would make her one of the most influential women in American history. Here she reflects on her thoughts during the 1880s as she searched for her calling. Read the passage, taken from her memoir *Twenty Years at Hull House* (1911), and answer the questions that follow.

I gradually reached a conviction that the first generation of college women had taken their learning too quickly, had departed too suddenly from the active, emotional life led by their grandmothers and great-grandmothers; that the contemporary education of young women had developed too exclusively the power of acquiring knowledge and of merely receiving impressions; that somewhere in the process of "being educated" they had lost that simple and almost automatic response to the human appeal, that old healthful reaction resulting in activity from the mere presence of suffering or of helplessness; that they are so sheltered and pampered they have no chance even to make "the great refusal." . . .

I remember a happy busy mother who, complacent with the knowledge that her daughter daily devoted four hours to her music, looked up from her knitting to say, "If I had had your opportunities when I was young, my dear, I should have been a very happy girl. I always had musical talent, but such training as I had, foolish little songs and waltzes and not time for half an hour's practice a day."

The mother did not dream of the sting her words left and that the sensitive girl appreciated only too well that her opportunities were fine and unusual, but she also knew that in spite of some faculty and much good teaching she had no genuine talent and never would fulfill the expectations of her friends. She looked back upon her mother's girlhood with positive envy because it was so full of happy industry and extenuating obstacles, with undisturbed opportunity to believe that her talents were unusual. The girl looked wistfully at her mother, but had not the courage to cry out what was in her heart: "I might believe I had unusual talent if I did not know what good music was; I might enjoy half an hour's practice a day if I were busy and happy the rest of the time. You do not know what life means when all the difficulties are removed! I am simply smothered and sickened with advantages. It is like eating a sweet dessert the first thing in the morning."[8]

1. What did Addams conclude about the deficiencies of the first generation of college women? _____

_____

_____

_____

2. What does Addams mean by "the great refusal"? _____

_____

_____

3. In what sense does Addams view the mother of the 1880s as ambivalent regarding the position of her daughter? _____

_____

_____

_____

4. In what sense does the daughter envy her mother? _____

_____

_____

_____

5. Identify three points that the Addams passage has in common with the Gilman passage in Exercise 5.

a. _____

_____

_____

b. _____

_____

_____

c. _____
_____
_____

6. Gilman talks about a broader range of women than does Addams. In what way is this so?
_____
_____
_____
_____

Exercise 7: Cartoons as Social Satire

In Chapter 1 you analyzed a political cartoon from the Reconstruction era to distinguish between past and present. Here you will evaluate a cartoon that constitutes social satire. Social satire employs sarcasm, irony, or ridicule to denounce a group's values or way of doing things. The cartoon in Figure 2.2 appeared during the early 1890s in *Harper's New Monthly Magazine*.

ANTE-POSTHUMOUS JEALOUSY.—Drawn by George du Maurier.

"Isn't Emily Firkinson a darling, Reginald?"
"A—ahem—no doubt. I can't say much for her singing, you know!"
"Ah! but she's so good and true—a perfect angel! I've known her all my life! I want you to promise me something, Reginald!"
"Certainly, my love!"
"If I should die young, and you should ever marry again, promise, oh! promise me that it shall be Emily Firkinson!"

FIGURE 2.2 *The Cartoon as Social Satire*

Questions on Figure 2.2

1. What group (class or gender) do you think is being satirized? _____

_____

2. How are the women and the man portrayed? _____

_____

3. What is the significance of the title and the setting of the cartoon? _____

_____

_____

4. See whether you can explain the cartoon's message. (*Hint:* Does it relate to changes discussed in Exercises 5 and 6?) _____

_____

_____

Exercise 8: Gender and Class, Sport and Courtship

We saw in Exercises 5, 6, and 7 how economic change altered the balance of indoor activities for women. In this exercise, we use a primary source to explore the expanded range of outdoor activities available to men and women alike, and we examine how this development influenced dress and courtship patterns.

With the increase in leisure time in late-nineteenth-century America, sporting activity grew sharply. Baseball became the most popular sport, and in the decade following the founding of the National League of Professional Baseball Clubs in 1876 it emerged as a major business enterprise. Baseball appealed primarily to men, but other sports, such as croquet, bicycling, and golf, attracted both sexes. These sports provided new ways for men and women to interact, thus affecting courtship patterns and, in the last two cases, ushering in major changes in women's dress. If a woman was to ride a bicycle comfortably or swing a golf club efficiently, she had to rid herself of constraining undergarments, particularly the corset. By 1900, when the population of the country stood at 76 million, there were over 10 million bicycles. For the most part, golf was reserved for the wealthy, but this group always influenced popular fashions well out of proportion to its numbers.

Figure 2.3, a drawing by Charles Dana Gibson, who produced many sketches for *Life* magazine during the 1890s, shows a man and a woman interacting in a setting very different from the setting portrayed in Figure 2.2. Think about those differences before responding to the questions that follow.

A LITTLE INCIDENT
SHOWING THAT EVEN INANIMATE OBJECTS CAN ENTER INTO THE SPIRIT OF THE GAME

FIGURE 2.3 *1890s Drawing of the "Gibson Girl"*

1. Given what is stated above, would the incident in Figure 2.3 or the incident in Figure 2.2 be more likely to have occurred before the 1890s? Explain. _____
   _____
   _____
   _____
   _____

2. How does the clothing of the principal women in Figures 2.2 and 2.3 differ? How do you explain the difference? _____
   _____
   _____
   _____
   _____

3. The man and the woman in Figure 2.3 are courting. How do you think the changes occurring in the late nineteenth century described above influenced courtship patterns?
   _____
   _____
   _____
   _____
   _____
   _____

4. What is the difference in demeanor of the two principal women in Figures 2.2 and 2.3? How do you explain the difference? Is one woman more traditional in her demeanor than the other? Which one? How do you explain the difference? What answer does the excerpt by Charlotte Perkins Gilman in Exercise 5 suggest? _____
   _____
   _____
   _____

_____

_____

_____

_____

5. Does the woman in Figure 2.3 fit the portrayal of young women of the 1880s described by Jane Addams in Exercise 6? Why or why not? _____

_____

_____

_____

_____

_____

6. The different portrayals of women in Figures 2.2 and 2.3 were made at roughly the same time. Some of the difference may be explained by the fact that the creators of the scenes were two different people. Can you think of one or two other explanations? What explanation do you think Gilman might offer? _____

_____

_____

_____

_____

_____

_____

Advertisements as Historical Documents

Although primitive advertisements existed centuries before the birth of Christianity, scholars usually say that the fifteenth century, when Europeans began to use movable type, or the seventeenth century, when newspapers first carried advertisements, marks the beginning of modern advertising. The first modern advertising agency did not appear until 1869 in the United States. That same year also saw the completion of the transcontinental railroad, a fact that was more than just a coincidence. The development of a national transportation network vastly increased the readership of newspapers and magazines. This growth, in turn, greatly expanded the market for advertising. By the end of the century, agencies not only were placing advertisements but preparing them as well.

Because advertisers try to convince consumers that a product will help them achieve desirable goals, advertisements are a useful source for identifying the prevailing values of a bygone age. One key to assessing the implications of individual advertisements is to identify their intended audience. Usually they are directed toward one or two groups of people rather than toward the population as a whole. Only by examining advertisements aimed at a wide variety of groups can historians draw definitive conclusions about the values of an entire society. Yet analyzing advertisements directed toward one group can be extremely suggestive, especially if that group has substantial influence in a society.

Exercise 9: Advertisements and Attitudes Toward Gender

This exercise asks you to analyze two advertisements. Both of them appeared in the June 1895 issue of *The Chautauquan*, a monthly magazine, and sought to appeal to people who wanted their children to attend a private school. These people constituted a small portion of the adult population, but, because of their above-average wealth and social standing, they wielded considerable influence on contemporary values.

Examine closely the advertisements shown in Figure 2.4. Notice that one school is a boys' school and one is for girls only. Pay particular attention to how this difference influences the advertisements' content and how the contents reflect attitudes toward gender roles in American society at the time. Then answer the questions that follow.

A.

Berkeley
School,

Nos 18 20, 22 and 24 West 44th Street,

New York,

Named to commemorate the work of BISHOP GEORGE BERKELEY, the greatest benefactor of early education in America, was opened in 1880.

"THE OVAL COTTAGE"

In 1891 it took possession of its new building, one of the largest and most beautiful school buildings in the world. The schoolhouse is absolutely fire-proof, is heated by hot water, and all the rooms are supplied with fresh air by a system of enforced ventilation carried on by means of fans.

The full course of the school is eight years, ages 10 to 18 with a preparatory department for little boys, 7 to 9. The school has a staff of twenty-six able masters and assistants (an average of one instructor for every ten pupils), and affords thorough preparation for the leading colleges and scientific schools, two hundred and thirty graduates having been sent to college in fifteen years. Besides an admirable equipment for manual training, the school employs the military drill, using its own armory and gymnasium, measuring 85 by 100 feet, the members being organized into two battalions of three companies each. It has systematic instruction in gymnastics, supplemented by unequalled opportunities for out door exercise, possessing ten acres of playgrounds at Morris Heights, called the Berkeley Oval, fifteen minutes distant by train from 42nd street. Seventeen resident pupils are received in the school building on 44th street, and seventeen more in the new cottage at the Oval. Tuition $250 to $350 per annum. Boarding pupils see JOHN S. WHITE L.L. D., *Head Master.* J. CLARK READ A. M., *Registrar.*

B.

Lasell Seminary for Young Women, Auburndale, Massachusetts, (ten miles from Boston).

Suggests to parents seeking a good school consideration of the following points in its method:

1st. Its special care of the health of growing girls.

Resident nurse supervising work, diet, and exercise; *abundant food* in *good variety* and *well cooked;* early and long sleep; a fine gymnasium furnished by Dr. Sargent, of Harvard; bowling alley and swimming-bath; no regular or foreknown examination, etc.

2d. Its broadly planned course of study.

Boston proximity both necessitates and helps to furnish the best of teachers, including many specialists; with one hundred and twenty pupils, a faculty of thirty. Four years' course; *in some things equal to college work; in others, planned rather for home and womanly life.* Two studies required, and two to be chosen from a list of eight or ten electives. One preparatory year. Special students admitted.

3d. Its home-like air and character.

Training in self-government; limited number (many declined every fall for lack of room); personal oversight in habits, manners, care of person, room, etc.; comforts not stinted.

4th. Its handiwork and other unusual departments.

Pioneer school in scientific teaching of Cooking, Millinery, Dress-cutting, Business Law for Women, Home Sanitation, Swimming.

Regular expense for schol year, $500. For illustrated catalogue address (mentioning THE CHAUTAUQUAN) C. C. Bragdon, Principal.

Jennie June says: "It is the brightest, most home-like and progressive boarding-school I ever saw."

Mary J. Safford, M.D. of Boston, says: "I believe you are honestly trying to *educate and not veneer* young women for life's duties."

FIGURE 2.4 *Advertisements for Children's Private Schools*

Questions on Figure 2.4

1. How do the drawings in the advertisements differ? _____
   _____
   _____

2. How might the difference between the drawing in B and that in A be explained by the fact that Lasell Seminary was exclusively for females and the Berkeley School was for males?
   _____
   _____

3. What are the differences in the advertisements regarding the curriculum and activities offered at the schools? _____
   _____
   _____

4. How do you think these differences are related to gender attitudes? _____
   _____
   _____

5. What other differences in the advertisements could reflect attitudes toward gender roles in America? _____
   _____
   _____

6. When placed in the context of materials in Exercises 5 through 8, what do these advertisements suggest about change and continuity in gender roles in late-nineteenth-century America? _____
   _____
   _____
   _____
   _____
   _____
   _____

Exercise 10: Synthesizing Primary Sources in a Paragraph

Now we ask you to use the material in Exercises 5 through 9 as the basis for a synthesis on change and continuity in the status of middle-class women at the end of the nineteenth century. *Synthesis* is defined as "the combination of separate elements or substances so as to form a whole."[9] Like the history you read in a book, synthesis involves condensing a body of material—attempting to capture its essence rather than its totality.

To help you structure your effort, we set the following ground rules. Your synthesis must be in the form of a single paragraph containing between four and six sentences and written (or typed) on a separate sheet of paper. The paragraph must have a clear topic sentence at the beginning. (A topic sentence states the main idea you seek to communicate.) As you write, make sure that you constantly refer to your topic sentence to see whether it covers what you are saying. If it does not, you must change either the topic sentence or what you are saying.

Pieces of historical evidence have much in common with objects you encounter in your everyday life. Likewise, the way historians assemble data and decipher their meaning requires skills that you can use to solve problems in the present. In addition to interpreting and evaluating primary documents, historians must content with secondary sources, or accounts that they themselves produce. The skills you learned in Chapter 2 will prove of considerable use in Chapter 3, which introduces you to these products of historians' labors.

Notes

[1] J. C. Furnas, *The Americans: A Social History of the United States*, 1587–1914 (New York: Putnam, 1969), 683.

[2] Nat Love, *The Life and Adventures of Nat Love* (New York: Arno Press, 1969), 66–67, 69.

[3] Harry Sinclair Drago, *Great American Cattle Trails* (New York: Bramhall House, 1965), 126–127.

[4] Fanny Gordon to Mrs. Rebecca L. Felton, August 27, 1877, Box 1, Rebecca L. Felton Collection, Georgia Room, University of Georgia Library, Athens, Ga.

[5] George F. Parker, ed., *The Writings and Speeches of Grover Cleveland* (New York: Casell, 1892), 67–68.

[6] Frederic Bancroft, ed., *Speeches, Correspondence and Political Papers of Carl Schurz*, vol. 3 (New York: Putnam, 1913), 494–495.

[7] Charlotte Perkins Gilman, *Women and Economics* (New York: Harper & Row, 1966), 151–155.

[8] Jane Addams, *Twenty Years at Hull House with Autobiographical Notes* (Urbana, Ill.: University of Illinois Press, 1990), 44–45.

[9] Copyright © 1996 by Houghton Mifflin Company. Adapted and reprinted by permission of *The American Heritage Dictionary of the English Language*, Third Edition.

3: The Historian's Work: Secondary Sources

American Expansion During the 1890s

The primary source is raw material for the historian; the secondary source is the product of his or her efforts. The distinction seems obvious, but the boundary between primary and secondary sources can get confusing. In Chapter 2, we defined primary sources as materials created during the period being studied. Typically, **secondary sources** are created after the period being studied. Yet oral histories and written memoirs are primary sources even if they are recorded years after the events recalled. There is one qualification, however: the testifier must have been involved in the events he or she discusses. What about sources that come from the period being studied but that are *not* created by someone actually involved in the events discussed? Such a person may recount the events shortly after they occurred, but only on the basis of testimony from others or of physical evidence from the scene. Should we classify a source by this person as primary or secondary?

This dilemma commonly applies to journalists' accounts. Consider the famous book *The Final Days*, written by *Washington Post* reporters Bob Woodward and Carl Bernstein. Published in 1976, the book came from the period of the Watergate scandals it described, but its authors did not actually participate in those events. They pieced together their story largely from the oral statements of participants, many of whom insisted that their identities not be revealed. We would place *The Final Days* in the category of primary sources because its authors reconstructed events within months, sometimes even days, of their occurrence and on the basis of direct contact with people who participated in them. Some historians would disagree, arguing that the failure to participate directly in or observe the event automatically disqualifies a person from being a primary source. Thus, although we define a secondary source as one created long after the events described and by someone who did not participate in them, others would drop the first qualification.

The distinction between primary and secondary sources becomes even more complex once we realize that some sources qualify as both, depending on how we use them. For example, more than a decade before Henry Kissinger became President Richard Nixon's leading adviser on foreign affairs, he wrote a book on European diplomacy in the aftermath of the Napoleonic Wars. Kissinger based his book on a wide array of documents surviving from the early nineteenth century. To a biographer of Kissinger analyzing Kissinger's attitudes toward international politics, this book is an important primary source. Yet if you took a course on nineteenth-century European diplomacy and found the book on your list of assigned reading, you would be using it as a secondary source.

Books and articles by historians also qualify as primary sources when they are the subject of studies of the evolution of historical thought we refer to such studies as **historiography.** If you wrote a paper on how historians have interpreted late-nineteenth-century American expansion, you would be doing historiography, and your primary sources would be books and articles by historians on that particular topic. But if you read an account by a historian of late-nineteenth-century American expansion to enhance your knowledge and understanding of that topic, you would be using the account as a secondary source.

Historiography can be an engaging and important endeavor, in part because over time historians have offered varying interpretations of the same events. Studying those interpretations can reveal a good deal about the personalities of individual historians as well as the times during which they wrote. Perhaps you already have picked up differences in interpretation between class lectures and your textbook. If so, your discovery may have produced a bit of anxiety. Who is right, you may have asked yourself, my instructor or my textbook author? The question probably has deeper roots than idle curiosity. After all, how are you supposed to answer an examination question if historians interpret events differently? We cannot answer the last question for you, although it is a fair one to ask your instructor. On the question of who is right, however, we can say that, on matters of interpretation, often no one is absolutely right or wrong. Different historians frequently read the same evidence in different ways, and there is no way to prove which view is correct.

Your anxiety may extend beyond concern over your course work. It would be comforting to know that, once you have established the credentials of a historian, you could place trust in his or her account. In truth, the vast bulk of the data presented in works by reputable historians can be relied on as accurate. When you move into the realm of interpretation, however, uncertainty becomes unavoidable.

This fact may bother you, but it hardly makes history unique as a discipline. Think, for example, of the field of medicine. Medicine qualifies as a science, and most people think of scientists as detached pursuers of truth. Yet physicians often disagree with each other. If they did not, there would be no reason to seek a second opinion about an illness or a treatment. Uncertainty pervades most aspects of human life, and more often than not we refuse to let it immobilize us. Although we should read secondary sources with a critical eye, always watching for bias and judgments based on incomplete information, our uncertainty should not prevent us from using these resources to study history.

Much of your reading and verbal communication in everyday life requires you to evaluate secondary sources. Think of articles or statements on television news programs about the past records of political candidates or of similar accounts of what caused a particular problem in the present. Because we do not have time to study primary sources on most of the issues we face, we look to others for assistance. The quality of our decisions often depends on whether we have chosen and evaluated our secondary sources wisely. In short, our skill in this area can be every bit as important as it is in judging primary sources.

The exercises in this chapter will develop your ability to evaluate secondary sources, just as those in Chapter 2 improved your skill in working with primary sources. Two of the exercises involve identifying passages from secondary writings as representative of particular schools and subfields in history. Then you will examine a selection from an important book on American imperialism during the 1890s to see how the historian used evidence to develop an interpretation. This exercise not only will help you to grasp how historians create secondary sources, but also will advance your ability to evaluate such sources critically.

Types of History

One method of categorizing secondary works is by subfield. Historians usually concentrate on particular aspects of the past, each of which has appropriate sources. A historian who decides to write political history will be very interested in election results, voting patterns in a legislature, or the letters of politicians but not so interested in the average age at which women give birth for the first time. A historian studying the changing American family will be very interested in childbirth and marriage statistics and not at all concerned about what politicians did or said. The types of history flow from the types of evidence the author has chosen, and the author in turn chooses types of evidence that fit his or her subject. Some of the different types of history are the following:

> *Political history:* the story of government, political leaders, electoral activities, the making of policy, and the interaction of branches of government
> *Diplomatic history:* the study of the relations between nations, diplomats, and ideas of diplomacy
> *Social history:* the study of ways and customs, family, education, children, demography (population change), and voluntary institutions (such as churches)
> *Cultural history:* the study of language and its uses, the arts and literature, sport, and entertainment
> *Economic history:* the study of how an entire system of production and consumption (or any of its parts) works, and of markets, industry, credit, and working people at all levels of the system

These conventional categories are neither airtight compartments nor are they exhaustive. For example, where does a history of newspapers belong—social, economic, or cultural history? An account of the founding and early years of Stanford University may be political as well as social and cultural history.

Exercise 1: Distinguishing Among Types of History

The following passages are examples of types of history. Write in the space at the end of each passage the type it best represents. Also write a brief explanation of your answer.

A The 1890s saw a burgeoning of sporting activity at the collegiate and even the professional level. In part, this development was an outgrowth of the economy's improved efficiency. With Americans having to spend less time producing the necessities of life, more and more activity could be devoted to other endeavors. Also, the rapid industrialization and bureaucratization of American life sparked concern about physical fitness that drew attention as never before to the positive dimensions of organized sport. Predictably, this concern generated new interest in recreational sport as well.

Type: _____ Explanation: _____
_____

B The 1896 election was a watershed in American history. The outcome ended the balance between the two parties that had existed in national politics over the past twenty years. Bearing the misfortune of holding the White House during the worst depression the nation had ever faced, the Democrats held only the solid South and the plains and mountain states while the Republicans swept the more populous Northeast and Midwest. Of the ethnic groups that previously had voted overwhelmingly Democratic, only the Irish retained their loyalty to the party of Jefferson. Republican domination of national politics would continue with only one interruption until the 1930s, when a depression even worse than that of the 1890s swept the GOP out of power.

Type: _____ Explanation: _____

_____

C Childbearing in America at the turn of the century revealed some interesting patterns. Overall, American families had become small, as women bore fewer and fewer children. The drop-off was not evenly distributed, however; women living on farms and in working-class families in the city gave birth to more children than did urban middle- or upper-class women. The reason for this was partly economic, as farm and urban working-class families often depended upon children to provide labor and income from an early age.

Type: _____ Explanation: _____

_____

Historical Schools

Another way to categorize historians is through their distinctive interpretations of particular events or subfields. Until recently, much writing in American history could be grouped into one of two schools. The first, which we label the **consensus school,** viewed our history in terms of broad continuities over time. Consensus historians believed that Americans agreed on basic ideas about politics and society—they argued over details but concurred on principles. To representatives of this tradition, American history is largely a success story. Although the school's leading practitioners criticize numerous incidents in our past, they generally approve of our nation's society, economy, and politics, and regard them as flexible enough to adapt to new realities without major internal disruption.

The consensus tradition had its roots in the mid-nineteenth century. Then, "amateur" historians—people who did not teach history or receive postgraduate training in the field—promoted the romantic vision of America as unique and special. In their view, our forebears were carrying out a spiritual mission to bring democracy to the world. The consensus school reached its heyday in the 1950s. Since then it has declined in influence, but historians who emphasize the country's pluralism carry forward its legacy today. For pluralisms, American history features interaction among a variety of groups and institutions, and major events grow out of a multiplicity of causes rather than single factors such as economics or ideology. The pluralists' link with the consensus school derives from their view that institutions in the United States, both public and private, have provided a framework within which conflict can be channeled without major social disruption.

The second school, which we call the **Left/Revisionist school,** views our nation's history predominantly as a series of conflicts between groups with different economic interests and stresses the way power and property have been used to repress weaker minorities at home and abroad. Representatives of this school tend to criticize capitalism and support a variety of reform causes. Blossoming shortly after the turn of the century, this school was initially labeled "Progressive" after the 1900–1920 era in which it appeared. Progressive historians flourished through the 1930s but fell into temporary eclipse during 'World War II and its aftermath, when sharp criticism of the United States' past was discouraged. This tradition resurfaced forcefully in the reform climate of the 1960s and often was labeled "New Left" to distinguish it from an older group of communist or socialist writers.

In addition to presenting a sharp critique of capitalism and emphasizing the prevalence of conflict throughout American history, members of the Left/Revisionist school drew new attention to many groups that were left out of conservative-consensus history, including immigrants, women, African-Americans, Native Americans, and the very poor. New Left historians generally portrayed these groups as victims of dominant elites, abused as cheap labor and denied equal treatment in the public arena. These historians also emphasized the role of economic motivation in the nation's politics and foreign policy. Although the New Left did not maintain its momentum in the more conservative trend that arose during the 1970s and 1980s, many of its central ideas, particularly the need to include minority and women's history in textbooks, have enriched every history survey course.

The current generation of historians does not show the dominance of any one or two doctrines. Indeed, a major complaint of older historians is that historical writing today is too fragmented and diverse. Yet ideas from the two schools continue to appear in many of the historical works of recent years.

Exercise 2: Identifying Schools of Interpretation: American Foreign Policy During the 1890s

The historiography of American foreign policy at the end of the nineteenth century is rich in differing opinions on why the United States went to war in 1898 and then expanded its overseas territories. Not all scholarship on these questions fits neatly into the two schools discussed earlier. Although the Left/Revisionist tradition is apparent among historians who emphasize economic motives in American expansion, opposing interpretations do not converge around something identifiable as consensus. In considering the following selections, therefore, we will keep **Left/Revisionist school** as one classification while adding several others:

Psychological-emotional: emphasizes a particular state of mind of a people at a given time

Reactive: views American action as a response to foreign influences

Domestic politics: dwells on public pressures at home on U.S. leaders

Nationalist: exalts the virtue of the United States in its actions abroad

Read the following example, note the "school" it falls into, and read the explanation of why.

. . . [war with Spain might have been avoided] if diplomacy could have been conducted in a vacuum. . . . But the tidal wave of war sentiment in America, especially after the *Maine* report, would not wait. Within the President's own Republican party a group of young jingoes [aggressive patriots] was making a commotion out of all proportion to its numbers.

The cry for blood was not confined to a few bellicose groups. Following the official report on the *Maine*, the masses were on fire for war. . . .

McKinley, an astute politician, was not blind to political realities. If he tried to thwart the popular will, he would jeopardize, perhaps ruin, his chances of reelection in 1900.[1]

School(s) of interpretation: <u>psychological-emotional and domestic politics</u>

Explanation: The passage combines the two interpretations by stressing, on the one hand, the psychological and emotional state of "a group of young jingoes" and "the masses" and, on the other hand, the impact of those groups on President William McKinley ("McKinley . . . was not blind to political realities") because of his political ambition ("reelection in 1900").

Now examine the following five selections and decide which school(s) of thought each reflects. Write your choice(s) in the space provided, and circle the key phrases or sentences that led you to your conclusion.

A. When the United States demanded the withdrawal of Spain from Cuba, it was with the declaration that "The United States hereby disclaims any disposition or intervention to exercise sovereignty, jurisdiction, or control over said island except for the pacification thereof, and asserts its determination, when that is accomplished, to leave the government and control of the island to its people." Never has a pledge made by a nation under such circumstances been more faithfully carried out. The administration of Cuba during the period of American military occupation was a model of its kind. General Leonard Wood, the military governor, and his associates . . . established order, relieved distress, organized hospitals and charitable institutions, undertook extensive public works, reorganized the system of public schools, and put Havana, Santiago, and other cities in a sanitary condition. In a hospital near Havana, Major Walter Reed, a surgeon in the United States army, demonstrated the fact that yellow fever is transmitted by the bite of a mosquito. This discovery was at once put to the test in Havana, and the city was rendered free from yellow fever for the first time in one hundred and forty years.[2]

School(s) of interpretation: _____

B. . . . It is often said that the 1890's, unlike the 1870's, form a "watershed" in American history. The difference between the emotional and intellectual impact of these two depressions [of the 1870's and 1890's] can be measured . . . by reference to a number of singular events that in the 1890's converged with the depression to heighten its impact on the public mind.

First in importance was the Populist movement, the free silver agitation, the heated campaign of 1896. For the first time in our history a depression had created a protest movement strong enough to capture a major party and raise the specter, however unreal, of drastic social convulsion. Second was the maturation and bureaucratization of American business . . . and the development of trusts on a scale sufficient to stir the anxiety that the old order of competitive opportunities was approaching an eclipse. Third . . . was the apparent filling up of the continent and the disappearance of the frontier line. . . . To the mind of the 1890's it seemed that the resource that had engaged the energies of the people for three centuries had been used up. The frightening possibility suggested itself that a serious juncture in the nation's history had come.[3]

School(s) of interpretation: _____

C. International fashions in thought and events on the world scene could have had a decisive influence on men of the establishment. . . . Knowledge of foreign thought affected their ideas about America's world mission and their understanding of Social Darwinism.

Observation of foreign experience suggested to them alternative methods of promoting national prosperity and dealing with social discontent. Above all, the foreign scene provided models for imitation (reference groups and reference idols, in social science jargon). The well-traveled and well-read American could select a position on the colonial issue by identifying it with, on the one hand, [such anti-imperialists as] Bright, Gladstone, Morley, and Richter or, on the other, [imperialists like] Roseberry, Chamberlain, Ferry, Bismarck, or Wilhelm II. Neither the American past nor an assessment of American economic needs nor Social Darwinism nor the domestic political scene offered such guidance.[4]

School(s) of interpretation: _____

D. The primary force producing the war against Spain was the marketplace-expansionist outlook generated by the agricultural majority of the country. . . . However they differed over the means—among themselves, and with their metropolitan counterparts—the form businessmen had never been thinking simply or only about Cuba. Cuba was but the temporary focus and symbol of their general, inclusive drive for overseas economic expansion.[5]

School(s) of interpretation: _____

E. . . . a cultural phenomenon—the renegotiation of male and female roles in the late nineteenth century—helped push the nation into war by fostering a desire for martial challenges—Gendered assumptions about citizenship and political leadership affected first jingoes' and then imperialists' abilities to implement their martial policies. . . . Imperialists wanted to build manly character not only because they were concerned about American men's standing relative to other nations and races but also because they were worried about American men's position vis-a-vis women.[6]

School(s) of interpretation: _____

Secondary Sources in Historical Context

It is possible to explain some of the differing interpretations of historians by looking at the period in which they lived. Current political and intellectual trends frequently influence the way people interpret the past and historians, after all, are just people. Not surprisingly, a school emphasizing the economic motives of elites in American history emerged during the first two decades of the twentieth century, when big business increasingly came under attack in our national politics. Yet America is a pluralistic society, and the historical profession mirrors that quality. So along with reform-minded historians, the early twentieth century produced conservative scholars as well, people who espoused the nationalist interpretation of American history mentioned in Exercise 2.

If personal experiences condition the way historians see the past, must we conclude that all historical writing is colored by the time and place in which it was produced? Those who would answer *yes*—that is, those who believe that all written history is conditioned, if not dictated, by the period in which the historian lives—are **historical relativists.** Others believe that scholars can approach, if never quite reach, objectivity in their writing and are **historical objectivists.**

The only way that we as readers can alert ourselves to a historian's point of view, hidden or overt, is to hone our critical skills: Does the historian's choice of words reveal bias, or is it balanced? Does the selection of primary materials appear one-sided, or is it thorough and appropriate? Does the construction of fact from evidence betray a slant, or is it sensible? Does the argument rest on prejudgment, or is it fully supported by the facts? These are the same kinds of questions we should ask in evaluating the platform of a political candidate, a legal brief, or a business report.

Exercise 3: Evaluating a Secondary Source

Now that you have been introduced to bias, interpretation, and various schools of historical thought, you are ready to try your hand at evaluating a secondary source. The selections that follow[7] are by a distinguished diplomatic historian, Ernest May of Harvard University. In them, May offers an explanation for President McKinley's decision to demand that Spain cede the Philippines to the United States. Each paragraph is lettered. **After each paragraph, write a one-sentence summary of the paragraph's major point**. The questions following the selection require you to identify May's overall argument, or thesis, and to consider the evidence on which he bases that thesis.

A. The President must have recognized at a very early date that he could not simply return to Spain ground that had been occupied by American troops. No voice in the land had spoken except against such a course.... Nearly all evidence filtering back to the White-House pictured Spanish rule as worse in the Philippines than in Cuba.... Hardly a popular magazine in either the United States or England failed to print someone's reminiscence or comment on Spanish iniquity.

Paragraph's major point: _____

_____

B. Nor could he have believed for long that sale or transfer was a feasible alternative. While the war was still in progress, the British and Japanese governments both said that if the United States did not want the islands, they did. The German ambassador in London told [U.S. ambassador to Great Britain John] Hay of Germany's desire for at least a base or coaling station. The New York *Herald* reported on July 3 a rumor that France and Russia had agreed to support Germany if she sought the whole archipelago. For the United States to offer the islands to any one power would surely bring protests, if nothing worse, from the rest. At home, the Germans and Irish would fight transfer to England, while others would oppose sale to anyone else. Moreover, as McKinley later observed, any such transaction might prove "bad business." The Philippines were reputed not only to offer advantageous bases for trade and navigation but also to possess rich resources, including quantities of gold. ...

Paragraph's major point: _____

_____

C. His one real option was to insist on independence for the islands, and he may have postponed [his] final decision partly in order to collect information on the character and disposition of the natives. Early data painted a depressing picture. John Foreman, an Englishman regarded as the foremost expert on the islands, wrote in the July *Contemporary Review*, "The Philippine islands ... would not remain one year peaceful under an independent native government. It is an utter impossibility." McKinley saw this article, for he obtained a copy from his private secretary. ... He may also have read other, similar writings, of which magazines and newspapers were full. At any rate, he saw little to contradict Foreman; hardly anyone claiming firsthand knowledge disputed his conclusions. . . .

Paragraph's major point: _____

_____

D. . . . If doubt lingered in his mind, it was because his thoughts were not really rational alternatives. His advisors talked of what would be wise, statesmanlike, and in the national interest. He did not.

Paragraph's major point: _____

_____

E. In his explanation to the French ambassador of why he could not offer precise armistice terms, the President said, "The American people would not accept it if we did not obtain some advantage from our great victories at Manila and from the sacrifices we have made in sending to the Philippines a large body of troops." When Oscar Straus advised him early in August not to take the islands, "he seemed," Straus noted in his diary, "to fear public opinion would not approve such a course." When McKinley first drafted a final directive to his commissioners, he did not mention information newly come or any other such consideration. He wrote simply, "There is a very general feeling that the United States, whatever it might prefer as to the Philippines, is in a situation where it can not let it go . . . , and it is my judgment that the well-considered opinion of the majority would be that duty requires we should take the archipelago." The sole concern of the President was with the mood and whim of public opinion. . . .

Paragraph's major point: _____

_____

F. In order to [gauge public sentiment] . . . , he arranged a speaking tour that would carry him through Indiana, Illinois, and Iowa, three states whose electoral votes had made the difference between victory and defeat in 1896, and through Nebraska and Missouri, where he had lost narrowly to Bryan. Considered either in terms of the contest for the House of Representatives or the approaching 1900 campaign, these were the areas that mattered. [See Figure 3.1.]

Paragraph's major point: _____

_____

G. In the course of each speech, McKinley said something that could be interpreted as referring to the Philippines. At Tama, Iowa, on October 11, he asserted, "We want to preserve carefully all the old life of the nation,—the dear old life of the nation and our cherished institutions—;" there was scattered clapping. He went on, "but we do not want to shirk a single responsibility that has been put upon us by the results of the war;" and there was great applause. Yet at Arcola, Illinois, on October 15, he won a similar rousing response with these words: "We have had great glory out of the war, and in its settlements we must be guided only by the demands of right and conscience and duty."

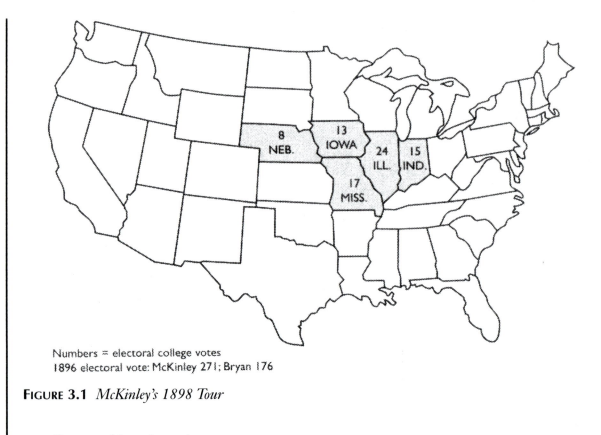

Numbers = electoral college votes
1896 electoral vote: McKinley 271; Bryan 176

FIGURE 3.1 *McKinley's 1898 Tour*

Paragraph's major point: _____

_____

H. He tried imperialism out at Ames, Iowa, from whence had come innumerable petitions to Congress in favor of pacifist causes. He experimented with anti-imperialism in Denison, the home of the state's war-hawk governor, Leslie M. Shaw. On each occasion, a stenographer made careful notes on the intensity and duration of applause. McKinley's own ears presumably registered the more subtle sounds.

Paragraph's major point: _____

_____

I. By the time he had circled to Omaha, Nebraska, and started back through Iowa, the President had found his answer. At the Trans-Mississippi Exposition in Omaha, he asked, "Shall we deny to ourselves what the rest of the world so freely and so justly accords to us?" From the audience came a loud cry of "No!" He went on amid great applause to speak of "a peace whose great gain to civilization is yet unknown and unwritten" and to declare, "The war was not more invited by us than were the questions which are laid at our door by its results. Now as then we will do our duty."

Paragraph's major point: _____

_____

J. . . . After the reception given these words, he virtually ceased to sound the cautious note. . . . The President had heard the voice of the people. There can be no doubt that this was what he had waited for. . . . Earlier, when dealing with the Cuban issue, he had sought to escape public clamor and pursue safe, cautious courses defined by himself and conservative statesmen and businessmen around him. After the crisis that brought on the war, he wanted only to hear the wishes and obey.

Paragraph's major point: _____

_____

The following eight questions include five multiple choice and three short answer. For the multiple-choice questions, circle the letter(s) beside the answer(s) that correctly complete(s) the statement or respond(s) to the question. For the short-answer questions, write your response in the space provided.

1. May's thesis is that McKinley supported annexation of the Philippines
   a. for economic reasons.
   b. because of public opinion.
   c. because he feared that Germany would take over the islands.
   d. because he was a racist.

2. A piece of evidence in paragraph B that could be used to support a thesis other than May's is that
   a. the Germans and Irish in the United States would not tolerate annexation of the Philippines by England.
   b. France and Russia supported German annexation of the islands.
   c. the Philippines supposedly would provide good bases for trade and navigation.
   d. the Spanish treated Filipinos harshly.

3. May presents *direct* evidence to support his thesis for the first time in paragraph
   a. E.
   b. A.
   c. C.
   d. H.

4. Why is it fair to assume that in October 1898 McKinley was *more* concerned about public opinion than he was at the same time during the previous year?
   a. The year 1898 was a congressional election year; 1897 was not.
   b. A presidential election was just around the corner in October 1898.
   c. Public opinion naturally tends to be more emotional after a war has started than before.
   d. The Republican party was weaker in the fall of 1898 than it had been the year before.

5. Why, according to May, did McKinley choose on his speaking tour (paragraphs G–I) to visit states such as Indiana, Illinois, Iowa, Missouri, and Nebraska?
   a. These states all had hotly contested races in the upcoming congressional elections.
   b. McKinley had lived in all these states at one time or another.
   c. All these states were likely to be important in McKinley's bid for reelection in 1900.
   d. Several key U.S. senators were from these states, and McKinley was trying to influence their votes on a peace treaty with Spain by shaping public opinion in their states.

6. Does May believe that McKinley went on a speaking tour to the Midwest and Plains states primarily to gauge public opinion or to shape it? _____

_____On what basis do you reach your conclusion? _____
_____

On what evidence does May reach his conclusion? _____
_____

7. Copy a sentence in which May clearly goes beyond—but does not contradict—the evidence he presents in attributing a motive or a reaction to McKinley during his speaking tour._____
_____
_____

8. Do you think that May draws a reasonable inference from his evidence here? _____ _____ Explain. _____
_____
_____

You are now familiar with some of the ways in which historians interpret the past and some of the critical methods with which you should approach their works. You probably considered Exercise 3 as requiring a meticulous examination of a secondary source, yet there are other steps you could take to evaluate the selection. For example, you could go to the primary sources cited by May and read them to determine whether or not he characterized them accurately and interpreted them wisely. You also could compare his interpretation of McKinley's decision with other secondary sources. Such a comparison might bring to light evidence that May chose not to include. In executing such tasks, you would need first to know your way around the library. Only then could you find the primary and secondary sources you needed. In the next chapter, we take you on a journey through the library to familiarize you with its many resources for the historian.

Notes

[1] Thomas A. Bailey, *A Diplomatic History of the American People*, 6th ed. (New York: Appleton-Century-Crofts, 1958), 460–461.

[2] John Holladay Latane and David W. Wainhouse, *A History of American Foreign Policy*, 2nd ed. (New York: Odyssey Press, 1940), 511.

[3] Richard Hofstadter, *The Paranoid Style in American Politics* (New York: Knopf, 1966), 148–149.

[4] Ernest R. May, *American Imperialism* (New York: Atheneum, 1968), 228–229.

[5] William Appleman Williams, *The Roots of the Modern American Empire* (New York: Random House, 1969), 408, 432.

[6] Kristin L. Hoganson, *Fighting for American Manhood: How Gender Politics Provoked the Spanish-American and Philippine-American Wars* (New Haven: Yale University Press, 1998), 14 and 139.

[7] Excerpt from Ernest R. May, *Imperial Democracy: The Emergence of America as a Great Power*, (Chicago: Imprint Publications, 1991), 253–260.

4: *Finding Evidence: Library Skills*

The Far West and the Metropolis, 1876–1920

The library is the most crucial resource on any college campus. It houses the vast range of materials you will need in your coursework, provides space for individual or group study, and offers basic information on local and regional activities—political, cultural, and recreational—that may occupy your time outside academic pursuits. This resource will remain useful to you, both in the workplace and during leisure time, throughout your adult life. The acquisition of library skills is thus an important part of your college experience.

Such skills are best developed not by reading about them in a textbook but by exploring library holdings. Students may now engage in some of this activity by sitting in front of a computer in their dorm or in a campus computer lab rather than by actually going to the library, as most libraries make available an increasing portion of their holdings to off-site users. This chapter provides a series of exercises designed to take you through the library and show you how to benefit from its offerings. It does so with two different, but interrelated developments in U.S. history: the settlement and economic expansion into the Far West and the rise of the metropolis – a densely populated urban area that marked the arrival of industrialized, commercialized, modern America.

Libraries possess a wide array of primary sources, from published materials such as books, magazines, and newspapers, to unpublished manuscript collections. The greatest library in the world today is the Library of Congress complex in Washington, D.C. There was a time not long ago when every historian of the United States relied on its collections. Today the Jefferson, Madison, and Adams buildings in the heart of official Washington, along with two more distant repositories for films and books, contain over 144 million items, including first editions of the Gutenberg Bible and other rare works, medieval hand written and decorated books, and other treasures. Indeed, the library is one of the world's great treasures. The library is the copyright repository and its cataloguing system is widely adopted all over the world. Because the Copyright Act of 1870 required the library had to have a copy of every copyrighted work, "in 1873 Congress authorized a competition to design plans for the new Library. In 1886, after many proposals and much controversy, Congress authorized construction of a new Library building in the style of the Italian Renaissance . . . The Library of Congress Building opened its doors to the public on November 1, 1897, it was hailed as a glorious national monument."[1]

Your college or university library does not have as much space for materials as the Library of Congress, but there are even limits to its space just as there are limits to your library's space. To save space, and to make materials available to users, all libraries are resorting to electronic media collections. The Library of Congress is scanning its collections and making the results available "digitally." These image versions of books and other materials can be accessed easily, on line. The first of these on line sources is the catalogue. Once upon a time, librarians very carefully typed card catalogue entries for the books and other individually bound additions to the collection. Magazine and journal articles for each year were bound in their own cloth bindings and they too were catalogued. Electronic cataloguing became popular in the 1990s, and with the Web, catalogues from libraries were accessible remotely—you, sitting at your computer can find the catalogues of major research libraries all over the country. That is your first exercise.

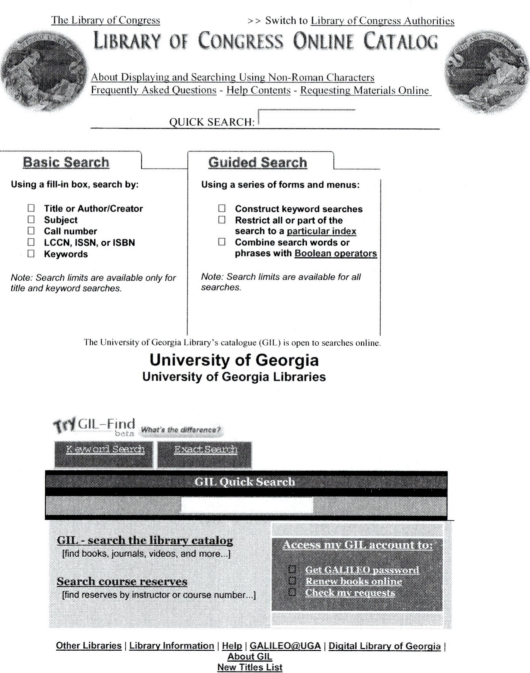

The Library of Congress >> Switch to Library of Congress Authorities

LIBRARY OF CONGRESS ONLINE CATALOG

About Displaying and Searching Using Non-Roman Characters
Frequently Asked Questions - Help Contents - Requesting Materials Online

QUICK SEARCH:

Basic Search

Using a fill-in box, search by:

☐ Title or Author/Creator
☐ Subject
☐ Call number
☐ LCCN, ISSN, or ISBN
☐ Keywords

Note: Search limits are available only for title and keyword searches.

Guided Search

Using a series of forms and menus:

☐ Construct keyword searches
☐ Restrict all or part of the search to a particular index
☐ Combine search words or phrases with Boolean operators

Note: Search limits are available for all searches.

The University of Georgia Library's catalogue (GIL) is open to searches online.

University of Georgia
University of Georgia Libraries

Try GIL–Find beta *What's the difference?*

Keyword Search   Exact Search

GIL Quick Search

GIL - search the library catalog
[find books, journals, videos, and more...]

Search course reserves
[find reserves by instructor or course number...]

Access my GIL account to:

☐ Get GALILEO password
☐ Renew books online
☐ Check my requests

Other Libraries | Library Information | Help | GALILEO@UGA | Digital Library of Georgia |
About GIL
New Titles List

The West

In 1893, at the Chicago World's Fair, historian Frederick Jackson turned read a scholarly paper entitled "In Influence of the Frontier on American History." His thesis was that the vast expanse of relatively cheap western lands for farming made Americans more individualistic, practical, and equal to one another. Historians explored his ideas for the next half century, and have largely discredited them, but the spur for this paper was a report in the Census of 1890 that the frontier no longer existed. The Far West had become so populated that it no longer resembled a frontier.

In fact, by 1890 the trans-Mississippi west was home to many more activities than farming. Vast herds of cattle roamed the grasslands. Copper, silver, and gold mines, along with iron ore and other mining operations, were transforming the landscape. Railroad lines crisscrossed this "new west," enabling ranchers to bring their cattle to market and mine owners to move their ores to smelters and factories in the East. By 1920, oil rigs added to that transformation. Western land was an economic resource making some individuals incredibly rich, the very opposite of Turner's vision of the frontier.

There were losers in this competition for the wealth of the Far West. Farmers, pushed to the edges of low rainfall short grass areas, found themselves between the rock of the dry weather and the hard place of rising haulage and storage costs. Homesteaders responded by creating new kinds of social groups called "Grange" societies. These were voluntary associations of farm families. The Granger movement turned political in the 1870s, seeking aid from state legislatures limiting what farmers had to pay railroads and grain elevator owners. When in the 1890s "People's Party" candidates promised to alleviate the farmers' woes the Granger movement went national.

Plains Indians suffered even more than the family farmers without the possibility of political action to aid their cause. The buffalo herds on which they depended were depleted by drought, competition with range cattle, the germs that sheep and cattle brought with them (to which the buffalo had no immunities) and buffalo hunters' market-driven slaughter of the animals. Federal officials, sometimes in violation of older treaties, attempted to force the Indians off traditional lands and onto "reservations." Some Indians rejected this step, and warfare on the plains erupted.

Exercise 1: Using the Catalogue in a Subject Search

The first step in developing library skills is to learn how to use the catalogue. It is the gateway to all searches. This exercise utilizes the computer-assisted search terminal and the card catalog to help locate books in the stacks or shelving area of the library. The Library of Congress has created a series of indexes to help students find books. One of the categories of this index is "subjects," another is "titles" and another is "authors." Using the catalogue of your library, find a book on each of the following people and events from the Far West. After listing the author and title of each book, enter the "call number" of the book, where it can be located on the shelves of the library (sometimes called the "stacks"). The task is going to get a little harder as you move down the list. Don't be discouraged.

1. A book on the Far West that includes material on cattle drives. _____

2. A book about "Custer's Last Stand." _____

3. A book about "homesteaders." _____

4. A book about the "Comstock Load." _____

The on-line catalogue also lists scholarly journals. These journals feature articles and book reviews by historians. Your next task is to find a journal that focuses on the history of the Far West.

1. What is its title? _____

2. Where on the shelves can bound volumes of it be found? (Just the call number will do.)
_____
_____

A trip to the stacks is now in order. Books will be shelved according to their call numbers. Your library will have maps with the various call number batches, that is, the various subjects, on every floor. Find the E and F sections. These have the bulk of books and journals on American history (although the history of women may be in the H's and the history of law in the K's, and so on.) Find your four books on the Far West on the shelves. Let's get some information on each of them: in particular, what press published them? When (look for the copyright date)? Do they have notes (either footnotes or endnotes)? Do they have bibliographies or bibliographical essays at the end? _____

1. _____
2. _____
3. _____
4. _____

Exercise 2: Using Electronic Sources

Most college libraries now either subscribe to or purchase electronic resources. These include finding aids, e-journals, and electronic (digital) versions of entire books. In addition, some commercial web sites allow you to read portions of printed books. Google has scanned and digitalized many older books, and Amazon allows you to read some of the pages of the books it is selling. If the image of the book says "look inside" you can search for keywords within the book, but the extent of the search is limited.

One of the best e-journal collections available in most libraries is JSTOR. It contains recoverable journal articles from hundreds of scholarly journals. It can be browsed or searched by keywords. "JSTOR is a not–for–profit service that helps scholars, researchers, and students discover, use, and build upon a wide range of content in a trusted digital archive of over one thousand academic journals and other scholarly content. We use information technology and tools to increase productivity and facilitate new forms of scholarship."

One of the journals archived on JSTOR is the *Journal of American History*. It is the journal of the Organization of American Historians. Your next exercise will take you to the JSTOR site in your library to search for articles by keywords. **From Exercise 1 pick four key words. List them below.**

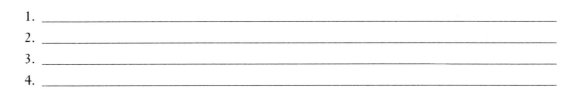

1. _____
2. _____
3. _____
4. _____

For each of these key words, find one article in the journal that includes the key word. On the lines below, give the author, the title of the article (in quotation marks please), the date and volume of the article, and the page numbers of the article (pp. x-y) inclusive.

1. _____
2. _____
3. _____
4. _____

There are other electronic sources in your library. Some of these are called "finding aids" and they are also searchable through key words. An old and reliable finding aid is the America: History and Life bibliography. When it began, it was a series of bound volumes contain every article, dissertation, master's thesis, and book published on any subject in American history each year. Then it became a CD. Now it is entirely on-line and part of the Ebsco family of finding aids. It allows the user to perform an "advanced search" and that is what you will do next. The "fields" for the keywords can be "all text" "title" "author" and "subject" and you can provide up to three keywords of these types to narrow your search. We are going to allow you to select three general keywords having to do with the Plains Indian wars of the period 1875–1900. List them below:

1. _____
2. _____
3. _____
4. _____

Next go to the America: History and Life or some other journal articles database for history available from your library and find the advanced search. Insert the three key words, one per dialog box and choose the field for each of them. Hit the search button. List below three articles that your search found. If you cannot find three articles. Select one or more different key words and search again. When you find three articles, list them by author, article title, and name of the journal in which they appeared, along with the page numbers, the volume number, and the date.

1. _____
2. _____
3. _____

The Urban Age

In the half century after the Civil War's end, the population of the United States increased from 33 million people to 92 million, but the population of the large cities grew even faster—metropolises as they were now called grew 700 percent. By 1910, a largely rural nation had become more than half urban. Cities like New York and Chicago sprawled into the surrounding land. New York (Manhattan) incorporated the four surrounding counties of Richmond, Bronx, Kings (the city of Brooklyn) and Queens into a new city of millions. Cities in the Midwest like Milwaukee and in the South, like Nashville and Atlanta recovered from wartime problems and joined booming West Coast cities like Los Angeles. Railroads knit these cities together, and industry, for example oil in Texas, allowed new cities like Dallas and Houston to grow even faster than the old metropolises.

City growth had environmental effects. The expansion of Chicago and Philadelphia brought former wetlands into the orbit of the city. On the plains and in the South, sprawl turned prairie grasslands and forests into suburbs. Factories, railyards, and stockyards polluted the cities, turning the sky and the new skyscrapers' facades black with soot.

The cities were also magnets to immigrants seeking jobs in factories. Chinese in San Francisco and Italians in New York found instead crowded tenement housing, corrupt city governments, and low pay for long hours. Approximately 30 million of these newcomers, mostly young and male, provided unskilled and semi-skilled labor for industry.

In response to the health and welfare problems the flood of immigrants from abroad and from rural areas brought to the city, city governments began to invest in mass transportation, sewer and drinking water improvements, and health regulations. Replacing gas and coal fuel use with electricity and introducing new forms of building construction also meant a cleaner (if not always a safer) city. This coincided with the rise of the Progressive Movement in politics, a largely urban phenomenon. City government run by "bosses" who did favors in return for graft and votes was the prime target of the reformers, but the bosses did not surrender their power. As one or another might be dislodged by a good government movement, another would take his place.

The city was also a site for cultural improvement. Many cities invested in public education on a scale that dwarfed ante-bellum schooling. High School, once a rarity, became the norm for native and newcomer. Cities were also home to the new universities, larger and more diverse than the pre-Civil War colleges. The universities like Columbia in New York City, the University of Chicago, and the University of Pennsylvania gave graduate degrees, attracted scholars and scientists from all over the world, and carried on research in medicine, physics, chemistry, and the humanities. The urban scene was also the setting for theater, ballet, art museums, and other "high brow" entertainments.

Exercise 3: Using the City Newspaper

One resource easily found in your library is newspapers. Once upon a time every library bought old newspapers on reels of microfilm or on microfiche. Your library might still have these older versions of source storage. More recently, libraries have invested in on-line digitalized collections of newspapers. For example, Pro-Quest has digitalized the Historic New York Times, Wall Street Journal, and Washington (D.C.) Post. The University of Georgia Library has digitalized the Atlanta Constitution back issues. Your first task in this exercise is to find an urban newspaper run (that is, all the back issues) from the year 1900 in your library either physically or on-line. Examining these, what three issues or problems seemed most important to the editor of the paper—what did he put on the front page?

1. _____

2. _____

3. _____

Your next assignment is to find a story about city government. In the space below, give the title of the newspaper story (the headline), the author (if there was a by-line for the story), and the name and date of the newspaper. Then, in your own words, summarize the story. _____
_____

Next, go to the back pages of the newspaper or to any other section with advertisements. What businesses or individuals advertised in your paper?

How are these advertisements different from the ones with which you are familiar? In particular, what seems to be missing from them? What items are advertised that you are unlikely to see advertised today? _____

_____

_____

Reference Works at the Library

While much at the library is on line, you should not ignore some of the golden oldies—the bound reference works. They were the result of painstaking labor by both scholars and librarians, and they cover older materials than may not have been digitalized.

Review the following list and brief description of some useful secondary works in American history. Some of these offer basic data in American history; others are bibliographies. Notice the date of publication of these tools for historical research. **Put the call numbers of the ones in your library in the margin to the left.** More recent editions are acceptable.

Historical Dictionaries and Encyclopedias

American National Biography (New York: Oxford University Press, 1999), eds., John A. Garraty and Mark C. Carnes. This work of 24 volumes includes short biographies of over 18,000 men and women who helped to shape American society, culture, and politics.

An Encyclopedia of World History (Boston: Hougton Mifflin, 1972), ed. William Langer. This is an impressive compilation of facts from ancient times to the modern world. In American history, it is useful primarily in dealing with U.S. involvement in major world events.

Dictionary of American Biography (New York: Charles Scribner's Sons, 1928–1988). This multivolume work provides invaluable information on more than 18,000 important Americans who died before 1970.

Dictionary of American History, 3rd ed. (New York: Thomson Learning, 2003), ed. by Stanley I. Kutler. This is an up-to-date alternative to the *Encyclopedia of American History* cited below.

Notable American Women (Cambridge, Mass.: Harvard University Press, 1971–1980), ed. Edward T. James. Three of the four volumes in this set appeared in 1971 and covered prominent American women who died before 1951. The fourth volume appeared in 1980 and included women who died between January 1, 1951, and December 31, 1975. The volumes include many more women than does the *Dictionary of American Biography*.

Encyclopedia of American History, *7th ed.* (New York: HarperCollins, 1982), eds. Richard B. Morris and Jeffrey B. Morris. You used this source in Exercise 5. It is extremely useful for basic facts in American history.

A note about historical dictionaries and encyclopedias: these sources frequently overlap in the information they provide, yet they always have different emphases. Some are extremely broad in their coverage but provide limited detail on any given topic. Others cover a relatively narrow area but in considerable detail. Sometimes you can get a good idea of the depth of information provided merely by looking at the title and length of the source. The narrower the subject matter covered in the title and the lengthier the source, the more detailed is the information you are likely to find there. In other cases, however, you will need to go to the source itself. Two historical dictionaries of World War I, for example, might be of relatively equal length, but one might place emphasis on military events while another centers on politics and diplomacy. To discover this difference, you might have to read the preface of each source or perhaps even study their contents.

Statistical Compilations

Historical Statistics of the United States, ColonialTimesto 1970 (Washington, D.C.: Bureau of the Census, 1976).

Statistical Abstract of the United States (Washington, D.C.: Government Printing Office, 1878-present). Annual.

Indexes and Bibliographies

American History and Life. This is a wonderful source for periodical literature on American history published since 1954. It includes articles and book reviews. Multiple volumes have appeared annually since 1974, the last being an index to all the others. It is now, as we have seen, on line.

Arts and Humanities Citation Index. This source is especially useful in finding reviews of books.

Book Review Digest. This annual volume has been published continuously since 1905 and provides a particularly good list of the short book reviews that appear within a year of a book's publication.

Book Review Index. Since 1965 this source has listed book reviews, mostly those that have appeared within a year of a book's publication.

Harvard Guide to American History, 2 vols. (Cambridge, Mass.: Harvard University Press, 1974), ed. Frank Friedel and Richard Showman. This is a standard bibliographical guide to American history, but it needs updating.

Humanities Index. Since 1974 this series has provided a monthly index to scholarly American and British journals, including book reviews. Previous titles of this index were *Readers Guide to Periodical Literature Supplement* (1907–1919), *International Index* (1920–1965), and *Social Sciences and Humanities Index* (1965–1974).

Index to Book Reviews in the Humanities. Since 1960 this source has indexed several hundred English-language periodicals, including history titles and book reviews.

Writings in American History. This series began in 1903, skipped 1904 and 1905, but then was published continuously through 1961. Each volume covers books and articles on American history published over the one- or two-year period included in the volume title. Suspended after 1961 for financial reasons, it resumed publication in 1974 with a volume covering articles published on American history during 1973 and 1974. A four-volume set appeared listing articles published between 1962 and 1973.

Comprehensive Guides to Reference Sources in History

Jules R. Benjamin, *A Student's Guide to History*, 4th ed. (New York: St. Martin's Press, 1991). See especially Chapter 4, "How to Research a History Topic;" Appendix A,

"Basic Reference Sources for History Study and Research;" and Appendix B, "Useful Information for the Historian."

Helen J. Poulton, *The Historian's Handbook: A Descriptive Guide to Reference Works* (Norman: University of Oklahoma Press, 1972). Chapter 3, "Guides, Manuals, and Bibliographies of History;" Chapter 4, "Encyclopedias and Dictionaries;" Chapter 8, "Biographical Materials;" and Chapter 11, "Government Publications," are particularly useful.

In what often seems like an attempt to confuse users, some libraries do not place all volumes of reference sources in the same place. If you become frustrated in your search for some of these, ask a librarian for help.

Exercise 4: The Reference Section Revisited

This two-part exercise exposes you to some of the differences among various historical dictionaries and encyclopedias. Your instructor may give you the option of doing Part I or Part II.

Part I

Jane Addams, Carrie Chapman Catt, and Margaret Sanger all contributed mightily to reform in the city during the Progressive era and the 1920s. Choose *one* of these three prominent Americans and look up her biography in the *Dictionary of American Biography, Notable American Women*, and either the *Encyclopaedia Britannica* or the *Encyclopedia Americana*. After reading the biographical sketch, answer the following questions.

1. Outline two things that the articles have in common, besides being about the same individual.

   a._____

   b._____

2. Outline two ways in which the pieces differ. For example, do they differ in the amount of information provided?

   a._____

   b._____

You now have some familiarity with the three reference sources. You might have to complete the two following assignments in a future history class. Which source would you begin with in each case, and why?

3. A term paper on woman's suffragist Carrie Chapman Catt

   Source:_____

   Why?_____

4. A five-page paper providing sketches on a dozen leading politicians during the Progressive era.

   Source:_____

   Why?_____

Part II

Take the *Encyclopedia of American History* and any of the individual city encyclopedias (both New York City and Chicago have their own encyclopedias off the shelf. Open each to the section that discusses the rise of the city. Read through the sections and answer the following questions.

1. Which source helps you more in understanding U.S. cities during the Progressive Era (1900–1920) ?
   Source:_____
   Explain:_____

2. Which source gives you a better sense of the struggle to reform city government during the Progressive Era?
   Source:_____
   Explain:_____

3. Which source gives you a better sense of problems that still faced city reformers at the end of the Progressive Era?
   Source:_____
   Explain:_____

4. Which source gives you a better sense of the politics of the city overall?
   Source:_____
   Explain:_____

5. After doing this assignment, which of the two sources would you consult first if you were looking for basic facts on the city in the first years of the twentieth century?
   Source:_____
   Explain:_____

Evaluating Secondary Sources

The books and articles you have found to do the exercises in this chapter may vary in quality. One way to judge quality is to read the materials yourself. There are certain standards by which historians normally judge each other's work. Although historians often disagree, they generally accept originality and persuasiveness of argument, adequacy of research, and clarity and felicity of writing style as key elements in any evaluation. The significance of the topic covered also is important. A book or article may be outstanding in all the criteria mentioned above and still be a minor contribution to the literature because of its limited scope.

Historians spend a good deal of time evaluating each other's work. Such evaluations can help you not only to judge the quality of secondary sources but also to comprehend the debates that occur among historians. The book review is a major source of historians' evaluations of each other. Exercise 5 asks you to find two book reviews and examine them as instruments of evaluation and debate.

Exercise 5: Locating and Examining Book Reviews

Find two reviews *of one* of the books in the following list. You may go to the stacks to look at bound volumes or go online to find electronic versions. Project Muse, for example, has the online version of *Reviews in American History*, a journal devoted to book reviews. For the most part, reviews appear within two years of a book's publication, so check listings in *America: History and Life* or JSTOR or other like database for the year of publication and the three years following. *Each review you choose must be at least 400 words long, and you should give priority to longer reviews.*

Alfred D. Chandler, Jr., *The Visible Hand: The Managerial Revolution in American Business* (Cambridge: The Belknap Press of Harvard University Press, 1977).
William Cronon, *Nature's Metropolis: Chicago and the Great West*, (New York: W. W. Norton & Company, 1992).
Patricia Nelson Limerick, *The Legacy of Conquest: The Unbroken Past of the American West* (New York: W. W. Norton & Company, 1987).
Robert Wiebe, *The Search for Order, 1877–1920* (New York: Hill and Wang, 1967).

Reviews:

1. _____
2. _____

Go to the journals, find the reviews, and photocopy or print them off. Read each review carefully, highlighting each statement that constitutes a judgment about one of the five categories of evaluation mentioned earlier: originality, persuasiveness, adequacy of research, writing style, and significance. Be prepared to discuss the reviews in class and to hand them in if your instructor desires.

We hope that these exercises have familiarized you with your library. The thought of going there to find something should be a bit less intimidating than before. Now you can enter the library feeling like a veteran detective seeking information that will solve a puzzle, rather than like a person stranded for the first time in a new city. Searching for materials in a library represents an early stage in producing history, however; only after you write about what you found is your task completed.

Note

[1] History of the Library of Congress, www.loc.gov/about/history.html.

5: The "New History": Borrowing from the Social Sciences

America in the Progressive and New Eras, 1890–1929

Historians of the Progressive and New Eras focus on a variety of subjects. They study the reform movements that transformed American politics, the tidal wave of immigration from eastern and southern Europe, the rise of the metropolis, and the introduction of mass produced consumer items and the department stores and mail order houses that brought these goods to people's doorsteps. Historians follow progressive reformers as they exposed corruption, regulated food and drug safety, and gained women the vote. Historians also note how Progressive reformers played a role in reform of domestic life, for example improving post-natal care of children, inventing separate courts for children accused of crimes, and requiring schooling for all children.

Scholars also study the negative developments of that period: the growing divide between the very rich and the very poor; the struggles of working people to gain some control over their lives; the rise of Jim Crow segregation; and the impact of two wars on American life. In the Progressive Era attempts to end child labor in the mines and factories failed; the Klu Klux Klan revived itself; prohibition of alcoholic beverages spurred the rise of organized crime, the sharp increase in cigarette smoking set the stage for sharp increases in lung cancer and other fatal diseases, and a "lost" generation of young men returning from World War I renounced the idealism that had led America into the war.

The Progressives also welcomed the rise of a new kind of knowing. It was called "social science," and it probed the workings of politics, society, culture, and economics. The social sciences made their appearance in the 1870s and 1880s, with economics the first to form a professional organization in 1885, followed in 1902 by anthropology, 1903 by political science, and 1905 by sociology. Political scientists, sociologists, anthropologists, and economists trained in the new graduate departments of universities like Johns Hopkins, Columbia, Wisconsin, and Chicago and published their findings in scholarly journals created for that purpose. Experts in these disciplines found jobs in government and colleges, and they tutored the next generation of social scientists. Although they had different subject matter interests, all of the social sciences focused on method and sought regularities and uniformities, much like the hard sciences of biology and chemistry, rather than the historians' focus on singular events and leading figures' actions. Social scientists moved away from religious explanations and moral judgments toward what they saw as more objective, secular explanations of human behavior. The Social Science Research Council that these social scientists created in 1923 fostered and funded this approach to the study of human behavior.

Many of the social scientists of the Progressive Era were themselves interested in social and political reform. Lester Frank Ward, the first president of the American Sociological Association in 1905, advocated worker's rights, women's equality, and the end of segregation. Edward A. Ross, another sociologist, was not a liberal on racial issues, but strongly supported freedom of expression and academic freedom in the university, investment in urban infrastructure, and legislation to close the gap between the rich and the poor. Economics professor Thorstein Veblen, who may have been the most talented of the social scientists, introduced the term "conspicuous consumption" (the chief occupation of the leisure classes was showing off how much money they had and could spend) and argued for regulation of giant corporations and financial institutions.

Historians not only watched these developments in the social sciences with interest, they began to borrow from the social sciences to analyze historical trends and events. Columbia historian James Harvey Robinson's The New History; Essays Illustrating the Modern Historical Outlook (1912) called on historians to focus on the everyday life of ordinary people, "the vague and comprehensive science of past human affairs." He was also a reformer. "Society is today engaged in a tremendous and unprecedented effort to better itself in manifold ways." Social history contributed to that effort by revealing how to "promote rational progress." Robinson's colleague at Columbia, Charles Beard, used the findings of the economists to rewrite the history of the United States. Beard was a little less starry-eyed and a little more hard-headed than Robinson, but his view of history was similarly influenced by social science ethos. In his high school textbook, History of the United States (1921), he dwelt upon "the social and economic aspects of our history," for these were the material facts that young readers must first master.[1]

In this chapter we will explore the most important topics of the Progressive Era using the tools of the social sciences, and at the same time explore how the social sciences influenced the thought and actions of the Progressives. Each of the social sciences is matched with a corresponding historical topic. First, however, it is necessary to recognize that the social sciences of the Progressive Era were a product of their time, imbued with its enthusiasms and constrained by its prejudices.

The Social Sciences and Race

The 1890s were a heady time for the sciences. New discoveries in physics and chemistry transformed technologies, allowing inventors like Thomas Alva Edison and Charles Westinghouse to transform everyday living. The allure of laboratory science, with its experimental method, and the practical applications of scientific discoveries hinted at a future without poverty, disease, or war. The home of the new science was the university, a place where research in pure and applied science brought prestige to institutions like the Massachusetts Institute of Technology and the California Institute of Technology.

But the underside of the rage for science was a new interest in race. For some, scientific racism supported the theory that there was a ruling race, destined by blood to rule the world. Variously associated with Anglo-Saxon or Teutonic heritage, this race had ingrained characteristics that bred true. Other races, distinguished by color or place of origin, were supposedly inferior in character and intellect to the ruling race. Race mixing was disdained as a form of "mongrelization."

Exercise 1: Science or Prejudice?

At the same time as the sciences were raising the standard of living and offering more precise ways to measure phenomena, the new science of race provided ammunition for those who wanted to restrict or eliminate immigration to the U.S. of peoples from Asia and Southern Europe; for the Eugenics movement to limit reproduction of "inferior" peoples and increase reproduction of "superior" peoples; and in the rigid enforcement of Jim Crow segregation laws in the American South. In the following selections, writers applied what they saw as scientific ideas to defend this notion. They based this on the superior knowledge of the expert.

Your task is to find the hidden prejudices behind the argument. Look for key words or phrases that revealed these prejudices and **underline** them. In the write-on spaces after each passage, **explain** your choices.

A In 1909 Senator Henry Cabot Lodge of Massachusetts, with a Ph. D. in history, explained why the U.S. should restrict immigration to those who could read and write English.

> It is found, in the first place, that the illiteracy test will bear most heavily upon the Italians, Russians, Poles, Hungarians, Greeks, and Asiatics, and very lightly, or not at all, upon English-speaking emigrants, or Germans, Scandinavians, and French. In other words, the races most affected by the illiteracy test are those whose emigration to this country has begun within the last twenty years and swelled rapidly to enormous proportions, races with which the English speaking people have never hitherto assimilated, and who are most alien to the great body of the people of the United States. On the other hand, immigrants from the United Kingdom and of those races which are most closely related to the English-speaking people, and who with the English-speaking people themselves founded the American colonies and built up the United States, are affected but little by the proposed test.[2]

_____

_____

_____

_____

B Edward A. Ross was a progressive social scientist who not only favored restriction of immigration, but supported the Eugenics movement. The idea of insuring racial purity of the ruling race was widely approved by leading Americans. Ross explained himself in his 1920 textbook, The Principles of Sociology.

> In American experience we find certain matters in which the intellectuals saw the truth before the-plain people, and the latter learned to see through their eyes. Such are the upholding of the public credit, the conservation of natural resources, the promotion of scientific research, civil service reform, appreciation of the expert in the public service, efficiency in government, the isolation of contagious diseases, public-health protection, compulsory vaccination, scientific charity, and eugenics. Vision in such matters calls for a fuller knowledge or a wider range of observation than the average uneducated person possesses.[3]

_____

_____

_____

_____

C In 1921 Madison Grant, a Columbia trained lawyer and popularizer of Nordic race theory, linked the ruling race theory to the basis for Jim Crow legislation mandating the separation of the races. He scorned the idea that the "melting pot" in the Americas enabled many peoples to live together and progress.

> What the Melting Pot actually does in practice can be seen in Mexico, where the absorption of the blood of the original Spanish conquerors by the native Indian population has produced the racial mixture which we call Mexican and which is now engaged in demonstrating its incapacity for self-government. The world has seen many such mixtures and the character of a mongrel race is only just beginning to be understood at its true value . . .
>
> It must be borne in mind that the specializations which characterize the higher races are of relatively recent development, are highly unstable and when mixed with generalized or primitive characters tend to disappear. Whether we like to admit it or not, the result of the mixture of two races, in the long run, gives us a race reverting to the more ancient, generalized and lower type. The cross between a white man and an Indian is an Indian; the cross between a white man and a Negro is a Negro; the cross between a white man and a Hindu is a Hindu; and the cross between any of the three European races and a Jew is a Jew.
>
> In the crossing of the blond and brunet elements of a population, the more deeply rooted and ancient dark traits are preponderant or dominant. This is matter of every-day observation and the working of this law of nature is not influenced or affected by democratic institutions or by religious beliefs. Nature cares not for the individual nor how he may be modified by environment. She is concerned only with the perpetuation of the species or type and heredity alone is the medium through which she acts.[4]

Grant's ideas would soon become the racial program of the Nazis in Germany, and fortunately (if ironically), the Nazi abuses of human rights would lead American leaders away from racism and toward a clearer idea of human rights. The United Nations Charter of 1945 and the Civil Rights movement repudiated the fake science of Grant and his comrades.

Political Science and Political Reform

The Progressives worked for political reform at every level of government. In municipalities, in state government, and in national politics they argued for clean government. They sponsored legislation that would recall erring government officials and allow referendums on unpopular measures. By the twentieth century's opening decade, however, they had split into two movements, one branch favoring a return to a perceived past time when individual enterprise was the norm and giant corporate interests did not exist, and the other branch favoring regulation of big business in the name of public interest. Both of these branches of Progressive reformers called on the ideas of political science to support their programs.

Political scientists seek the general principles beneath surface political ideas, movements, events, and systems. The American Political Science Association was formed in 1903 to foster the scientific study of politics, perfectly fitting the aims of Progressive reformers seeking help with their movement. Indeed, the leaders of the new organization were themselves progressives, and had one foot in government (while the other was firmly planted in the universities). Not every APSA president or member believed that politics could be reduced to a science, but all believed that the systematic study of politics could improve governance.

Exercise 2: A Science of Politics

The Progressives were eager to explain themselves in books, articles, and speeches. Can you spot the references to science-like ideas in the passages of political ideologies that follow the paragraphs describing the individual authors? In the lines following each passage, **summarize** in your own words what the author writes about the underlying regularities and uniformities in politics. Hint: look for general statements.

A Emma Goldman was a reformer of a more radical sort than the mainstream Progressive. She was born in Russia and came to New York City in 1885, at the age of 16. She was instrumental in peaceful anarchism (a movement opposed to any kind of ordered society), but, when violent anarchists began throwing bombs during and after World War I, she was deported to Russia. There she saw the evils of Soviet totalitarianism and reported them. She spoke and wrote against the oppression of women, organized religion, and homophobia. She died in Canada, in 1940.

> In politics, naught but quantity counts. In proportion to its increase, however, principles, ideals, justice and uprightness are completely swamped by the array of numbers. In the struggle for supremacy, the various political parties outdo each other in trickery, deceit, cunning, and shady machinations, confident that the one who succeeds is sure to be hailed by the majority as the victor. That is the only god–success.[5]

_____

_____

_____

B Randolph Bourne was a journalist who saw an intimate connection between politics and war. He strongly opposed American entry into World War I, but based his views on political science, not personal opinion. He died in the Spanish Flu epidemic of 1918. He believed in a robust democracy, feared the tyranny of an all-powerful government, and favored isolationism.

> The State is the country acting as a political unit. It is the group acting as a repository of force, determiner of law, arbiter of justice. International politics is a "power politics" because it is a relation of states and that is what states infallibly and calamitously are, huge aggregations of human and industrial force that may be hurled against each other in war.[6]

_____

_____

_____

C Herbert Croly was a New York City editor, publisher, and in his time a public intellectual much respected by other progressives. His <u>New Republic</u> magazine of opinion is still must reading for many intellectuals. In <u>The Promise of American Life</u> (1909), he espoused the "new nationalism" of Theodore Roosevelt and others in the Progressive Party, calling on government to help ordinary citizens by regulating trusts and other powerful private institutions and by helping labor unions. Here he writes about Progressive reform of state politics.

> The chief executive, when supported by public opinion, would become a veritable "Boss"; and he would inevitably be the sworn enemy of unofficial "Bosses" who now dominate local politics. He would have the power to purify American local politics, and this power he would be obliged to use. The logic of his whole position would convert him into an enemy of the machine, in so far as the machine was using any governmental function for private, special, or partisan purposes. The real "Boss" would destroy the sham "Bosses"; and no other means, as yet suggested, will, I believe, be sufficient to accomplish such a result. After the creation of such

a system of local government the power of the professional politician would not last a year longer than the people wanted it to last. The governor would control the distribution of all those fruits of the administrative and legislative system upon which the machine has lived. There could be no trafficking in offices, in public contracts, or in legislation; and the man who wished to serve the state unofficially would have to do so from disinterested motives. Moreover, the professional politician could not only be destroyed, but he would not be needed.[7]

Exercise 3: Historians and Political Scientists

Historians and political scientists view these reform movements and reformers in different ways. The passages that follow discuss the rise of the U.S. national government. Your job is to determine which of the authors are historians and which are political scientists. In the write-on lines following each passage, **indicate** your choice and then **explain** the reason for your choice. As usual feel free to underline tell-tale words, phrases, and/or sentences in the passage.

A Over the following pages, the modern American state will be traced to its origins in the unique developmental challenge that conditioned the rise of our modern bureaucratic apparatus. The distinguishing features of this state will be found in the specific forms new administrative institutions took, in the special place they claimed in the government as a whole, and in the peculiar problems officials faced in reestablishing a semblance of governmental order and political authority in their presence. The path taken in modern American institutional development has now fully eclipsed the sense of statelessness that so clearly marked our early politics, but that past was not without consequence for our present difficulties. Its impact is uncovered in the political and institutional struggles that attended the formation of the state in which we now live.[8]

B By the closing years of the nineteenth century, four approaches to governmental organization were available to Americans. One was that of majoritarian democracy, inherited from the Jacksonians and still robust despite its failures and critics. A second was the application of antislavery moral precepts; although these principles addressed many late nineteenth-century problems either ambiguously or not at all, they did provide guidance for some problems, and former antislavery advocates who found themselves in positions of power after the war were eager to implement them. A third approach, generated by reformers and intellectuals who were aware of the inadequacies of both majoritarian democracy and antislavery morality, was the study of history to identify the social preconditions of moral government; once those preconditions were adequately understood, reformers hoped to reestablish them and thereby restore morality to government. The fourth approach, also generated by those dissatisfied with the first two, allocated narrowly defined problems to various institutions, each of which was to resolve those problems by expert analysis and categorization of the facts.[9]

C The advance of the policy state is a narrative of organizational evolution and bureaucratic entrepreneurship. Operating within the rigid confines of the American institutional order – the primacy of elected officials, the constraints of American political culture, and the dominance of parties – administrative leaders in the USDA [U.S. Department of Agriculture] and the Post Office Department slowly carved out pockets of limited discretion by starting small experimental programs. By nurturing local constituencies and by using their multiple network affiliations to build broad support coalitions among professionals, agrarians, women's groups, moral crusaders, and congressional and partisan elites, they won for their young programs both political currency and administrative legitimacy. Fledgling experiments with dubious survival prospects at the turn of the century became, by the close of the 1920s, established policies. At almost every step in the development of these programs, the institutional authorities of the American order – Congress, the president, the parties, the courts, and organized interests – assented to greater and greater administrative innovation. Through reputation building, federal agencies won the capacity to innovate. In American political development, bureaucratic autonomy was not captured but earned.[10]

D Some states did regulate various forms of personal morality, but only on very rare occasions before the Civil War did Congress pass moral legislation. That changed after the war because the Christian lobby convinced the federal government to accept a far greater role in regulating moral behavior. The story of the lobby's campaigns in Congress and the subsequent debates over the bills they presented thus forms part of a larger story, that of the reconstruction of the American state in the years between the Civil War and World War I. Thomas R. Pegram makes the case that Prohibition was part of the expansion of the State, and Morton Keller shows how various campaigns to regulate moral behavior helped expand governmental power. Keller's important work, in fact, describes the old polity much as it is here. Most scholars, however, have focused on the role of liberal and economic regulation in expanding the size and functions of government, not moral reform. Giving appropriate attention to the role played by conservative Christians adds complexity to the historical narrative of the creation of the twentieth-century state.[11]

Sociology, Immigration, and the Rise of the City

Along with war and economic depression, immigration is a subject of continuing concern to American leaders and ordinary Americans. At no time was immigration seen as a more pressing issue than in the Progressive and New Eras. Then intellectuals and politicians tried to understand the impact on America of relatively open doors to those who wanted to relocate to the United States. This effort, like the application of social science to race, was affected by the interests and perceptions of the time. In Immigration (1918), for example, New York University sociologist Henry Fairchild, writing in the city of initial destination of most European immigrants, announced that he sought "to regard immigration, not simply as an 'American problem,' but as a sociological phenomenon of world-wide significance." He went on to assert a problematic relationship between "immigration and strikes, child labor, and education." Immigration of poor people from Eastern and Southern Europe and from Asia was the cause of social evils in Fairchild's mind. "Modern immigrants have but slight commerce with anything that is calculated to inculcate American ideas or contribute to any real American influence," he declared. By American, Fairchild meant attitudes, ideas, and behaviors in the U.S. that pre-dated the post-Civil War surge in immigration from areas other than Northern and Western Europe. The claim was problematic cultural history, but Fairchild was not a cultural historian. He depended instead on the social statistics that filled his pages.[12]

The rise of sociological science and the flood of new immigration were co-incident. Indeed, it may be said that the latter gave special impetus to the development of the former. Sociologists asked whether immigrants could be assimilated in the "melting pot," a metaphor for the creation of one people out of many. They asked also if immigrant success depended on individual traits of thriftiness, industry, and talent. They compared the immigrant family to the American family, generalizing in the manner of social science about the loss of ethnic uniqueness as the generation that came to the U.S. passed away and the generations born in the U.S. grew to adulthood. In his classic study <u>The City</u> (1925), for instance, University of Chicago sociologist Robert Parks asserted that the first generation of immigrants refused to turn to public assistance, did not contribute to the crime wave of the 1920s, and learned to read English because they wanted to know about their new land. Park's sociology was the opposite of Fairchild's because Park began with different assumptions. He did not see immigration as a problem. He saw assimilation as a process that took place in the city, a natural process similar to internal migration patterns.[13]

The differences in views of Fairchild and Park suggest that the new "science" of sociology was as subject to bias as any human intellectual endeavor. That is, individuals in the discipline could differ just as much in perspective as could other members of American society during the Progressive and New Eras.

Exercise 4: The Influence of Ideas on Politics

The 1920s saw a sharp break with the largely unrestricted immigration policy of the federal government in the past. In your textbook or on the Internet, look up the immigration act passed by Congress in 1924. After reading a description of it, identify below whether the ideas expressed by Park or Fairchild were the most influential in its basic approach. Explain your choice.

_____
_____
_____
_____

Exercise 5: Reading the Data of Progressive Era Immigration

Some sociologists studying immigration relied on data–numerical and categorical. Examples of the former were numbers of immigrants by years. Examples of the latter were the home countries of the immigrants. Other sociologists from the Progressive Era preferred to theorize. The key elements in their work were sets of ordered ideas. The following selections include both approaches. After each, **answer** the questions in the spaces provided.

A Another circumstance which affects the ability of the country to assimilate immigrants, and in which there has been a marked change during the history of immigration, is the ratio of men to land, upon which much emphasis has already been laid. As the amount of unappropriated and unsettled land diminishes in any country, the need of new settlers also diminishes, while the difficulty of assimilation and the possible evils resulting from foreign population proportionally increase. In the case of the United States the first and simplest comparison to make is that between immigration and the total territory of the nation. In this, as in the subsequent comparisons, it will be desirable to leave Alaska out of consideration. The enormous extent of that inhospitable region, to which practically none of our immigrants ever find their way, if included in the reckoning, would simply confuse the issue. The gross area of the United States, exclusive of Alaska and Hawaii, at the time of the different censuses, has been as follows: 1790 and 1800, 827,844 square miles; 1810, 1,999,775 square miles; 1820, 2,059,043 square miles; 1830 and 1840, the same; 1850, 2,980,959 square miles; 1860 down to the present, 3,025,600 square miles. Estimating the immigration before 1820 at 10,000 per year, and using the official figures after that date, we find that the immigration [for 1870s was 2.8 million newcomers, for the 1880s was 5.2 million, for the 1890s was 3.7 million and for the decade 1901–1910, 8.8 million] . . . Combining these two sets of figures, it appears that for each immigrant coming to this country during the decades specified, there was at the close of the decade the following number of square miles of territory in the United States . . . In 1860 there were, as nearly as can be estimated, 939,173,057 acres of land lying unappropriated and unreserved in the public domain. In 1906 there were 424,202,732 acres of such land, representing the leavings, after all the best land had been chosen. In other words, for each immigrant entering the country during the decade ending 1860 there were 374 acres in the public domain, at least half of it extremely valuable farm land. In 1906, for each immigrant entering during the previous ten years, there were 68.9 acres, almost wholly arid and worthless.[14]

1. Give an example of numerical data from this passage. _____
2. Give an example of categorical data from this passage._____
3. What is the key mathematical term in this passage? _____
4. What are the two sets of figures the author compares? _____
5. In your own words, what conclusion does the author reach from these calculations? _____
6. In what kind of place might the immigrants have decided to live that would make the author's analysis misleading? _____

_____

_____

B If we take up, one by one, the forms of union that are mighty and spreading in these days, we can see that each of them owes its existence to something else than the charm of like for like. It is a commonplace of history that the unceasing agglomeration of communities has never been due to the mutual attraction of peoples, but always to conquest or to combination for defence. Not sentiment, but invariably force or the dread of force, has called into being that most extensive of cooperations, the State. Again, certain types of voluntary association that thrive mightily in our time, the industrial corporation and the labor union, are often cited as the work of the "spirit of association." But a moment's consideration shows that these unions testify to interlacing interests, rather than to the sociable instinct.

Or take that wonder of our age, the growth of cities. The modern commercial or industrial city, with its lack of neighborliness, its mutual indifference, its mingling without fellowship and its contact without intercourse, its absence of communal opinion, its machinal charities, its vicarious philanthropy, its dismal contrasts of wealth and poverty, its wolfish struggle for personal success, its crimes, frauds, exploitations, and parasitism—surely this strange agglomeration is the work of the economic man, not the social man![15]

1. According to the author, what factors motivate human beings? _____
2. What function or functions do cities serve? _____
3. What evidence does the author use to substantiate these conclusions? _____

_____

4. Are these conclusions limited to a particular time and place or are they universal? Explain. _____

_____

_____

5. What is the hidden bias of this author, in your opinion? _____

_____

6. Would the arrival of a technology like the telephone change the analysis? Why or why not? _____

_____

Economics and the New Consumer

In 1924, Macy's department store in the Herald Square section of downtown New York City became the biggest retail vender in the world. It occupied an entire city block and it offered clothing, furniture, dishware, and just about everything any shopper could want. For the emphasis was on shopping. The store advertised its wares, its sales, and its customer service in the city's many newspapers. It was truly a palace of consumerism. And it was not alone. Marshall Fields in Chicago, Wannamaker in Philadelphia, Hudson's in Detroit and their clones in all the major cities were elegant examples of the post-World War I prosperity.

What urban mansions were to the magnates of the Gilded Age, department stores were to the middle classes. Lured in by elegant window displays and greeted by doormen in the store's gold-braided livery, shoppers could meander along wide aisles of merchandise made in America and imported from all over the world. Sales men and women courteously answered questions, allowed the shoppers to handle the goods, or pointed out changing rooms where clothing could be "tried on." A restaurant served the hungry shopper full meals at bargain prices. Customers could "lay away" their purchases on easy credit terms or simply enjoy shopping and leave empty handed.

Beneath the spotless surface of the great halls of consumer palaces, a furnace of activity roared. In the Progressive Era, America became an industrial giant second to none in the world.

In the 1890s and early 1900s, immigration averaged over 500,000 newcomers a year, totaling more than twenty million in the forty year period 1880 to 1920. Stepping off the rudely appointed ships, they seemed the embodiment of Emma Lazarus's "huddled masses, yearning to breathe free." Most immigrants came to the cities. By 1900 four-fifths of Chicago residents were foreign born. African Americans had moved in large numbers from the rural south to New York City and Chicago, as well as into former border state cities like Cincinnati, St. Louis, and Baltimore. From 1860 to 1900 rural population doubled; the cities' population increased sevenfold. By 1900 one-third of America lived in its cities.

Cities were more than just densely packed warehouses of people. They flaunted their size vertically and horizontally. Innovations in construction like the all steel frame and the electric elevator enabled builders to invent the skyscraper, "a soaring thing, rising in sheer exultation" according to one turn of the century architect. From the top floor of these twenty-plus story towers one could see how the cities' "suburbs" sprawled into the countryside.

The city boasted huge manufacturing plants as well. Nothing so embodied the material ambition of the nation as its factories. Carnegie's Homestead Steel Works on the outskirts of Pittsburgh employed over 7000 workers in mills and furnace works. The new wealth from manufacturing spawned a new class of super rich–the number of millionaires grew to 4000 from perhaps 300 over the years from 1860 to the 1890s. Some fortunes made in speculation were lost in the collapse of 1893, but men like John D. Rockefeller of the Standard Oil Company and Andrew Carnegie, whose holdings became U.S. Steel, did not fear recession.

Their companies were octopi, controlling every step of the manufacturing and distribution process. With the aid of bankers like J.P. Morgan, the industrial giants built financial empires large enough to match their industrial capacities.

The corporation had become the preferred legal shield for giant business ventures. And they too grew larger. Between 1897 and 1904, 4,227 firms merged to form 257 corporations. By 1904, 318 companies controlled about 40 percent of the nation's manufacturing output. A single firm produced over half the output in 78 industries. At the top of these pyramids of industry was the trust, holding companies that enabled the tobacco, sugar, oil, steel, and other industries to reduce competition and control the labor market. Against such "combinations" that restrained free trade Congress passed the Sherman Antitrust act of 1890, but the law had to be tested in court.

The other side of the story of bigness with its accumulation of wealth in a few hands was labor unrest and poverty on a hitherto unimagined scale. Economic progress rested upon cheap labor. To increase workplace safety and gain higher wages and shorter hours, workers organized, but the companies had enough clout with local and state government, and enough wealth, to beat down the unions. The Homestead Strike of 1892 and the Pullman strike of 1894 were proofs that the state had to intervene as broker or conciliator if labor and capital were to avoid all out war. When the federal courts applied the Sherman Act to labor unions, Congress stepped in with the Clayton Antitrust Act of 1914, but the federal courts still barred unions from engaging in a wide variety of collective actions against employers. Federal courts also upon injunctions against unions when railroad, steel, and coal company lawyers convinced the courts that the strike injured the public good. As it happened, many of the federal judges had worked for the same business enterprises as now came before the court seeking the injunction.

Under President Theodore Roosevelt, the federal government joined the state governments in economic reform efforts. His "Square Deal" included regulation of food and drugs, rail freight rates, and monopolistic industrial combinations. He was directly responsible for the National Park Service and National Park system to set aside wilderness areas and conserve national resources. Although he was friendly to unions, he did seek legislation to protect labor organizations. He did, however, support state regulation of health and safety in the workplace.

Exercise 6: The Muckrakers

Roosevelt had mixed feelings about journalistic exposés of the worst industrial abuses. As he said in a 1908 Washington D.C. speech, "There are in the body politic, economic and social, many and grave evils, and there is urgent necessity for the sternest war upon them. There should be relentless exposure of and attack upon every evil man, whether politician or business man, every evil practice, whether in politics, business, or social life. I hail as a benefactor every writer or speaker, every man who, on the platform or in a book, magazine, or newspaper, with merciless severity makes such attack, provided always that he in his turn remembers that the attack is of use only if it is absolutely truthful." Were they truthful, or did they exaggerate for effect and for sales of their copy? In some of the first and finest examples of investigative journalism, reporters like Ida Tarbell and Ray Stannard Baker and writers like Frank Norris and Upton Sinclair seemed to have it in for the rich. Though not themselves radicals who condemned the entire system of capitalism, they found their motives fully within the Progressive ideology. They believed that it was only necessary to find and reveal all the facts for the American system to reform itself. **Answer** the questions that follow each of the selections.

A Ida Tarbell was an unusual woman for her times. Born in poverty, she worked her way through Allegheny College and in 1876 began her career as a teacher of science and a journalist. Her history of the Standard Oil Company became an instant classic in 1904, the year it was published. It is still in print. The founder of the company, John D. Rockefeller, was one of the most successful businessmen of his time, and one of the richest.

Although Mr. Rockefeller was everywhere, and heard everything in these days, he rarely talked. "I remember well how little he said," one of the most aggressively independent of the Titusville refiners told the writer [Tarbell]. "One day several of us met at the office of one of the refiners, who, I felt pretty sure, was being persuaded to go into the scheme which they were talking up. Everybody talked except Mr. Rockefeller. He sat in a rocking-chair, softly swinging back and forth, his hands over his face. I got pretty excited when I saw how those South Improvement men were pulling the wool over our men's eyes, and making them believe we were all going to the dogs if there wasn't an immediate combination to put up the price of refined and prevent new people coming into the business, and I made a speech which, I guess, was pretty warlike. Well, right in the middle of it John Rockefeller stopped rocking and took down his hands and looked at me. You never saw such eyes. He took me all in, saw just how much fight he could expect from me, and I knew it, and then up went his hands and back and forth went his chair.'[16]

1. What kind of evidence did Tarbell use for this account?_____

2. What impression did the anecdote leave on you?_____

3. Do you find any evidence of bias in her account?_____

4. What technique did she employ to persuade you that the company was acting in the wrong? _____

_____

B Ray Stannard Baker's 1900 <u>Our New Prosperity</u> was an eye-opening attack on the new wealth. Unlike Tarbell, whose views were expressed through her selection of stories and facts, Baker let his own opinions show. Like Tarbell, Baker was a college graduate, but law rather than science attracted him, and then the bustling world of Chicago newspapers. He died in 1946, the same year as Tarbell. **Answer** the questions following the selection.

It is curious and wonderful to see how exactly the industries of the world tread in lock-step, and how the man of the soil, the farmer, towers huge and powerful at the head of the line. When his tread is slow and heavy, the iron master, the trans-porter, the miner, the manufacturer, must also tread slowly—and depression and hard times are abroad in the land. But when the man of the soil increases his speed, those behind him move more rapidly; for he represents the world's primary need—food. Indeed, this farmer is a wonderful and a powerful force in the United States. There are upwards of 8,500,000 of him as against 5,000,000 man-ufacturing workers and only 368,000 mining producers. Much is heard of the immensity of America's manufacturing industries, and yet the farmer has an invested capital of nearly three times that of the manufacturer, and more than twelve times that of the miner, although the manufacturer does produce a much greater value of commodities per capita.[17]

1. What comparison does Baker make between the farmers of America and the manufacturers?

_____

_____

2. What point is he trying to make with the comparison? _____

3. Do you find any bias in the selection? If so, what is it? _____

_____

The emergence of these social sciences greatly changed the course of American life. Through the institution of departments dedicated to each of these fields, college graduates took courses in these disciplines. Those who enjoyed what the classes offered majored in the subject taking its approaches to knowledge with them as they entered the work-world or taught it themselves as teachers or professors. Some of the best of these men, and the most courageous and dedicated of the women who fought sexism at every turn, then dedicated themselves to the Progressive movement. But, their contribution did not end there. We live today in the academic houses these social scientists built.

For historians, the contribution is no less important for the way we study the past. None of the histories written at present or in the future can claim to be uninfluenced by the work or social scientists for good or ill. Sociology, anthropology, economics, and political science all exert a profound impact on how we view the societies, cultures, economies, and politics of the past. With this brief introduction to these disciplines and some exercises to go with them, we hope you have gained some understanding of this impact on the reading and writing of history.

Notes

[1] James Harvey Robinson, *The New History* (New York: Walden, 1912), 1, 23, 24; Charles Beard and Mary Beard, *The History of the United States* (New York: Macmillan, 1921), vi.

[2] Henry Cabor Lodge, Speech on the Immigration Act of 1909, *Speeches and Addresses, 1884–1909* (Boston: Houghton, Mifflin, 1909), 247.

[3] Edward A. Ross, *Principles of Sociology* (New York: Century, 1920), 691.

[4] Madison Grant, *The Passing of the Great Race* (New York: Scribners, 1921), 18.

[5] Emma Goldman, *Anarchism and Other Essays* (New York: Mother Earth, 1910), 75

[6] Randolph Bourne, "The State" [1918] in Bourne, *Untimely Papers* (New York: Huebsch, 1919), 67.

[7] Herbert Croly, *The Promise of American Life* (New York: Macmillan, 1909), 340.

[8] Stephen Skowronek, *Building a New American State: The Expansion of National Administrative Capacities, 1877–1920* (New York: Cambridge University Press, 1982, 1995), 5.

[9] William E. Nelson, *The Roots of American Bureaucracy, 1830–1900* (Cambridge: Harvard University Press, 1982), 113.

[10] Daniel P. Carpenter, *The Forging of Bureaucratic Autonomy: Reputations, Networks, and Policy Innovation in Executive Agencies, 1862–1928* (Princeton: Princeton University Press, 2001), 6.

[11] Gaines M. Foster, *Moral Reconstruction: Christian Lobbyists and the Federal Legislation of Morality, 1865–1920* (Chapel Hill: University of North Carolina Press, 2002), 6.

[12] Henry Pratt Fairchild, *Immigration* (1918), iii, viii, 375.

[13] Robert E. Park, *The City* (Chicago: University of Chicago Press, 1925), 25.

[14] Fairchild, *Immigration*, 370–371.

[15] Edward A. Ross, *Social Control* (1915), 18–19.

[16] Ida M. Tarbell, *The History of Standard Oil* (New York: McClure, 1904), 1:104–105.

[17] Ray Stannard Baker, *Our New Prosperity* (New York: Doubleday, 1900), 22.

6: Narrative and Exposition: Telling the Story

The Great Depression

Narrative, according to one dictionary, is "an orderly, continuous account of an event or series of events." **Exposition** is "an explanation" of or "commentary" on an event, series of events, or issue. Most historical writing combines the two: it both tells a story and explains events.

Writing can be fun, but it is nearly always hard work. You cannot avoid the latter, but this chapter offers some guidelines and exercises that, along with the analytical skills you have already learned in this book, will improve the final product of your efforts. Because the rest of this volume includes substantial writing assignments, it is critical that you develop basic writing skills here.

Making Your Point

A historical essay must have an identifiable beginning, middle, and end. The beginning, or *introduction,* should tell the reader what the essay is about. In a short essay of the kind you would write for an examination, the introduction should be no more than one short paragraph. In a longer essay, such as one you might write as a term paper in an upper-level class, the introduction might be a page or slightly longer. In addition to informing readers, the ideal introduction will engage them, enticing them to read on.

The middle, or *body,* of the essay should continue to engage readers, but primarily it develops the major theme. A theme is the writer's argument or interpretation of an event. In an essay on the origins of the Great Depression, for example, the theme would explain why that event occurred. If the essay author subscribed to the monetarist interpretation, he or she would center the theme on the ill-advised policies of the Federal Reserve Board. The essay's body contains both descriptive and explanatory detail; thus it is normally several times as long as each of the other sections.

The end, or *conclusion*, pulls together the material in the body. In some cases, it merely summarizes key points made in the body; in other cases, it goes beyond anything stated explicitly in the body to develop the full implications of the material covered. Although the conclusion should be much shorter than the body, it is not as restricted in length as the introduction.

One thing common to beginnings, middles, and ends is that they are divided into paragraphs. Paragraphs contain the basic units of thought in an essay and carry the reader forward in a logical sequence from one point to the next. In turn, the central organizing device in a paragraph is the *topic sentence*, which states the paragraph's main idea. Sometimes the topic sentence offers a generalization that takes two or even several paragraphs to discuss. The third paragraph in this chapter, for instance, begins with a topic sentence about essays that serves three paragraphs. We could have combined the third, fourth, and fifth paragraphs into one, but we thought that dividing up the material on the beginnings, middles, and ends of essays would help you understand the material more easily.

Our choice demonstrates the fact that writers possess a good deal of freedom within broad guidelines. Topic sentences usually cover one paragraph and come at the beginning of paragraphs, but there are exceptions. We prefer to keep our paragraphs from a quarter to a third of a page in length, long enough to develop a thought but not so long as to tire or confuse the reader. Yet some paragraphs in this workbook are shorter than that, and others are longer. Furthermore, when we write for an audience of fellow professional historians, we use somewhat different rules than we do here. Guidelines are not hard and fast: sometimes they are broken or adapted to different circumstances. Nonetheless, you need to keep them in mind and remember that the fundamental purpose of writing is to communicate with your audience.

The first four exercises in this chapter give you some practice in analyzing paragraphs. They will help you to distinguish among paragraphs that appear at the beginning, middle, or end of narratives; to identify information that does or does not fit together; to grasp the conclusions that may be drawn from a narrative; and to spot qualifiers, or statements that limit generalizations. By the end of the chapter, you will be ready to write an essay that combines narration and exposition.

Exercise 1: Beginnings, Middles, and Ends

The following excerpts from a book by a distinguished historian are chosen to help you learn about narrative. Each comes from the introduction, the body, or the conclusion of a book on the Depression and the New Deal. Comparing them reveals some of the differences between beginnings, middles, and ends, as well as some of the characteristics of good historical writing.

A The following excerpt is the first paragraph in *The Crisis of the Old Order, 1919–1933*, by Arthur M. Schlesinger, Jr. The book focuses on American politics from the end of World War I to Franklin D. Roosevelt's assumption of the presidency in March 1933. **Read** the passage and **answer** the questions that follow.

> The White House, midnight, Friday, March 3, 1933. Across the country the banks of the nation had gradually shuttered their windows and locked their doors. The very machinery of the American economy seemed to be coming to a stop. The rich and fertile nation, overflowing with natural wealth in its fields and forests and mines, equipped with unsurpassed technology, endowed with boundless resources in its men and women, lay stricken.

"We are at the end of our rope," the weary President at last said, as the striking clock announced the day of his retirement. "There is nothing more we can do."[1]

1. Why do you suppose Schlesinger opens with a scene from 1933, chronologically the termination point of the book? _____

_____

2. The topic sentence of the paragraph is the third sentence, not the first. Why do you think Schlesinger chose to place that sentence third rather than first? _____

_____

_____

3. Do you find the paragraph engaging? Why or why not? _____

_____

4. What role does the quotation at the end of the paragraph play? _____

_____

5. What effect does Schlesinger seek by referring to Herbert Hoover as the "President" rather than using his name? _____

_____

6. What qualities does the paragraph possess that mark it as a beginning? _____

_____

B The next paragraph is from the middle of Schlesinger's book. **Read** it and **answer** the questions that follow.

At the breadlines and soup kitchens, hours of waiting would produce a bowl of mush, often without milk or sugar, and a tin cup of coffee. The vapors from the huge steam cookers mingling with the stench of wet clothes and sweating bodies made the air foul. But waiting in the soup kitchen was better than the scavenging in the dump. Citizens of Chicago, in this second winter, could be seen digging into heaps of refuse with sticks and hands as soon as the garbage trucks pulled out. On June 30, 1931, the Pennsylvania Department of Labor and Industry reported that nearly one-quarter of the labor force of the state was out of work. Clarence Pickett of the Friends found schools where 85, 90, even 99 per cent of the children were underweight, and, in consequence, drowsy and lethargic. "Have you ever heard a hungry child cry?" asked Lillian Wald of Henry Street. "Have you seen the uncontrollable trembling of parents who have gone half starved for weeks so that the children may have food?"[2]

1. Does the paragraph capture your interest? Why or why not? _____

_____

2. What are some of the words Schlesinger uses that help capture your attention? _____

_____

_____

3. Schlesinger uses direct quotations at the end of paragraphs A and B. What purpose do they serve? _____

_____

_____

4. There is no topic sentence in paragraph B. Do you think the paragraph is strengthened or weakened by the absence of a topic sentence? _____

   Why? _____

   _____

5. Write a topic sentence for the paragraph. _____

   _____

   Where would you put it? _____

   Why? _____

6. Do you think paragraph B could be used effectively at the beginning or end of an article or book? Explain your answer. _____

   _____

C The following passage is the last paragraph in Schlesinger's book. **Read** it and **answer** the questions that follow.

Many had deserted freedom, many more had lost their nerve. But Roosevelt, armored in some inner faith, remained calm and inscrutable, confident that American improvisation could meet the future on its own terms. And so on March 4, as he took the silent ride in the presidential limousine down the packed streets to the Capitol, he was grim and unafraid. Deep within, he seemed to know that the nation had resources beyond its banks and exchanges; that the collapse of the older order meant catharsis [purging and cleansing] rather than catastrophe; that the common disaster could make the people see themselves for a season as a community, as a family; that catastrophe could provide the indispensable setting for democratic experiment and for presidential leadership. If this were so, then crisis could change from calamity to challenge. The only thing Americans had to fear was fear itself. And so he serenely awaited the morrow. The event was in the hand of God.[3]

1. Which is the topic sentence of the paragraph? _____

   _____

   Why doesn't Schlesinger place it first?_____

   _____

2. What distinguishes this paragraph as a last rather than a first paragraph? If you wish, compare this paragraph with paragraph A. _____

   _____

3. Although this paragraph serves as the book's conclusion, the book is the first in a multivolume study entitled *The Age of Roosevelt*. In what way does the paragraph serve as both an end to one volume and a lead-in to another? _____

   _____

4. As in paragraphs A and B, Schlesinger paints a mental picture in paragraph C, an image in the reader's mind of a past situation. Identify one method he uses to create that picture.

   _____

   _____

5. Summarize the qualities that Schlesinger displays in the three quoted paragraphs that make him an effective writer. _____

   _____

Exercise 2: Detecting "Ringers"

Each paragraph of a narrative tells part of a story, and every part is the result of a series of decisions by the author about what to include and what to leave out. Think of a narrative as a dish of fine cuisine. Behind that dish is a recipe with a variety of ingredients in very precise amounts. If those ingredients changed, so would the flavors in the dish. If the amounts fluctuated, so would the balance of flavors. In crafting a narrative, you must constantly ask yourself what material belongs, what does not, and, for the material that does belong, what portion of it should be included. Every sentence in a narrative could be made longer by the insertion of more information. Every paragraph could be extended in the same way. You have to decide what kinds of information fit together, and in what proportion.

Read the following three passages on the Great Depression. Each one has a sentence that should be removed—a "ringer"—because it is not essential to the narrative or contradicts the other sentences. **Underline the sentence that should be deleted. Explain your answer in the space provided after each passage**. The first passage is completed for you as an example.

A. The United States of the 1930s remained a giant step from the nation that, in the aftermath of World War II, took over Great Britain's nineteenth-century role as international balancer. Early in the decade, Washington did little to stem the tide of economic collapse abroad. Indeed, the Hawley–Smoot tariff adopted in mid-1930 produced the highest barriers to imports into the United States of the entire twentieth century; the stubborn insistence on continuing payments on war debts into the following year played havoc with Europe's need for capital; and the refusal to cooperate with the British at the London Economic Conference during the summer of 1933 prevented any stabilization of exchange rates. Politically, the United States did little to cultivate a multilateral response to the aggressions of Japan, Germany, and Italy. <u>Mussolini's rise to power in the last country in the 1920s produced only a marginal response in Paris, London, and Washington.</u> Even with the outbreak of war in Europe in September 1939, American policymakers remained determined to avoid direct involvement on the eastern shores of the Atlantic.

Explanation: The sentence deals with the 1920s rather than the 1930s and involves the responses of Great Britain and France as well as the United States.

B. Americans in the early 1930s yearned for a dynamic, self-assured leader in the White House, a man who could restore the nation's confidence in the aftermath of the stock market crash and the subsequent nose dive of the economy. Herbert Hoover proved unequal to the task. An engineer by training and an introvert by disposition, he lacked the intellectual flexibility and the personal flair to guide a democratic, pluralistic nation through its time of trial. To him, the ideal vacation was a weekend of fly fishing in a trout stream in the Virginia mountains. Only after Franklin D. Roosevelt, a seemingly shallow New York patrician, took the oath of office in March of 1933 did the national mood begin to shift.

Explanation:

_____

_____

_____

C. The most powerful political asset that African-Americans and women held in Washington, D.C., during the New Deal years was the president's wife, Eleanor. An activist in a variety of reform causes since World War I, Eleanor Roosevelt was determined as First Lady to be more than the keeper of her husband's social calendar. During the 1940s, she would become an enthusiastic supporter of U.S. involvement in the United Nations. She called her own press conferences and permitted entry only to female reporters. She met frequently with relief administrator Harry Hopkins, taking special interest in jobs for women and African-Americans. She nudged FDR leftward on appointments for these underrepresented groups. For her efforts, she gained a special place in the hearts of the downtrodden, but she also sparked criticism and nasty rumors, especially among tradition-minded white southerners.

Explanation:

_____

_____

_____

Exercise 3: Drawing Inferences

In the end, the purpose of an essay is to persuade the reader to accept the author's point. To do so, a story has to make sense. The following exercise asks you to determine whether a passage supports a series of inferences, or conclusions, drawn from evidence. If we know that a river flows from north to south, for example, we can infer that most boats traveling on the river will move faster when going southward than when going northward. This conclusion might not turn out to be true, but it still would be reasonable, given the available evidence.

After each of the following passages, you will find four statements. Each statement purports to be true. Decide which can be sustained by the passage. If you think that the statement follows logically from the narrative, write *true* in the space provided. If the statement is contradicted by what you have read, write *false*. If there is no evidence one way or the other, write *cannot determine*. Be prepared to justify your answers in class.

A. As late as 1940 there were still 1,250,000 women seeking work, and another 450,000 women were employed on public emergency work. Along with unemployment, women workers had to face the additional obstacle of prejudice and discrimination on the part of their prospective employers and coworkers. The antagonism toward the woman worker, which had always been present, even in times of prosperity, was greatly intensified by the Depression. Its most severe impact was felt by the white-collar woman worker, especially if she happened to be married.[4]

1. During the Depression, more women than men were seeking work. _____
2. Antagonism toward married women in the workplace was greater than antagonism toward unmarried women. _____
3. Antagonism toward women in the workplace was greater during the Depression than during previous times of prosperity. _____
4. During the Depression, more women were employed in the private than in the public sector. _____

B. Watching the bureaucratic history of [Civilian Conservation Corps] camps for unemployed women was a frustrating experience for Hilda Washington Smith and her colleagues in the [women's] network. Expectations for camps for women were always far below the scale proposed for camps for men. Hilda Smith felt this discrepancy keenly: "The CCC camps with their millions of dollars for wages, educational work, travel, and supervision constantly remind me of what we might do for women from these same families. *As [is] so often the case, the boys get the breaks, the girls are neglected.* Even though similar plans for women are more difficult to develop, I do not believe they should be discarded as impossible" [emphasis added]. Yet as a result of the efforts of women like Smith, Eleanor Roosevelt, and other prominent women administrators, the government at least made a token effort to meet the needs of these young women. While not a stunning achievement in numbers (8,500 women compared to 2.5 million men), the camps might not have materialized at all without the dedication and persistence of certain members of the network.[5]

1. During the 1930s, well-connected women played a crucial role in getting some government assistance for less fortunate women. _____

2. New Deal programs provided just as many benefits for women as for men. _____

3. Civilian Conservation Corps camps for women were less well equipped than those for men. _____

4. The New Deal served more men than women, but those women who did get government aid got just as much as their male counterparts. _____

Exercise 4: Qualifiers

It is difficult to know why one narrative is more convincing than another. Certainly, detail and logic are important. So is a graceful style of storytelling. Most important, however, is conveying to your readers a sense that you have given all the points of view on your subject a fair hearing. You cannot take all of them equally into account; if you did, your narrative would degenerate into a mass of conflicting statements. The challenge is to choose among them while reassuring your reader that you have not ignored the ones you ultimately reject. One way to convince your reader that your account is balanced and reasonable is through the use of *qualifiers*, words that modify or limit your claims. *Many, few, some, usually, sometimes, increasing, decreasing, liberal, conservative,* and the like are all qualifiers. Phrases as well as single words can serve as qualifiers. The following passage on unemployment during the Depression is filled with qualifiers. Three of them are underlined. **Underline six more.**

Men of <u>old-fashioned</u> principles <u>really</u> believed that the less said about the unemployed, the faster they would get jobs. They really believed that public relief was bad for the poor because it discouraged them from looking for work or from taking it at wages that would tempt business to start up again. <u>According to their theory</u>, permanent mass unemployment was impossible, because there was work at some wage for every able-bodied man, if he would only find and do it. Charity was necessary, of course, for those who were really disabled through no fault of their own, but there could never be very many of these, and they should be screened carefully and given help of a kind and in a way that would keep them from asking for it as long as possible. Those who held this view were not necessarily hardhearted or self-interested. Josephine Lowell, a woman who devoted her life to the poor, issued the bluntest warning: "The presence in the community of certain persons living on public relief has the tendency to tempt others to sink to their degraded level." That was in 1884, when cities were smaller, and fewer people depended on the ups and downs of factory work.[6]

Some Qualities of Good Writing: A Review

Good writing is not always easy to define, but the first four exercises in this chapter provide some guidelines. In general, a well-written essay has an identifiable structure—an introduction, body, and conclusion—as well as paragraphs containing clear topic sentences. The structure helps the reader follow the development of the story or argument. A well-written essay also contains words and phrases that capture and hold the reader's attention. Active verbs, colorful quotations from primary sources, and short, crisp sentences all engage the reader. A plausible thesis based on the logical presentation of evidence is also important. Opinions develop from the evidence presented and, although they need not be restricted to a narrow interpretation of the facts, are qualified sufficiently to prevent the reader from suspecting excessive bias. Keep these points in mind as you work on Exercise 5.

Exercise 5: Writing an Essay

This exercise provides the documents from which you will write an essay. The topic has been chosen for you, but the story is yours to write, and your choice of themes and emphasis makes it your own. We do suggest, however, that you be as comprehensive as possible in integrating material from the sources provided. Do not be afraid to reach your own conclusions. Originality is an important part of any essay, whether written by a historian or by a student of history.

Following is a series of documents from the 1930s by people who lived through that decade. **Read** the introductory materials and the documents carefully, thinking about how you can use them to construct a narrative on the experience of the Great Depression. The questions that accompany the documents will help you to focus your thoughts. As you read, **highlight** passages in each document that suggest a theme or that you could use to enliven your narrative. In the space provided at the end of each passage, jot down some notes for future reference: What theme does the document suggest? How does the document relate to the other passages? Do not hesitate to write ideas in the margins.

A The son of a West Virginia coal miner, Tom Kromer spent three years in college but never finished for lack of funds. Twenty-three years old in 1930, Kromer became a vagrant during the Depression, traveling from city to city across the country on freight trains, begging for a few dimes for a meal or a flop (a bed on which to sleep the night). As often as not, he wound up sleeping on a park bench and going for days without food. Figure 6.1 conveys the hopelessness of many men (and women) in his situation. Eventually Kromer found work for fifteen months with the Civilian Conservation Corps, a New Deal agency. In 1935 he was able to publish an autobiographical novel, *Waiting for Nothing*, from which the following is excerpted.

It is night, and we are in . . . a garbage heap. Around us are piles of tin cans and broken bottles. Between the piles are fires. A man and a woman huddle by the fire to our right. A baby gasps in the woman's arms. It has the croup. It coughs until it is black in the face. The woman . . . pounds it on the back. It catches its breath for a little while, but that is all. You cannot cure a baby of the croup by pounding it on the back with your hand.

The man walks back and forth between the piles of garbage. His shoulders are hunched. He clasps his hands behind him. Up and down he walks. Up and down. He has a look on

FIGURE 6.1 *Hoboes During the 1930s*
Courtesy of Dorothea Lange Collection, Oakland Museum
of California, City of Oakland. Gift of Paul S. Taylor.

his face. I know that look. I have had that look on my own face. You can tell what a stiff is thinking when you see that look on his face. He . . . wishes to Jesus Christ he could get his hands on a gat [gun]. But . . . a gat costs money. He has no money. He is a lousy stiff. He will never have any money.

Where are they going? . . . They do not know. He hunts for work, and he is a damn fool. There is no work. He cannot leave his wife and kids to starve to death alone, so he brings them with him. Now he can watch them starve to death. What can he do? Nothing but what he is doing. If he hides out on a dark street and gives it to some bastard on the head, they will put him in and throw the keys away if they catch him. . . . So he stays away from dark streets and cooks up jungle slop for his wife and kid between the piles of garbage.

I look around this jungle filled with fires. They are a pitiful sight, these stiffs with their ragged clothes and their sunken cheeks. They crouch around their fires. They are cooking up. They take their baloney butts out of their packs and put them in their skillets to cook. They huddle around their fires in the night. Tomorrow they will huddle around their fires, and the next night, and the next. It will not be here. The bulls [police] will not let a stiff stay in one place for long. . . .

We are five men at this fire I am at. We take turns stumbling into the dark in search of wood. . . . I am groping my way through the dark in search of wood when I stumble into this barbed wire fence. A couple of good stout poles will burn a long time. What do I care if this is someone's fence? . . . We are five men. We are cold. We must have a fire. It takes wood to make a fire. I take this piece of iron pipe and pry the staples loose.

This is good wood. It makes a good blaze. We do not have to huddle so close now. It is warm, too, except when the wind whistles hard against our backs. Then we shiver and turn our backs to the fire and watch these rats that scamper back and forth in the shadows. These are no ordinary rats. They are big rats. But I am too smart for these rats. I have me a big piece of canvas. This is not to keep me warm. It is to keep these rats from biting a chunk out of my nose when I sleep. But it does not keep out the sound and the feel of them as they sprawl all over you.[7]

Questions to Consider

What group of people does Kromer describe? What sets them apart from other poor people? Did traditional gender roles survive the harsh conditions that these people faced? How can you tell from the document? How do these people feel about the law? Why? Is their view of the law similar to that of poor people today? Why or why not? _____

_____

_____

_____

_____

B Born in Iowa in 1900, Meridel Le Sueur grew up in an atmosphere of political radicalism. During the 1920s, she joined the Communist Party of the United States. An essayist, novelist, and poet, Le Sueur published extensively during the 1920s and 1930s, especially on the lives of middle- and lower-middle-class women. The next excerpt is from "Women Are Hungry," which appeared in 1934 in the journal *American Mercury*. Le Sueur spent most of the 1930s in Minneapolis raising two children, writing, and working in a variety of menial jobs. Partly from her personal experiences and partly from extensive interaction with other poor women, she creates a poignant vision of the Depression's impact on her gender and the family.

When you look at the unemployed women and girls you think instantly that there must be some kind of war. The men are gone away from the family; the family is disintegrating; the women try to hold it together, because women have most to do with the vivid life of procreation, food, shelter. Deprived of their participation in that, they are beggars.

. . . poverty is more personal to them than to men. The women looking for jobs or bumming on the road, or that you see waiting for a hand-out from the charities, are already mental cases as well as physical ones. A man can always get drunk, or talk to other men, no matter how broken he is in body and spirit; but a woman, ten to one, will starve alone in a hall bedroom until she is thrown out, and then she will sleep alone in some alley until she is picked up.

When the social fabric begins to give way it gives way from the bottom first. . . . The working-class family is going fast. The lower-middle-class family is also going, though not so fast. It is like a landslide. It is like a great chasm opening beneath the feet and swallowing the bottom classes first. The worker who lives from hand to mouth goes first, and then his family goes. The family rots, decays and goes to pieces with the woman standing last, trying to hold it together, and then going too. The man loses his job, cannot find another, then leaves. The older children try to get money, fail, and leave or are taken to the community farms. The mother stays with the little children helped by charity, until they too are sucked under by the diminishing dole and the growing terror.

Where are the women? There is the old woman who has raised her children, and they have all left her now, under the lash of hunger. There is the unattached woman, and the professional one, and the domestic servant. The latter went down two years ago. The professional woman began going down only recently. They are the young school girls—more than a million of them—who were graduated into unemployment two or three years ago. Many of them, particularly those coming from the industrial centers, who never went beyond grammar school, are now hoboes riding on the freights. Their ages run from eight to eighteen.[8]

Questions to Consider

How does this document compare to the three others authored by women (documents C, D, and F)? How does Le Sueur compare in status, occupation, residence, and political outlook (insofar as you can tell) to the other women authors? Can you envision Le Sueur writing any of the other three documents? _____

_____

_____

_____

_____

C The following letter, dated January 2, 1935, was addressed to First Lady Eleanor Roosevelt by a woman in Troy, New York, a small city near the state capital at Albany.

About a month ago I wrote you asking if you would buy some baby clothes for me with the understanding that I was to repay you as soon as my husband got enough work. Several weeks later I received a reply to apply to a Welfare Association so I might receive the aid I needed. . . .

Please Mrs. Roosevelt, I do not want charity, only a chance from someone who will trust me until we can get enough money to repay the amount spent for the things I need. As a proof that I really am sincere, I am sending you two of my dearest possessions to keep as security, a ring my husband gave me before we were married, and a ring my mother used to wear. Perhaps the actual value of them is not high, but they are worth a lot to me. If you will consider buying the baby clothes, please keep them [rings] until I send you the money you spent. It is very hard to face bearing a baby we cannot afford to have, and the fact that it is due to arrive soon, and still there is no money for the hospital or clothing, does not make it any easier. . . .

If you still feel you cannot trust me, it is allright and I can only say I do not blame you, but if you decide my word is worth anything with so small a security, here is a list of what I will need—but I will need it very soon. . . . [There follows a list of eleven different pieces of infant clothing.]

If you will get these for me I would rather no one knew about it. I promise to repay the cost of the layette as soon as possible.[9]

Questions to Consider

Why do you suppose the woman wrote to Mrs. Roosevelt instead of to the president? Why did the wife rather than the husband write for help? Why doesn't the woman want charity? Why does she not want others to know about her approaching Mrs. Roosevelt? Do this woman's values appear to differ from those of Le Sueur in document B? If so, how do they differ? _____

_____

_____

_____

_____

D The next document also was addressed to Mrs. Roosevelt. The letter was from a woman living in Winnsboro, a small town in Louisiana. It was dated October 29, 1935. Figure 6.2 shows a woman posing for the photographer with her husband, children, and mother.

> I read your letter telling me to write to the relif office for help I did they wrote me that they was puting people off the relif now instead of takin them on and I dont want on the relif if I can help it I want to work for my livin but the last thing we have is gone my cow that I ask you to send me some money to save her for my little children to have milk has bin taken and we only ge $17.50 on our debt for her we picked cotton at 40 cents per 100 lbs till it was all gone now there isnt one thing here that we can do to get bread to eat my sick child is still livin and takin medicine but the Dr says he cannot keep letting us have medicine unless we pay him some for he is in debt for it and the man that has let us have a house and land to work wont let us stay in the house if we cant get a mill plow the land with. . . . dont you know its aful to have to get out and no place to have a roof over your sick child and noting to eat I cant tell all my troubles there isnt any use we only have a few days to stay here in the house. . . . please send me some money and please dont write me like you did before my Husban is in bad condishion and if you write me a letter like you did before it will hurt him so much so wont you please send it and say nothing about it.[10]

Questions to Consider

What is the most noticeable difference between this letter and document C? Can you explain this difference? If so, how? Like the woman in document C, the writer of this letter does not want others to know that she has written to Mrs. Roosevelt. Are their reasons similar? Does this suggest anything about American values at the time? Do you think such values continue to prevail today? _____

_____

_____

_____

_____

E The following letter to President Roosevelt, dated October 19, 1935, was from an unidentified person living in Reidsville, Georgia. Figure 6.3 shows three generations of an impoverished rural family posing for the photographer.

> Would you please direct the people in charge of the relief work in Georgia to issue the provisions + other supplies to our suffering colored people. I am sorry to worrie you with

FIGURE 6.2 *Poor Farmers in the Deep South During the 1930s*

this Mr. President but . . . the relief officials here are using up most every thing that you send for them self + their friends. they give out the releaf supplies here on Wednesday . . . and give us black folks, each one, nothing but a few cans of pickle meet and to white folks they give blankets, bolts of cloth and things like that . . . the witto Nancy Hendrics own lands, stock holder in the Bank in this town and she is being supplied with Blankets cloth and gets a supply of cans goods regular this is only one case but I could tell you many.

Please help us mr President because we cant help our self and we know you is the president and a good Christian man we is praying for you. Yours truly cant sign my name Mr President they will beat me up and run me away from here and this is my home[11]

Questions to Consider

Do you think the letter is by a man or a woman? Why? What is similar in the actual texts of documents D and E? How do you explain the similarity? What is different about the writers of the two letters? Is the author of document E concerned about townpeople discovering his or her appeal to the president for the same reason that the authors of documents C and D don't want others to know of their appeals to Mrs. Roosevelt? How is the appeal in document E different from that in documents C and D? Can you explain the difference? If so, how? _____

_____

_____

_____

_____

FIGURE 6.3 *A Rural Family in the South During the 1930s*
Courtesy of Alamy Ltd.

F The following letter to Mrs. Roosevelt, from a woman in Mancelona, Michigan, was dated August 6, 1934.

> I am writing you to ask you to help me and my old Father to live I am in a farm which he owns and has planted or farmed all he was able to do we havnt any stock nothing to feed them untill his corn is through growing we have a fuw chickens this is what I would like to ask of you and the President if I could have a small pinsion each month so we would not starve my father is seventy six to old to work at the Antriim Co furnace I cant go away and leave him alone to look for work and to stay here in such poverty I am so disturbed trying to know what to do.[12]

Questions to Consider
What do the authors of documents D and F have in common? In what ways are the two letters similar? What group of people is introduced in this document? How has the condition of most people in that group changed since the 1930s? Why has the change occurred?

_____
_____
_____
_____
_____

FIGURE 6.4 *A Soup Kitchen in Chicago During the 1930s*
Courtesy of Corbis Images.

G The following letter to the president was from a boy living in Chicago, Illinois, and was written sometime in February 1936. Figure 6.4 shows men down on their luck in Chicago receiving a free meal.

I'm a boy of 12 years. . . . My father hasn't worked for 5 months. He went plenty times to relief. . . . They won't give us anything. I don't know why. Please you do something. We haven't paid 4 months rent, Everyday the landlord rings the door bell, we don't open the door for him. We are afraid that we will be put out, been put out before, and don't want to happen again. We haven't paid the gas bill, and the electric bill, haven't paid grocery bill for 3 months. My brother goes to . . . High School. . . . hasn't gone to school for 2 weeks because he got no carfare. I have a sister she's twenty years, she can't find work. My father is staying home. All the time he's crying because he can't find work. I told him why are you crying daddy, and daddy said why shouldn't I cry when there is nothing in the house. I feel sorry for him. That night I couldn't sleep. The next morning I wrote this letter to you. . . . Please answer right away because we need it. will starve Thank you.[13]

Questions to Consider

How does the father in this document differ from the author of document C? How do you think the father would react if he knew about his son's letter? How are the conditions described in this document similar to those described in the other documents? Would the family described in document G find it easier to get help today? If so, from whom?

_____

_____

_____

H Not everyone suffered during the Great Depression, as this and the next document reveal. Both are excerpts from oral histories recorded in the late 1960s of people who either got rich or stayed rich during the 1930s. The first speaker is William Benton, who, after his business successes of the 1930s, became a United States senator from Connecticut.

> I left Chicago in June of '29. . . . Chester Bowles and I started a business with seventeen hundred square feet, just the two of us and a couple of girls. . . .
>
> I was only twenty-nine, and Bowles was only twenty-eight. . . . We didn't know the Depression was going on. Except that our clients' products were plummeting, and they were willing to talk to us about new ideas. They wouldn't have let us in the door if times were good. So the Depression benefited me. My income doubled every year. . . .
>
> . . . I contributed enormously to the "Maxwell House Show Boat," which later became the Number One program in broadcasting. . . .
>
> "Show Boat" went on in 1933, really the bottom of the Depression. Maxwell House Coffee went up eighty-five percent within six months. And kept zooming. . . . The chain stores were selling coffee that was almost as good—the difference was indetectable—for a much lower price. But advertising so gave a glamor and verve to Maxwell House that it made everybody think it was a whale of a lot better.[14]

Questions to Consider

How do you explain Benton's success in the 1930s in contrast to the failure of others? What percentage of the American people do Benton and Martin DeVries, the author of document I, represent? What does the success of Maxwell House Coffee during the 1930s suggest? _____

_____

_____

_____

_____

I Martin DeVries, a wealthy businessman, showed limited sympathy for those who suffered in the Depression.

> People were speculating. Now who are they gonna blame aside from themselves? It's their fault. . . . If you gamble and make a mistake, why pick on somebody else? It's your fault. . . .
>
> It's like many people on the bread lines. I certainly felt sorry for them. But many of them hadn't lived properly when they were making it. They hadn't saved anything. . . . Way back in the '70s, people were wearing $20 silk shirts and throwing their money around like crazy. If they had been buying Arrow $2 shirts and putting the other eighteen in the bank, when the trouble came, they wouldn't have been in the condition they were in. . . .
>
> Most people today are living beyond their means. They don't give a damn. The Government'll take care of them. People today don't want to work. . . .

These New Dealers felt they had a mission to perform. . . . My friends and I often spoke about it. . . . Here we were paying taxes and not asking for anything. Everybody else was asking for relief, for our money to help them out. . . . A certain amount of that is O.K., but when they strip you clean and still don't accomplish anything, it's unfair.[15]

Questions to Consider

Do you think the people about whom DeVries complains represent a large percentage of the American people? Do you think they are characteristic of the people writing and being described in documents A through G? How do DeVries's values compare with those of the people represented in those documents? How do you explain any differences?

_____

_____

_____

_____

_____

Exercise 6: Write an Essay

Now that you have read the documents, it is time to write the first draft of your essay. In following the steps below, keep in mind a length limit. All writing involves making decisions about what material to include and what to omit. This assignment is no different. Your final essay should be no longer than three typewritten (double spaced) pages or nine handwritten (single spaced) pages.

Step 1. Look over your notes for each passage, and think about a theme that you would like to develop. What would you like to say about life during the Great Depression? Write your theme in one sentence below.

_____

_____

_____

Step 2. How will you support your theme? In the space provided, list the points that you will use to support your argument. After each point, include some details, taken from the documents, that will flesh out the point. These points, with their details, will form the paragraphs of your essay's body.

_____

_____

_____

_____

_____

_____

_____

_____

_____

_____

_____

Step 3. On a separate sheet of paper, write the introduction to your essay. Remember that the introduction should do three things: grab the reader's attention, state your theme, and briefly preview the supporting points that you will cover in your essay body.

Step 4. Draft the body of your essay. Look at your list from Step 2 and expand each point into a full paragraph. Be sure that each paragraph begins with a clear topic sentence that announces the paragraph's main point. Also check that each paragraph contains interesting details that support the topic sentence. Finally, be sure that each paragraph flows smoothly into the next paragraph.

Step 5. Write the conclusion of your essay. Recap your main points, and firmly restate your theme. If you wish, raise any larger questions that may have come to mind as you thought about the Depression.

Step 6. Set aside your first draft for a few hours or for a day or two.

Step 7. Reread your essay, asking yourself the following questions:

Does my introduction state my thesis?

Will it grab the reader's attention?

Does each paragraph in the essay body contain only one main idea, and does that main idea back up my thesis?

Does each paragraph have enough supporting, interesting details to flesh out the topic sentence?

Does each paragraph flow smoothly into the next one?

Throughout my essay, do I express my ideas clearly and vividly?

Will my readers want to keep reading my paper?

Does my paper end in a satisfying conclusion that restates my thesis?

You may want to have a friend read your first draft, too, and give you his or her impressions.

Step 8. Revise your essay to resolve any problems that came up in Step 7. Do not hesitate to make extensive changes; most authors revise their work several times before being satisfied.

Step 9. Read through your second draft again, and correct any spelling, punctuation, or grammatical errors.

Step 10. Hand in your final essay with pride.

You have completed the first major writing assignment in this book. Rather than emphasizing style and organization, the assignments in the remaining chapters will center on more specific aspects of historical writing. For example, Chapter 7 focuses on causation, or the question of why events occur. Still, to complete these assignments, you will have to read and take notes on primary documents, organize an essay, and then write several paragraphs of clear and lively prose, just as you did in this chapter. All this effort devoted to writing is not wasted. Good writing takes much practice, but these skills will prove valuable to you for the rest of your life. Whether you become a historian, a novelist, a journalist, a businessperson, a doctor, or a teacher, your ability to communicate persuasively and engagingly through the written word will have considerable impact on your attainments.

Notes

[1] Excerpts from *The Crisis of the Old Order* by Arthur M. Schlesinger. Copyright © 1957 by Arthur M. Schlesinger. By the Houghton Mifflin Company.

[2] Ibid., 171.

[3] Ibid., 485.

[4] Winifred D. Wandersee, *Women's Work and Family Values, 1920–1940* (Cambridge, Mass.: Harvard University Press, 1981), 97.

[5] Susan Ware, *Beyond Suffrage: Women in the New Deal* (Cambridge, Mass.: Harvard University Press, 1981), 114.

[6] Caroline Bird, *The Invisible Scar* (New York: McKay, 1966), 30–31.

[7] Text by Tom Kromer from *Waiting for Nothing & Other Writings*, edited by Arthur D. Casciato and James L. West. Copyright © 1986 by the University of Georgia Press.

[8] The article was republished in Meridel Le Sueur, *Ripening Selected Work, 1927–1980*, edited with an introduction by Elaine Hedges (Old Westbury, N.Y.: Feminist Press, 1934), 144–157.

[9] From *Down and Out in the Great Depression: Letters from the "Forgotten Man"* by Robert S. McElvaine. Copyright © 1983 by the University of North Carolina Press.

[10] Ibid., 69–70.

[11] Ibid., 83.

[12] Ibid., 100–101.

[13] Ibid., 117.

[14] Studs Terkel, *Hard Times: An Oral History of the Great Depression* (New York: Pantheon, 1970), 60–62.

[15] Ibid., 74–75.

7: *Causation: Why Events Happen*

World War II and the Origins of the Cold War

E. H. Carr wrote in his widely acclaimed book *What Is History?* that "the study of history is the study of causes. The historian . . . continuously asks the question: Why?; and so long as he hopes for an answer, he cannot rest."[1] Although historians often substitute for *causes* words such as *roots, origins, influences, foundations,* and *factors,* causal analysis continues to play a central role in their enterprise. Indeed, the same can be said for the rest of us as well. Rarely do we go through a day without asking why something happened the way it did.

The study of causation, though important, is complicated. Historians usually divide causes into the underlying and the immediate. Underlying causes are long-term factors that tend to move events in a particular direction, such as toward war or peace between nations. Immediate causes are short-term factors that spark an event. In analyzing the Cuban missile crisis of 1962, for example, historians generally identify the long-standing tension and competition between the Soviet Union and the United States as an underlying cause and the impulsive personality of Soviet leader Nikita Khrushchev as an immediate one. Deciding how much weight to give to these two types of causes is one of the primary tasks that historians face in explaining the past. This challenge is also essential for anyone attempting to anticipate the future.

To understand this principle, imagine a person, Jane Doe, who recently inherited a portfolio with thousands of shares of stock in oil companies that have major holdings in the Middle East. The date is August 3, 1990, and Iraqi forces just invaded Kuwait, sending the region into a state of heightened uncertainty. Should Jane sell her oil stocks? Chances are, Jane will base her decision on an assessment of what caused past fluctuations of her stocks' value and how likely those forces are to arise in the future, in both the short and the long term. If her oil stocks are showing a long-term upward trend, despite occasional downward shifts, and if her financial needs are mainly long-term, then she probably will hold on to those investments. If, however, her needs are primarily short-term, and if past crises in the Middle East led to sharp dips in the value of her stocks, she is likely to sell them quickly.

The nature of the event or phenomenon being analyzed may further complicate the study of causation. The Cuban missile crisis is a readily identifiable event with a limited duration; but other phenomena are more diffuse, both in character and in duration. The Cold War, of which the Cuban missile crisis was a part, is a prime example.

You have seen and heard the phrase "Cold War" many times, usually to refer to the intense and often bitter competition between the United States and the Soviet Union that ended in the late 1980s. Historians sometimes disagree over when the Cold War started, although they acknowledge that it emerged in the aftermath of World War II and to some degree as a result of that most monumental of conflicts. Tensions subsided temporarily during the mid-1950s and again in the early 1970s, but not until Mikhail Gorbachev rose to leadership in the Soviet Union and American president Ronald Reagan welcomed his overtures did relations between Moscow and Washington relax to a point where the two countries' leaders could consistently negotiate major issues short of crisis conditions.

Despite the high level of animosity characteristic of the Cold War, actual fighting between American and Soviet forces never occurred. For a long time, historians studying the conflict's causes preoccupied themselves with explaining Soviet-American enmity. More recently, scholars have devoted greater attention to the absence of a "hot" war between the two nations. Whatever the emphasis, the peculiar nature of the Cold War has presented numerous challenges to historians asking *why?* This chapter focuses on historical causation, with the Cold War serving as the example and World War II as the background. For additional information on these events, consult your textbook.

The following exercises provide you with the opportunity to hone your skills, first in comprehending the historical background leading up to a major event, second in summarizing and categorizing causal statements, and third in developing your own causal explanation based on primary sources.

FIGURE 7.1 *World War II in Europe and Africa*
Reproduced from A History of the American People, Second Edition, Volume II, (1993), by permission of the Houghton Mifflin Company. Copyright © 1993 by D.C. Heath and Company.

FIGURE 7.2 *Communism's Advance in Europe As a Result of World War II*

Exercise 1: Western Strategy in World War II and the Political Configuration of Europe and Asia Later On

The great nineteenth-century Prussian strategist Karl von Clausewitz once characterized war as "politics by other means." In fact, whether intended or not, military events and strategies in wartime usually play a major role in determining subsequent political developments. By studying the maps in Figures 7.1 through 7.4, you should be able to make this connection in the context of World War II. Section A deals with the European theater, section B with Asia and the Pacific. Section C asks you to integrate the two.

A The United States and its ally, Great Britain, pursued a Europe-first strategy in World War II, believing that Germany was a greater threat to their interests than was Japan. Yet Japan's attack on American possessions in the Pacific and British possessions in Southeast Asia in December 1941 meant that these two nations had to fight in Asia and the Pacific as well as in Europe. The Soviet Union, in contrast, did not enter the war against Japan until August 1945. Thus its entire war effort until Germany surrendered on May 8, 1945, was in Europe.

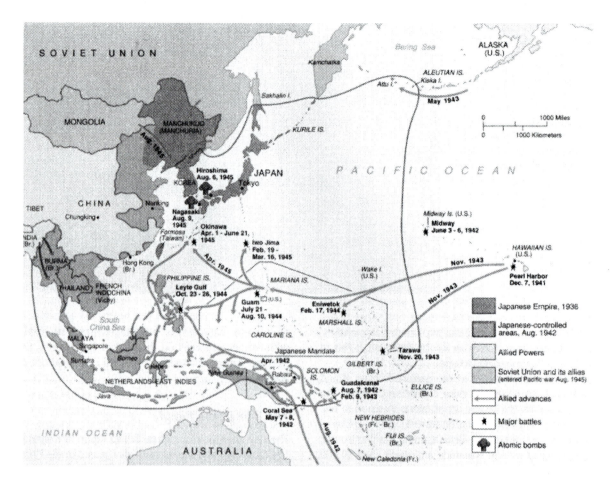

FIGURE 7.3 *World War II in the Pacific*
Reproduced from *A History of the American People*, Second Edition, Volume II, (1993), by permission of the Houghton Mifflin Company. Copyright © 1993 by D.C. Heath and Company.

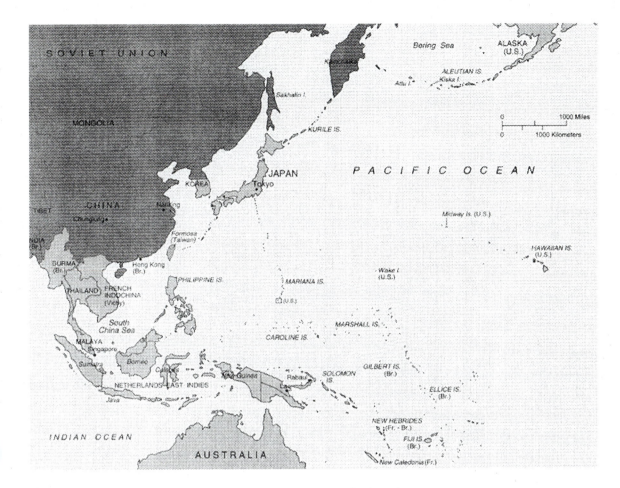

FIGURE 7.4 *Communist-governed territories in 1950 (darkened)*

Examine the map in Figure 7.1 carefully. How do you think the movement of forces against Germany was influenced by the fact that the United States and Great Britain were fighting in Asia and the Pacific at the same time while the Soviet Union was fighting only in Europe?

_____

_____

_____

_____

Now compare the movements of Allied forces in Figure 7.1 with the map in Figure 7.2, which shows Soviet territorial expansion and the emergence of Communist governments during and after the war. What pattern does this comparison suggest? _____

_____

_____

_____

_____

Outside the eastern front against the Soviet Union, the main concentration of German military power was in France and Belgium in the west. Keeping this in mind, examine the dates of the military movements of Anglo-American forces on the map in Figure 7.1. Do these help to explain the positions of British and American forces in relation to Soviet at the end of the war? If, so how? _____

_____

_____

_____

_____

_____

B Although the United States and Great Britain emphasized the European theater of operations in World War II, they put considerable effort into the struggle against Japan. The map in Figure 7.3 shows the dates and places of major allied military operations in the Pacific and Asian theaters. What do these operations suggest to you about allied military strategy against Japan and its empire? _____

_____

_____

_____

_____

Notice where the Soviet Union moved its forces in August 1945 when it declared war against Japan. Now examine the map in Figure 7.4, which shows areas governed by Communists at the beginning of 1950. What does this comparison suggest to you about the connection between military operations in wartime and political developments later on?

_____

_____

_____

_____

C Write a paragraph below pulling together conclusions you reached in sections A and B about the linkage between military events during World War II and political developments in its aftermath. _____

_____

_____

_____

_____

_____

_____

_____

_____

_____

_____

_____

_____

_____

Exercise 2: Identifying Causal Statements

An event as complicated as the Cold War is bound to generate disagreement among historians. In fact, scholars have offered a wide variety of explanations as to why the Cold War developed as it did. The following excerpts present a few of those explanations. Read the excerpts and in the space provided summarize in no more than two sentences the author's causal statements about the Cold War. Also indicate whether the causal statement is essentially long-term or short-term. If you are not sure, write *uncertain*.

A Washington policymakers mistook [Soviet leader Joseph] Stalin's determination to ensure Russian security through spheres of influence [in eastern Europe, Iran, and northeast Asia] for a renewed effort to spread communism outside the borders of the Soviet Union. The Russians did not immediately impose communist regimes on all the countries they occupied after the war, and Stalin showed notoriously little interest in promoting the fortunes of communist parties in areas beyond his control. But the Soviet leader failed to make the limited nature of his objectives clear.[2]

The Cold War occurred because _____

Is this a long-term or a short-term cause? _____

B . . . the fundamental explanation of the speed with which the Cold War escalated . . . lies precisely in the fact that the Soviet Union was not a traditional national state . . . : it was a totalitarian state, endowed with an all-explanatory, all-consuming ideology, committed to the infallibility of government and party, . . . and ruled by a dictator who . . . had his paranoid moments. . . .

Stalin and his associates . . . were bound to regard the United States as the enemy not because of this deed or that, but because of the primordial fact that America was the leading capitalist power and thus, by Leninist syllogism, unappeasably hostile, driven by the logic of its system to oppose, encircle, and destroy Soviet Russia.[3]

The Cold War occurred because _____

_____

_____

Is this a long-term or a short-term cause? _____

C Stalin's effort to solve Russia's problem of security and recovery short of widespread conflict with the United States was not matched by American leaders who acceded to power upon the death of Roosevelt. The President bequeathed them little . . . beyond the traditional outlook of open-door expansion. They proceeded rapidly . . . to translate that conception of America and the world into a series of actions and policies which closed the door to any result but the cold war. . . . [Fundamental to their thinking] was the fear that America's economic system would suffer a serious depression if it did not continue to expand overseas.[4]

The Cold War occurred because _____

_____

_____

Is this a long-term or a short-term cause? _____

Causal Statements and Historical Schools

Now that you are familiar with some theories about what caused the Cold War, you are ready to examine how they fit into interpretive schools.

Most causal statements in history, particularly about phenomena as large and as recent as the Cold War, derive in part from their authors' political or ideological attitude. Political orientation—reactionary, conservative, liberal, radical, revolutionary—affects how a historian determines cause. During the 1950s, conservatives and liberals usually agreed on the origins of the Cold War. Members of these groups argued intensely over specific issues, but they accepted the broad view that the Cold War grew out of a necessary U.S. response to Soviet expansionism—that is, the Soviet Union started the conflict, and the United States reacted. Behind this **traditional explanation** of the Cold War was a consensus that applauded capitalism and democracy as practiced in the United States and that rejected the authoritarian, socialist system of the Soviet Union.

Only a few radicals departed from this traditional interpretation. These **revisionist** thinkers were extremely critical of American capitalism, and, if not advocates of the Soviet system in its entirety, they were at least sympathetic to aspects of its government-controlled economy. During the 1960s, with the rise of the opposition to U.S. involvement in Vietnam, revisionist historians became more numerous. Radicals gained a substantial following, and many liberals and moderates began to question the Cold War consensus of the 1950s. Revisionists argued that American leaders sometimes had overreacted to Soviet moves abroad and on occasion had held the Soviets to standards of behavior that they themselves did not always uphold.

The challenge to the traditional view led not to a new consensus rallying around the revisionists but to an effort to pull together aspects of both interpretations into a **postrevisionist synthesis**. Subscribers to this approach, which emerged in the more conservative 1970s, refused to place sole blame for the Cold War on one side and were keenly sensitive to post–World War II conditions that sparked tension between the Soviet Union and the United States.

Given the pluralism of political views within American academe, all three of these interpretations are likely to continue to be well represented.

Exercise 3: Categorizing Causal Statements

Go back to the selections in Exercise 2 and, using the discussion of Cold War historiography in the preceding section, categorize them as *traditionalist, revisionist,* or *postrevisionist.* In each case, explain your choice.

Selection A

Interpretation: _____

Explanation: _____

_____

Selection B

Interpretation: _____

Explanation: _____

_____

Selection C

Interpretation: _____

Explanation: _____

_____

The Atomic Bomb: A Causal Analysis

Exercises 2 and 3 focused on the work of others. With the experience gained in examining and categorizing causal statements, you are now ready to do some causal analysis of your own. Exercise 4 introduces you to this task through a selection of primary documents relating to the American decision to use the atomic bomb against Japan in 1945. Before you plunge into the exercise, read the following background information. You may want to supplement this material by reading pertinent sections in your textbook or in an encyclopedia. Historians have long argued over why President Truman used the bomb against Japan, and in the mid-1990s controversy spilled over into the public arena over an exhibit on the event at the Air and Space Museum in Washington, D.C. On the surface, the reason seems obvious: to induce Japan to surrender quickly, thus eliminating the need for an American invasion of its home islands and the hundreds of thousands of U.S. casualties that would result. This was the most popular explanation in the United States for the first generation after the dropping of the bomb. In the mid-1960s, another interpretation emerged—namely, that Truman ordered the bomb's use against Japan primarily to impress the Soviets. Relations between Washington and Moscow had deteriorated after President Franklin D. Roosevelt's death in April, and, by demonstrating the power of the new weapon, Truman hoped to increase his bargaining power on a variety of unresolved issues.

During the 1970s, as new documentation pertinent to the bombing became available, scholars began to acknowledge that there may have been a number of reasons driving Truman's decision. For one thing, historians pointed out that the desires to save American lives and to influence the Soviets were not mutually exclusive. Both may have entered Truman's calculations. Emotion and momentum also may have played a role. Americans had not forgotten Japan's surprise attack on Pearl Harbor in 1941 or the atrocities of Japanese soldiers during the ensuing war in the western Pacific and China. To most Americans of the time, the Japanese seemed to be an alien people with devious and barbarous inclinations. The desire for revenge against what many believed to be a lower order of human beings was deeply ingrained in people's minds. Furthermore, virtually everyone involved with the Manhattan Project since its inception in 1942 had been assuming that the bomb would be used against the enemy as soon as it was ready. For Truman, a decision not to use the weapon against Japan would have required a reversal of the past thinking of responsible officials. The new president, who did not even learn of the Manhattan Project until late April 1945, was not in a strong position to adopt such a course.

Whatever cause or causes one chooses to emphasize, it is clear that the final decision to drop the bomb came only after much deliberation. In early May 1945, the president approved the establishment, under Secretary of War Henry L. Stimson, of an Interim Committee of top scientists and government officials. This group was to make recommendations on possible use of the weapon once it was ready. (An atomic device was not actually tested in the New Mexico desert until July 16.) On June 1 the committee recommended using the bomb against Japan, without warning, a decision that reflected what Stimson and Truman already believed. Later in June, in response to a plea from scientists directly involved in the Manhattan Project, the committee considered providing the Japanese with a technical demonstration of the weapon's power before using it on a live target. However, the committee remained unpersuaded that anything other than its actual deployment against the enemy would have the desired effect. There is no evidence that Truman subsequently reconsidered his view that the bomb should be used as soon as practicable. With the technical and logistical tasks completed around August 1, all that remained was to wait for clear weather over a target city. The United States dropped one bomb on Hiroshima on August 6 and one bomb on Nagasaki three days later.

Exercise 4: Writing a Causal Analysis

The excerpts from the primary sources that follow include evidence as to why President Truman decided to use the atomic bomb against Japan. Examine this evidence and make up your own mind about what caused Truman to take the course he did. A brief introduction precedes each excerpt to place it in context. Figure 7.3 shows a map of the western Pacific. After each excerpt space is provided for you to comment on the significance of the passage. Think about which of the reasons outlined earlier fits each document. Specifically, does the document support the interpretation that Truman bombed Japan to end the war or to impress the Soviets, or for one or any of the reasons previously mentioned? Do any other explanations not discussed seem plausible? Ask yourself how important each document is in explaining Truman's decision. Remember that, in the end, the decision was the president's alone to make.

Consider the author of the source and the circumstances under which it was produced, as well as its content. Did the author possess an obvious bias in recounting events the way he did? Was he in a good position to describe the events mentioned? How long after the event was the document created? Feel free to highlight portions of the documents and to write notes in the margins.

A This excerpt, dated May 15, 1945, is from the diary of Secretary of War Stimson. The excerpt relates a meeting held by the Committee of Three, a top-level group of U.S. officials that sought to coordinate policy among the War, Navy, and State departments. Winston Churchill was prime minister of the United Kingdom, and Joseph Stalin was Soviet premier and secretary of the ruling Communist party. The map in Figure 7.2 will help you to understand the concern over the Soviets' territorial gains. W. Averell Harriman was the U.S. ambassador to the Soviet Union.

> . . . the President has now promised apparently to meet Stalin and Churchill on the first of July and at that time . . . it may be necessary to have it out with Russia on her relations to Manchuria and Port Arthur and various other parts of North China, and also the relations of China to us. Over any such tangled wave of problems the S-1 [the code name for the atomic bomb] secret would be dominant and yet we will not know until after that time probably, until after that meeting, whether this is a weapon in our hands or not. We think it will be shortly afterwards, but it seems a terrible thing to gamble with such big stakes in diplomacy without having your master card in your hand. The best we could do today was to persuade Harriman not to go back until we had had time to think over these things a little bit harder.[5]

Questions to Consider

What does the excerpt suggest about the state of U.S. relations with the Soviet Union (Russia)? Do the meeting participants make a connection between the Soviet-American relationship and the atomic bomb? _____

_____

_____

_____

_____

B This excerpt is from the "Reminiscences" of Leo Szilard, a scientist in the Manhattan Project who doubted the prudence of using the atomic bomb against Japan. The meeting outlined in this excerpt occurred on May 28, 1945. James Byrnes was the president's representative on the Interim Committee. On July 3 he became secretary of state.

> Byrnes agreed that if we refrained from testing the bomb, people would conclude that its development did not succeed. However, he said that we had spent two billion dollars on developing the bomb, and Congress would want to know what we got for the money spent. "How would you get Congress to appropriate money for atomic energy research if you do not show results for the money which has been spent already?" . . .
>
> Byrnes thought that the war would be over in about six months, and this proved to be a fairly accurate estimate. He was concerned about Russia's postwar behavior. Russian troops had moved into Hungary and Rumania; Byrnes thought it would be very difficult to persuade Russia to withdraw her troops from these countries, and that Russia might be more manageable if impressed by American military might.[6]

Questions to Consider

Why is Byrnes concerned about views in Congress? Does his concern seem to be pushing him toward or away from using the bomb against Japan? Is Byrnes's concern about the Soviet Union an argument for or against using the bomb against Japan?

_____

_____

_____

_____

C Here is another excerpt from Stimson's diary, this time for June 6, 1945. The excerpt describes a meeting with President Truman.

> I then took up the matters on my agenda, telling him first of the work of the Interim Committee meetings last week. He said that Byrnes had reported to him already about it and that Byrnes seemed to be highly pleased with what had been done. I then said that the points of agreement and views arrived at were substantially as follows:
>
> That there should be no revelation to Russia or anyone else of our work in S-1 until the first bomb had been successfully laid on Japan.
>
> That the greatest complication was what might happen at the meeting of the Big Three. He told me he had postponed that until the 15th of July on purpose to give us more time. I pointed out that there might still be delay and if there was and the Russians should bring up the subject and ask us to take them in as partners, I thought that our attitude was to do just what the Russians had done to us, namely to make the simple statement that as yet we were not quite ready to do it.

Questions to Consider

Does a basic decision appear to have been made to use the atomic bomb against Japan? What was Truman's reason for postponing the meeting with the Soviet Union and Great Britain? _____

_____

_____

_____

_____

D The next excerpt is from a memo from Secretary of War Stimson to President Truman. The president read the memo during a meeting with Stimson on July 2 and, according to Stimson, "was apparently acquiescent with my attitude."

Proposed Program for Japan

1. The plans of operation up to and including the first landing have been authorized and the preparations for the operation are now actually going on. This situation was accepted by all members of your conference on Monday, June 18th.

2. There is reason to believe that the operation for the occupation of Japan following the landing may be a very long, costly and arduous struggle on our part. . . .

3. If we once land on one of the main islands and begin a forceful occupation of Japan, we shall probably have cast the die of last ditch resistance. The Japanese are highly patriotic and certainly susceptible to calls for fanatical resistance to repel an invasion. . . .

4. A question then comes: Is there any alternative to such a forceful occupation of Japan which will secure for us the equivalent of an unconditional surrender of her forces and a permanent destruction of her power again to strike an aggressive blow at the "peace of the Pacific"? I am inclined to think that there is enough such chance to make it well worthwhile our giving them a warning of what is to come and a definite opportunity to capitulate. . . .

We have . . . enormously favorable factors on our side. . . .

The problem is to translate these advantages into prompt and economical achievement of our objectives. I believe Japan *is* susceptible to reason in such a crisis to a much greater extent than is indicated by our current press and other current comment. Japan is not a nation composed wholly of mad fanatics of an entirely different mentality from ours.

On the other hand, I think that the attempt to exterminate her armies and her population by gunfire or other means will tend to produce a fusion of race solidity and antipathy which had no analogy in the case of Germany. We have a national interest in creating, if possible, a condition wherein the Japanese nation may live as a peaceful and useful member of the future Pacific community.

5. It is therefore my conclusion that a carefully timed warning be given to Japan by the chief representatives of the United States, Great Britain, China and, if then a belligerent, Russia, calling upon Japan to surrender and permit the occupation of her country in order to insure its complete demilitarization for the sake of the future peace. . . .

6. Success of course will depend on the potency of the warning which we give her. She has an extremely sensitive national pride and, as we are now seeing every day, when actually locked with the enemy will fight to the very death. For that reason the warning must be tendered before the actual invasion has occurred and while the impending destruction, though clear beyond peradventure, has not yet reduced her to fanatical despair. If Russia is a part of the threat, the Russian attack, if actual, must not have progressed too far.

Questions to Consider

In suggesting U.S. motives for using the atomic bomb against Japan, how does this document compare with selections A, B, and C? What is the major concern expressed by Stimson in the document? _____

_____
_____
_____
_____
_____
_____

E The following excerpts are from a collection called "MAGIC"—DIPLOMATIC SUMMARIES.[7] Early in the war the United States broke the code used in the electronic transmission of Japanese military and diplomatic messages. American translators were able to take intercepted and decoded messages, translate them into English, and then pass on summaries to military commanders in the Pacific and/or top policymakers in Washington, including the president. These summaries were critical in assessing Japanese intentions during the spring and summer of 1945. The first excerpt below is part of the "MAGIC"—DIPLOMATIC SUMMARY of July 13, 1945. The sections in quotes are directly from the translations of the Japanese decoded messages.

1. <u>Follow-up message on Japanese peace move</u>: On 12 July—the day after advising [Japanese] Ambassador [to the Soviet Union Sato] of Japan's desire to "make use of Russia in ending the war"—[Japanese] Foreign Minister Togo dispatched the following additional message on the subject, labeled "very urgent":

"I have not yet received a wire about your interview with [Soviet Foreign Minister] Molotov. Accordingly, although it may smack a little of attacking without sufficient reconnaissance, we think it would be appropriate to go a step further on this occasion and, before the opening of the Three Power Conference, inform the Russians of the Imperial will concerning the ending of the war. We should, therefore, like you to present this matter to Molotov in the following terms:

'His Majesty the Emperor, mindful of the fact that the present war daily brings greater evil and sacrifice upon the peoples of all belligerent powers, desires from his heart that it may be quickly terminated. But so long as England and the U.S. insist upon unconditional surrender the Japanese Empire has no alternative but to fight on with all its strength for the honor and the existence of the Motherland. . . .

"The Emperor's will, as expressed above, arises not only from his benevolence toward his own subjects but from his concern for the welfare of humanity in general. It is the Emperor's private intention to send Prince Konoye to Moscow as a Special Envoy with a letter from him containing the statements given above. . . .'"

The next excerpt is from the July 14 "MAGIC"—DIPLOMATIC SUMMARY.

1. <u>Messages from Sato on peace move</u>: Parts of three messages sent to Tokyo by Ambassador Sato on 12 and 13 July have been received; they disclose that (a) as of the morning of the 13th Sato intended to try to see Molotov for the purpose of presenting the Emperor's peace plea before Molotov should leave for Potsdam, and (b) Sato was pessimistic about the chances for success of Japan's peace move unless the Government were prepared to accept terms "virtually equivalent to unconditional surrender."

The first message was sent late on 12 July; at that time, Sato had read Foreign Minister Togo's 11 July messages instructing him to find out whether Russia might help Japan make peace on the basis of a surrender of all territory occupied during the war, but he had not yet received the 12 July message expressing the Emperor's desire for peace and outlining the plan to have Prince Konoye fly to Moscow. The available parts of Sato's message . . . read as follows:

"I received your [two] messages of 11 July immediately after I had reported to you on my 12 July interview with Molotov. I realize that the gist of your idea is a basic sounding out of the Russians on the possibility of using them in ending the war.

"In my frank opinion, it is no exaggeration to say that the Russians are not attracted by the proposals which former [Japanese] Premier Hirota made to [Soviet ambassador to Japan] Malik [for a non-aggression and mutual assistance pact in return for various concessions by Japan . . .] and that there is no hope that they will meet your terms. . . ."

The third excerpt is from the July 15 "MAGIC"—DIPLOMATIC SUMMARY.

. . . two earlier reports from Sato, parts of which have previously been reported, are now available in full. The first of the two, dated 12 July, was sent after Sato had received Togo's instructions to find out whether Russia might help Japan make peace on the basis of a surrender of all territory occupied during the war, but before he had read the message conveying the Emperor's peace plea. . . . The previously missing part of the message reads as follows:

"You state that 'Japan has not the slightest intention of annexing or keeping in its possession the occupied territories.' Now the fact is that we have already lost Burma and the Philippines, and even Okinawa which is at the very tip of our Empire has fallen into the hands of the enemy. How much of an effect do you expect our statements regarding the non-annexation and non-possession of territories which we have already lost or are about to lose will have on the Soviet authorities? . . .

"If the Japanese Empire is really faced with the necessity of terminating the war, we must first of all make up our own minds to do so. Unless we make up our own minds, there is absolutely no point in sounding out the views of the Soviet Government. . . ."

The final excerpt below is from the July 22 "MAGIC"—DIPLOMATIC SUMMARY.

In a message of 21 July, Foreign Minister Togo has now replied as follows:
"Special Envoy Konoye's mission will be in obedience to the Imperial Will.
He will request assistance in bringing about an end to the war through the good offices of the Soviet Government. In this regard he will set forth positive intentions, and he will negotiate details concerning the establishment of a co-operative relationship between Japan and Russia which will form the basis of
Imperial diplomacy both during and after the war. . . .

Togo's "next wire", sent the same day, reads as follows:

"With regard to unconditional surrender . . . we are unable to consent to it under any circumstances whatever. Even if the war drags on and it becomes clear that it will take much more bloodshed, the whole country as one man will pit itself against the enemy in accordance with the Imperial Will so long as the enemy demands unconditional surrender. . . .

Therefore, it is not only impossible for us to request the Russians to lend their good offices in obtaining a peace without conditions, but it would also be both disadvantageous and impossible, from the standpoint of foreign and domestic considerations, to make an immediate declaration of specific terms. . . ." Togo concluded by saying that he had read a long message of 20 July from
Sato, but that the decision he was communicating had been made by the Cabinet and that Sato should proceed accordingly.

The long message of 20 July from Sato . . . constitutes an impassioned plea to the Japanese Government to surrender to the Allies with the sole reservation that Japan's "national structure"—i.e., the Imperial House—be preserved.

Questions to Consider

What do the four excerpts indicate regarding the Japanese government's terms for ending the war? What is meant by "occupied territories?" What do you think American leaders concluded from reading the excerpts provided, which are representative of the "MAGIC"—DIPLOMATIC SUMMARIES during the period, regarding the Japanese government's intentions? _____

_____

_____

_____

_____

F The following selection is from President Truman's diary, which he kept intermittently during his White House years. He wrote this entry while in Potsdam, Germany, negotiating wartime and postwar issues with the Soviets and the British (see Figure 7.5) shortly after he had received a preliminary report of the successful test of an atomic device in the New Mexico desert.

July 17, 1945

Just spent a couple of hours with Stalin. [My adviser] Joe Davies called [Soviet diplomat Ivan] Maisky and made the date last night for noon today. Promptly a few minutes before twelve I looked up from the desk and there stood Stalin in the doorway. I got to my feet and advanced to meet him. He put out his hand and smiled. I did the same, we shook, I greeted [Soviet Foreign Minister] Molotov and the interpreter, and we sat down. After the usual polite remarks we got down to business. I told Stalin that I am no diplomat but usually said yes & no to questions after hearing all the argument. It pleased him. I asked him if he had the agenda for the meeting. He said he had and that he had some more questions to present. I told him to fire away. He did and it is dynamite—but I have some dynamite too which I'm not exploding now. He wants to fire Franco, to which I wouldn't object, and divide up the Italian colonies and other mandates, some no doubt that the British have. Then he got on the Chinese situation, told us what agreements had been reached and what was in abeyance. Most of the big points are settled. He'll be in the Jap War on August 15th. Fini Japs when that comes about. We had lunch, talked socially, put on a real show drinking toasts to everyone, then had pictures made in the back yard. I can deal with Stalin. He is honest—but smart as hell.[8]

FIGURE 7.5 *Photograph of Churchill, Truman, and Stalin at the Potsdam Conference* Courtesy of Corbis Images.

Questions to Consider

Does Truman hope to influence Stalin through his possession of the atomic bomb? Does Truman want the Soviets to enter the war against Japan? Why? Does the document suggest a single reason for using the bomb against Japan, or more than one reason? _____

_____

_____

_____

_____

G The next selection is from Stimson's diary of July 22, the day after top American officials in Potsdam received a detailed report of the successful test of an atomic device five days earlier. On July 21, Stimson described the report in his diary as follows: "It was an immensely powerful document . . . and revealed far greater destructive power than we expected in S-1." General Leslie Groves, the author of the report, was the director of the Manhattan Project.

At ten-forty [American delegate Harvey] Bundy and I again went to the British headquarters and talked to the Prime Minister and Lord Cherwell for over an hour. Churchill read Groves' report in full. He told me that he had noticed at the meeting of the Three yesterday that Truman was evidently much fortified by something that had happened and that he stood up to the Russians in a most emphatic manner, telling them as to certain demands that they absolutely could not have and that the United States was entirely against them. He said "Now I know what happened to Truman yesterday. I couldn't understand it. When he got to the meeting after having read this report he was a changed man. He told the Russians just where they got on and off and generally bossed the whole meeting." Churchill said he now understood how this pepping up had taken place and that he felt the same way.

Question to Consider

How does the report on the A-bomb test seem to have influenced Truman's behavior? _____

_____

_____

_____

_____

H The following excerpt is from Stimson's diary on July 23. The setting was still Potsdam. General George Marshall was the U.S. Army chief of staff.

At eleven o'clock I went down to the "Little White House" . . . and I asked for the President who saw me at once. . . . He told me that he had the warning message which we prepared on his desk . . . and that he proposed to shoot it out as soon as he heard the definite day of the operation. We had a brief discussion about Stalin's recent expansions and he confirmed what I have heard. But he told me that the United States was standing firm and he was apparently relying greatly upon the information as to S-1. He evidently thinks a good deal of the new claims of the Russians are bluff. . . .

After lunch and a short rest I received Generals Marshall and [Hap] Arnold, and had in McCloy and Bundy at the conference. The President had told me at a meeting in the morning that he was very anxious to know whether Marshall felt that we needed the Russians in the war or whether we could get along without them, and that was one of the subjects we talked over. Of course Marshall could not answer directly or explicitly. We had desired the Russians to come into the war originally for the sake of holding up in Manchuria the Japanese Manchurian Army. That now was being accomplished as the Russians have amassed their forces on that border, Marshall said, and were poised, and the Japanese were moving up positions in their Army. But he pointed out that even if we went ahead in the war without the Russians, and compelled the Japanese to surrender to our terms, that would not prevent the Russians from marching into Manchuria anyhow and striking, thus permitting them to get virtually what they wanted in the surrender terms.

Questions to Consider

What appears to be Truman's primary concern in his discussion with Stimson? In the later discussion, does Marshall seem to conclude that the Soviets are needed in the war against Japan or that they can be kept out through U.S. action? _____

_____

_____

_____

_____

I The following excerpt is from Stimson's diary on July 24.

At nine-twenty I went to "The Little White House" and was at once shown into the President's room. . . . He told me about the events of yesterday's meeting with which he seemed to be very well satisfied. I then told him of my conference with Marshall and the implication that could be inferred as to his feeling that the Russians were not needed. . . .

I then spoke of the importance which I attributed to the reassurance of the Japanese on the continuance of their dynasty, and I had felt that the insertion of that in the formal warning was important and might be just the thing that would make or mar their acceptance, but that I had heard from Byrnes that they preferred not to put it in.

Question to Consider

If the top priority of U.S. leaders was to keep the Soviets out of the war against Japan, should they have assured the Japanese that surrender would not require them to give up their emperor? _____

_____

_____

_____

_____

J This excerpt is from Truman's diary on July 25. The president was still in Potsdam.

This weapon is to be used against Japan between now and August 10th. I have told the Sec. of War, Mr. Stimson. . . . He & I are in accord. The target will be a purely military one and we will issue a warning statement asking the Japs to surrender and save lives. I'm sure they will not do that, but we will have given them the chance. It is certainly a good thing for the world that Hitler's crowd or Stalin's did not discover this atomic bomb. It seems to be the most terrible thing ever discovered, but it can be made the most useful.[9]

Questions to Consider

What attitude does Truman express toward the Japanese? toward the Soviet Union? Does Truman reveal anything regarding his motives for using the bomb? _____

_____

_____

_____

_____

K This excerpt is from Stimson's diary on August 9. The secretary of war was now back in Washington.

. . . I could see in my recent trip to Europe what a difficult task at best it will be to keep in existence a contented army of occupation and, if mingled with the inevitable difficulties there is a sense of [the army's] grievance against the unfairness of the government, the situation may become bad. Consequently the paper that we drew last night and continued today was a ticklish one. The bomb and the entrance of the Russians into the war will certainly have an effect on hastening the victory. But just how much that effect is or how long and how many men we will have to keep to accomplish that victory, it is impossible yet to determine. There is a great tendency in the press and among other critics to think that the Army leaders have no feeling for these things and are simply determined to keep a big army in existence because they like it, and therefore it is ticklish to run head on into this feeling with direct counter criticism. Therefore we tried to draft a paper which would make the people [public] feel that we appreciated their views as well as ours, and their difficulties as well as ours, and which would give us the confidence which we will have to have while we are solving these difficult problems.

Question to Consider

This document was written after the A-bombs were dropped on Japan and does not discuss a motive for that action. Do these facts eliminate the document's usefulness in determining U.S. motives? _____

_____

_____

_____

_____

L The following excerpt is from a telegram sent to President Truman on the evening of August 7 from Winder, Georgia. Its author, Senator Richard B. Russell (D, Ga.), is responding to press reports that Under Secretary of State Grew was pushing for a U.S. offer of surrender terms to the Japanese that would permit them to keep their emperor.

PERMIT ME TO RESPECTFULLY SUGGEST THAT WE CEASE OUR EFFORTS TO CAJOLE JAPAN INTO SURRENDERING IN ACCORDANCE WITH THE POTSDAM DECLARATION. LET US CARRY THE WAR TO THEM UNTIL THEY BEG US TO ACCEPT THE UNCONDITIONAL SURRENDER. THE FOUL ATTACK ON PEARL HARBOR BROUGHT US INTO WAR AND I AM UNABLE TO SEE ANY VALID REASON WHY WE SHOULD BE SO MUCH MORE CONSIDER-ATE AND LENIENT IN DEALING WITH JAPAN THAN WITH GERMANY. I EARNESTLY INSIST JAPAN SHOULD BE DEALT WITH AS HARSHLY AS GER-MANY AND THAT SHE SHOULD NOT BE THE BENEFICIARY OF A SOFT PEACE. THE VAST MAJORITY OF THE AMERICAN PEOPLE, INCLUDING MANY SOUND THINKERS WHO HAVE INTIMATE KNOWLEDGE OF THE ORIENT, DO NOT AGREE WITH MR. GREW IN HIS ATTITUDE THAT THERE IS ANYTHING SACROSANCT ABOUT HIROHITO. HE SHOULD GO. WE HAVE NO OBLIGATION TO SHINTOLISM [Shintoism]. THE CONTEMPTUOUS ANSWER OF THE JAPS TO THE POTSDAM ULTIMATUM JUSTIFIES A REVI-SION OF THAT DOCUMENT AND STERNER PEACE TERMS.

IF WE DO NOT HAVE AVAILABLE A SUFFICIENT NUMBER OF ATOMIC BOMBS WITH WHICH TO FINISH THE JOB IMMEDIATELY, LET US CARRY ON WITH TNT AND FIRE BOMBS UNTIL WE CAN PRODUCE THEM.[10]

Questions to Consider

Does Russell reveal an emotion in the telegram that could have been a factor in the decision to use the bomb against Japan (even though Russell himself did not have a direct role in the decision)? If so, what is that emotion? Is it likely that Russell's views were his own alone or representative of the views of many Americans at the time? _____

_____

_____

_____

_____

M The final document is Truman's reply on August 9 to the telegram above. Before Truman became vice president in March 1945, he had been a colleague of Russell's in the Senate.

Dear Dick:

I read your telegram of August seventh with a lot of interest.

I know that Japan is a terribly cruel and uncivilized nation in warfare but I can't bring myself to believe that, because they are beasts, we should ourselves act in the same manner.

For myself, I certainly regret the necessity of wiping out whole populations because of the "pigheadedness" of the leaders of a nation and, for your information, I am not going to do it unless it is absolutely necessary. It is my opinion that after the Russians enter into the war the Japanese will very shortly fold up.

My object is to save as many American lives as possible but I also have a humane feeling for the women and children of Japan.[11]

Questions to Consider

Does Truman indicate that he was influenced in his decision to use the bomb by considerations mentioned by Russell in his telegram? What reason does Truman give for using the bomb against Japan? _____

_____

_____

_____

_____

Exercise 5: Write an Essay

Now that you have finished reading and taking notes on the documents, write a brief essay (no more than three typewritten, double-spaced pages) stating your conclusions about why Truman used the atomic bomb against Japan and outlining the rationale behind your claims. You may quote the documents provided to develop your interpretation. When you use a document to make a particular point, whether you include a direct quotation or not, identify that document's letter in parentheses after the appropriate sentence.

The preceding excerpts represent only a small portion of the documentation that historians have used to explain why the United States used the atomic bomb against Japan. Yet the primary materials included in Exercise 4 alone present a complex picture of the factors that went into the American decision during the spring and summer of 1945. This exercise merely hints at some of the challenges of causal analysis.

Causal analysis is difficult in part because it often entails understanding personalities and their interaction with each other. It is people, after all, who make decisions, and it does not take much contact with them to discover that they are not all the same. With the importance of individuals in history in mind, we turn in the next chapter to the subject of biography.

Notes

[1] E. H. Carr, *What Is History?* (New York: Vintage, 1961), 113.

[2] John Lewis Gaddis, *The United States and the Origins of the Cold War, 1941–1947* (New York: Columbia University Press, 1972), 355.

[3] Arthur M. Schlesinger, Jr., "Origins of the Cold War," *Foreign Affairs* 46 (October 1967), 46–47.

[4] William Appleman Williams, *The Tragedy of American Diplomacy*, rev. ed. (New York: Norton, 1972), 229–232.

[5] The diary is in the Stimson Papers, Sterling Library, Yale University, New Haven, Conn. This and subsequent excerpts from the diary are from the microfilm edition.

[6] Donald Fleming and Bernard Bailyn, eds., *The Intellectual Migration: Europe and America, 1930–1960* (Cambridge, Mass.: Harvard University Press, 1969), 127–128.

[7] "MAGIC"—DIPLOMATIC SUMMARIES, Box 18, Record Group 457, National Archives II, College Park, Md.

[8] Box 333, President's Secretary's Files, Harry S Truman Papers, Harry S Truman Library, Independence, Mo.

[9] Ibid.

[10] Richard B. Russell Papers, Russell Library, University of Georgia, Athens, Ga.

[11] Ibid.

8: Biography: The Individual in History

Martin Luther King, Jr.

Historian John A. Garraty traces biography back to ancient Egyptian kings who, in their "search for immortality," had records of their lives and achievements placed in their tombs.[1] Despite the notable contributions of the Roman Plutarch in the first century of the Christian era and authors of lives of the saints after him, it was not until the publication in 1791 of James Boswell's *Life of Samuel Johnson* that such a work exhibited all the characteristics of what we call modern biography. Boswell's passion for accuracy drove him to do meticulous and exhaustive research. His grasp of biography as an art, his keen eye for the telling anecdote, and his determination to probe the inner life of his subject made his *Life* a model for later scholars. Though Boswell labored before the emergence of psychology as a field of study, with all its sparkling insights into human motivation, some call his masterpiece the greatest biography ever written.

English-language biographies during the next century failed to match Boswell's in quality, but they often served important didactic purposes. For example, some biographies provided moral instruction and cohesion in rapidly changing societies. In the United States, Parson M. L. Weems's *The Life of Washington*, published during the first decade of the nineteenth century, represented an extreme but popular manifestation of biography as moral exhortation. Laced with anecdotes concocted from the author's imagination, including the story of young George and the cherry tree, the book became an integral part of American folklore.

The twentieth-century trend toward professionalism throughout historical writing undermined the old enthusiasm for biography as an instrument of moral instruction but did not dampen the genre's popularity. Biographical or autobiographical works regularly appear on nonfiction bestseller lists. British scholar Alan Shelston offers two reasons for this: people's "curiosity about human personality" and their "interest in factual knowledge."[2]

The purpose of this chapter is to cultivate an appreciation for the aesthetic and functional values of biography. On the one hand, you can derive great pleasure from reading a finely crafted account of another person's life. On the other, you can develop important insights into human motivation that may help you in everyday life, as well as a sense of how individuals mold—and are molded by—the society around them. Finally, the study of biographers' techniques advances your own ability to capture your reader's attention with the written word.

121

In probing individual motivation and assessing their subjects' place in history, contemporary biographers often use imagination, just as Boswell did. As one historian of biography notes,

> the exact records of a life are, at best, desultory and fragmentary . . . [not to mention] ambiguous, To achieve the leap from the known to the possibly knowable makes imperative some degree of imaginative intervention, and to bring out the ultimate significance of the life thus recreated requires the exercise of personal judgment. Informed speculation . . . is not only permissable but indispensable if a coherent and meaningful story is to be fashioned from the shreds of fact.[3]

In sum, capturing the inner workings of an individual personality presents unique challenges.

At its best, biography tells a good deal not only about an individual, man or woman, but about the events, movements, and institutions of that person's times. Often the biographer's subject made a special contribution to a nation, to a culture, or to human beings in general, or represented a particular time and place or group of people. Biography never ignores the world around the individual. A biography centers on one person, but in tracing that person's interaction with others and penetrating to his or her inner core, it can—indeed it *should*—reveal much about life during a particular time.

The following exercises introduce you to the personality, intellect, and impact of Martin Luther King, Jr. The first two exercises show you how three biographers treated aspects of King's personality. The passages provided demonstrate both the potential appeal of descriptive narrative writing and biography's power to shed light on the times during which the subject lived. The exercises also require you to search passages for hints about the biographer's own values and assumptions.

Next you will examine King's intellectual development, with special attention to his adherence to the strategy of militant nonviolence in advancing the African-American cause. Again, you will see that biography can facilitate the understanding of a period of time as well as of an individual.

The last two exercises address the question of King's place in history. How important was he to the civil-rights movement? Had he not lived or had he made a different career choice in 1954—for example, taking a job in Detroit, Michigan, rather than Montgomery, Alabama—would the struggle for equality of African-Americans have been significantly affected? How should revelations about his behavior toward women and his plagiarism as a graduate student influence his stature? The exercises provide you with a better appreciation of the purposes of biography and with a deeper understanding of American life during the 1940s, 1950s, and 1960s. At the same time, they give you further practice evaluating secondary and primary sources, which you encountered in earlier chapters.

Personality, the Core of Biography

A major task of any biography is to construct a word portrait of an individual human being. The biographer must describe both a person's physical attributes and his or her behavioral patterns and qualities of mind. By evaluating the ways biographers execute this task, you can learn a good deal about effective writing and about how individuals relate to their environment.

Born on January 15, 1929, Martin Luther King, Jr., grew up in a middle-class African-American neighborhood in Atlanta, Georgia. Racial segregation pervaded the South during those years, in housing, schools, the workplace, and public transportation. African-Americans virtually always found themselves subordinated to whites. *Young* Martin suffered at the hands of prejudiced white people, whom he resented deeply. Yet he enjoyed a largely happy childhood under the watch of his stern, patriarchal father, a prominent Baptist minister, and his mild-mannered, polished mother, the daughter of a preacher.

Exercise 1: Catching the Reader's Eye and Ear

The following passages from two biographies of King offer partial portraits of King during his teens. Read the passages, underlining words and phrases that you find particularly effective in creating a mental picture of King's appearance and personality. **Circle any words or phrases that you find awkward or confusing**.

A. . . . M. L. was a sensuous youth who played a violin, liked opera, and relished soul food—fried chicken, cornbread, and collard greens with ham hocks and bacon drippings. Physically he was small and plump-faced, with almond-shaped eyes, a mahogany complexion, and expressive hands. But the most memorable thing about him was his voice. It had changed into a rich and resonant baritone that commanded attention when he spoke in class or held forth in a nearby drugstore.

He discovered something else about his voice: girls blushed and flirted when he spoke to them in his mellifluent drawl. A natty dresser, nicknamed "Tweed" because of a fondness for tweed suits, he became a connoisseur of lovely young women, many of them from the best Negro families in Atlanta. A. D. could not remember a time when his big brother was not interested in girls, and M. L. himself laughed that women and food were always his main weaknesses. "He kept flitting from chick to chick," A. D. said later, "and I decided I couldn't keep up with him. Especially since he was crazy about dances, and just about the best jitterbug in town."[4]

B. . . . Mike [Martin] developed early the aggressiveness typical of the short male. When he left Morehouse [College in Atlanta], he would be five feet seven inches tall and weigh slightly less than 170 pounds. He was healthy, agile, and solidly built. The young ladies he courted remember his short height only as an after thought. His sartorial fastidiousness and his confident charm and eloquence are the primary legacies of his enterprise among Atlanta's belles. Mike's selection of pretty girls was as careful as the choice of his wardrobe. . . . Lacking aquiline features and long straight hair—near-white attributes upon which black mothers placed a pathetically dogmatic value—Mike charmed with his mellifluent baritone. The genteel damsels of the black aristocracy were told of the Rubicons they caused to be crossed, of the calamitous Waterloos their mere existence created, of the Troys of whose destruction they were the source:

On desperate seas, long wont to roam,
Thy hyacinth hair, thy classic face,
Thy Naiad airs have brought me borne
To the glory that was Greece and the grandeur that was Rome.

One catches distinctly the cadences of that earnest, deep voice, the vowels distended three times their normal length. And one pictures the pleasure mirrored in the lovely face of a feminine listener. Mike King played hard, dressed well, and attempted to be a great lover.[5]

Now read the passages a second time. Which one most effectively captures and holds your attention? Use the space provided to explain your conclusion. Identify any principles for good narrative writing that could be drawn from your evaluation of the two passages.

_____

_____

_____

_____

_____

_____

_____

_____

_____

Go back and read the passages a third time, this time looking for indications of prevalent values of the society in which King grew up. List those values here.

_____

_____

_____

_____

1. Did King fit comfortably into the middle-class African-American community in Atlanta in which he was raised? _____

2. What are the indication in either passage of the biographer's values? Are there instances in which the biographer goes beyond merely presenting facts and expresses an opinion?

_____

_____

Fitting Individuals into Their Times

The year 1952 found King studying for a doctorate in theology at Boston University. He already possessed degrees from Morehouse College and Crozer Theological Seminary in Pennsylvania. King was also searching for a wife. As a minister in the African-American community, he knew that he would be expected to "marry sooner rather than later," that his choice would "affect his career" as well as his personal life, and that "he must look for certain objective qualities in prospective mates."[6]

Exercise 2: Courting in the 1950s

In the following selections, Pulitzer Prize–winning author Taylor Branch describes King's first encounter with his future wife. Read selection A, keeping in mind that a common purpose of the biographer is to describe his subject in the context of the world around him.

A. King was doing his best to marry. He and Philip Lenud double-dated frequently, and King met other possibilities in the churches where he preached. He had long since invented a coded rating system for eligible women, calling an attractive woman a "doctor" and a stunning one a "constitution," saying that she was "well-established and amply endowed." . . .

King's bachelor style fit the postwar fashion. He elbowed his male friends in the ribs if a "constitution" went by, collected phone numbers, and began each contact with a promising new lady by trying out his lines. Early in 1952, he called a woman blindly on the recommendation of a friend. After passing along a few of the friend's compliments as reasons why he had obtained the phone number, King threw out his opening line. "You know every Napoleon has his Waterloo," he said. "I'm like Napoleon. I'm at my Waterloo, and I'm on my knees."

"That's absurd," Coretta Scott replied. "You don't even know me." Unabashed, King continued with the melodrama and poetry, throwing in some comments about his course work that identified him quickly as a man of substance. His come-on crisscrossed between directness and caricature, authority and humor. When Scott did not hang up on him after his opening flourishes, it was only a matter of minutes until he persuaded her to have lunch with him the next day. He picked her up in his Chevrolet and took her to a cafeteria.[7]

1. Does Branch suggest that King's behavior toward women was commonplace or exceptional for unmarried men during the 1950s? _____

2. How would you describe King's behavior? _____
   _____

3. What is implied in King's behavior about his attitude toward women (their likes, their dislikes, and their role in society, for example)? _____
   _____

FIGURE 8.1 *Coretta Scott King and Martin Luther King Shortly After Their Marriage*
Courtesy of AP/Wide World Photos.

Coretta Scott was the daughter of an Alabama farmer who owned several hundred acres of land. Although a member of the local African-American elite, Obadiah Scott was far from wealthy. As a child, his daughter "had picked cotton in the fields and scrubbed clothes in a washtub," but she received enough education in a local church school to qualify for a partial scholarship at Ohio's recently integrated Antioch College. Graduating from Antioch in 1951, Coretta went to the New England Conservatory of Music in Boston, aspiring "to become a classical singer." She received only a small scholarship, hardly enough to support herself. So she worked "at a fashionable Beacon Hill boardinghouse in exchange for room and board."[8] Selection B, again from Branch's study, conveys her state of mind when she first met King and goes on to show how the two reacted to one another. See Figure 8.1.

B. Suffering from the compounded insecurities of race, poverty, and the competitive world of music, Scott struggled to keep her dignity and her optimism above her acute sense of realism. "The next man I give my photograph to is going to be my husband," she told herself. Nearly two years older than King, she would turn twenty-five that spring and was already past the prime marrying age of that era. In the absence of a career break or a prosperous suitor, she would soon be obliged to scale back her ambitions.

King knew all this. It would become one of his stinging jokes to tease her with the remark that she would have wound up picking cotton back in Alabama had he not come along. At their first lunch, however, he praised her looks, especially her long bangs, and launched into discussion of topics from soul food to [Walter] Rauschenbusch [a prominent American theologian]. To Coretta Scott, who had been put off at first sight by King's lack of height, he seemed to grow as he talked. As he drove her back to the Conservatory, he shocked her again by declaring that she would make him a good wife. "The four things that I look for in a wife are character, intelligence, personality, and beauty," he told her. "And you have them all. I want to see you again." She replied unsteadily that she would have to check her schedule.[9]

Read over the first paragraph in the passage above. In explaining Coretta's feelings of insecurity, Branch mentions her race, her poverty, and the competitive nature of her chosen field.

1. What else might he have mentioned? _____
2. What does this omission say about the author? _____
_____

Now look again at passage B as a whole. What does it say about the values of young Martin and Coretta and the society around them? Were they conforming to or rebelling against their society? _____
_____
_____
_____
_____
_____
_____
_____
_____

Connecting Personality and Ideas

Martin Luther King, Jr., was a complex man with a sharp, well-trained intellect. In the course of his academic preparation at Morehouse, Crozer, and Boston University, he encountered a wide range of ideas about religion, politics, and human society. By examining the connection between King's readings in school and his later activism on social issues, including his strategy of nonviolent resistance, we can evaluate the impact of King's surroundings on his ideas as well as the degree of originality in his thought.

King's academic readings included the work of American theologians Walter Rauschenbusch (1861–1918) and Reinhold Niebuhr (1892–1971) and of the Indian independence leader Mohandas Gandhi (1869–1948). The following paragraphs provide some background on the three men, followed by passages by each of them. Each passage addresses either the social activism of clergy or nonviolent resistance as a strategy for combating injustice.

A Baptist clergyman, Rauschenbusch had been a leader of the turn-of-the-century social gospel movement, which sought to liberate Protestant churches from a narrow focus on saving individual souls. According to Rauschenbusch and his allies, the clergy should become directly involved in ameliorating the ills of city and factory. Social gospelers believed that humankind had the capacity to Christianize society and to create a Kingdom of God on earth, but only through broad reforms, and Rauschenbusch inclined toward a radical conception of the changes required. He attacked capitalism for dividing "industrial society into two classes,—those who own the instruments and materials of production, and those who furnish the labor for it." In the inevitable struggle between the two classes, labor always held the weaker hand. Only a socialist system, he insisted, would eliminate this class division, restoring "the independence of workingmen by making him once more the owner of his tools and the [recipient] . . . of the full proceeds of his production."[10]

FIGURE 8.2 *Gandhi and His Followers in India*
Courtesy of Corbis Images.

Although Niebuhr criticized capitalism, he also rejected the social gospel's faith in the essential goodness of humankind. An activist in reform causes, he eventually became a prominent writer on Christian doctrine and its application to society's problems. With the publication in 1932 of his *Moral Man and Immoral Society*, he emerged as the key spokesman for what became known as neo-orthodoxy. According to this view, people were born in original sin and could never fully escape that fact. Because people were inherently selfish, they could not expect the coming of a Kingdom of God on earth. Nevertheless, they could (and should) seek changes in an unjust system, often by shifting power away from dominant groups.

American society in the early twentieth century may have been unjust, but at least it was not part of a foreign empire, as was Mohandas Gandhi's native land. Despite British oppression in India, Gandhi first became involved in reform causes while practicing law in South Africa's rigidly segregated society. After spending two decades there organizing Indians to resist discrimination, he returned to his homeland and soon became an agitator for change, including independence from British rule. Already an advocate of nonviolent resistance to injustice, which he called *Satyagraha*, he worked diligently to train his countrymen in the technique (see Figure 8.2). In 1930 he organized a march of some 200 miles in protest of the British Salt Acts, which were a particular burden on poor Indians. During World War II he used British desperation for assistance against Japan and Germany to campaign for independence. When the British finally granted India its independence in 1947, Gandhi turned all his efforts to the containment of strife between Hindus and Muslims in India. In January 1948 a Hindu extremist assassinated him in New Delhi.

Exercise 3: The Origins of King's Social Activism and Strategy of Nonviolent Resistance

Read the following passages from the works of Rauschenbusch, Gandhi, and Niebuhr. All three may be used to explain King's development of a strategy for advancing the African-American cause in the United States. Answer the questions following each passage.

A. [Rauschenbusch] The social gospel is the old message of salvation, but enlarged and intensified. The individualistic gospel has taught us to see the sinfulness of every human heart and has inspired us with faith in the willingness and power of God to save every soul that comes to him. But it has not given us an adequate understanding of the sinfulness of the social order and its share in the sins of all individuals within it. It has not evoked faith in the will and power of God to redeem the permanent institutions of human society from their inherited guilt of oppression and extortion. . . . The social gospel seeks to bring men under repentance for their collective sins and to create a more sensitive and more modern conscience.[11]

1. What is the difference between the "social gospel" and the "individualistic gospel"?

   _____

   _____

2. How would clergy who subscribe to the social gospel differ in their professional activities from clergy who subscribe to the individual gospel? _____

   _____

3. As an African-American and an aspiring clergyman, how might Martin Luther King, Jr., have used the passage above to define his mission in life? _____

   _____

B. [Gandhi] Satyagraha differs from Passive Resistance as the North Pole from the South. The latter . . . does not exclude the use of . . . violence for the purpose of gaining one's end, whereas the former . . . excludes the use of violence in any shape or form. . . .

Its root meaning is holding on to truth, hence truth-force. . . . In the application of Satyagraha I discovered in the earliest stages that pursuit of truth did not admit of violence being inflicted on one's opponent but that he must be weaned from error by patience and sympathy. For what appears to be truth to the one may appear to be error to the other. And patience means self-suffering. So the doctrine came to mean vindication of truth not by infliction of suffering on the opponent but on one's self.

But on the political field the struggle on behalf of the people mostly consists in opposing error in the shape of unjust laws. When you have failed to bring the error home to the lawgiver by way of petitions and the like, the only remedy open to you, if you do not wish to submit to error, is to compel him by physical force to yield to you or by suffering in your own person by inviting the penalty for the breach of the law. Hence Satyagraha largely appears to the public as Civil Disobedience or Civil Resistance. It is civil in the sense that it is not criminal.

The lawbreaker breaks the law surreptitiously and tries to avoid the penalty, not so the civil resister. He ever obeys the laws of the State to which he belongs, not out of fear of the sanctions but because he considers them to be good for the welfare of society. But there come occasions, generally rare, when he considers certain laws to be so unjust as to render obedience to them a dishonour. He then openly and civilly breaks them and quietly suffers the penalty for their breach. . . .

The beauty and efficacy of Satyagraha are so great and the doctrine so simple that it can be preached even to children. It was preached by me to thousands of men, women and children commonly called indentured Indians with excellent results.[12]

1. According to Gandhi, what is the difference between Passive Resistance and Satyagraha?

   _____

   _____

2. Why, under Satyagraha, may personal suffering prove essential? _____

   _____

3. How does the practice of Satyagraha differ from the actions of the average lawbreaker?

   _____

   _____

4. In the American South during the 1950s, to which laws might an African-American apply Satyagraha? _____

   _____

C. [Niebuhr] However large the number of individual white men who . . . identify themselves completely with the Negro cause, the white race in America will not admit the Negro to equal rights if it is not forced to do so. . . .

On the other hand, any effort at violent revolution on the part of the Negro will accentuate the animosities and prejudices of his oppressors. Since they outnumber him hopelessly, any appeal to arms must inevitably result in a terrible social catastrophe. Social ignorance and economic interest are arrayed against him. If the social ignorance is challenged by ordinary coercive weapons it will bring forth the most violent passions of which ignorant men are capable. Even if there were more social intelligence, economic interest would offer stubborn resistance to his claims.

The technique of non-violence will not eliminate all these perils. But it will reduce them. It will, if persisted in with the same patience and discipline attained by Mr. Gandhi and his followers, achieve a degree of justice which neither pure moral suasion nor violence could gain. Boycotts against banks which discriminate against Negroes in granting credit, against stores which refuse to employ Negroes while serving Negro trade, and against public service corporations which practice racial discrimination, would undoubtedly be crowned with some measure of success. Nonpayment of taxes against states which spend on education of Negro children only a fraction of the amount spent on white children, might be an equally efficacious weapon. . . .

There is no problem of political life to which religious imagination can make a larger contribution than this problem of developing non-violent resistance. The discovery of elements of common human frailty in the foe and . . . the appreciation of all human life as possessing transcendent worth . . . creates attitudes which transcend social conflict and thus mitigate its cruelties. . . . These attitudes of repentance which recognize that the evil in the foe is also in the self, and these impulses of love which claim kinship with all men in spite of social conflict, are the peculiar gifts of religion to the human spirit. . . . It is no accident of history that the spirit of non-violence has been introduced into contemporary politics by a religious leader of the orient.[13]

1. When Niebuhr says that "the white race in America will not admit the Negro to equal rights if it is not forced to do so," is he advocating violence by African-Americans to achieve their rights? _____ Explain. _____
   _____
   _____
   _____

2. Why does Niebuhr believe that Gandhi's ideas are especially applicable to the American South? _____
   _____

3. Is Niebuhr's judgment on the applicability of Gandhi's ideas in the American South primarily moral or practical? _____ Explain. _____
   _____

Passage D is from King's first book, *Stride Toward Freedom*, written during the year following his triumphant role in the Montgomery bus boycott of 1955–1956. This event began less than two years after King moved to that city to assume the pastorate at Dexter Avenue Baptist Church. Although King played no part in the incident leading to the boycott, he soon emerged as leader of the civil-rights campaign in Montgomery, largely because he had not lived there long enough to become associated with one of the many factions that divided the African-American community. The segregation of Montgomery buses provided ideal circumstances for the application of nonviolent resistance (see Figure 8.3), and King's success elevated him to national prominence. *Stride Toward Freedom* centered on the boycott itself but also included much information about King's life before moving to Montgomery. Read the following selection, from his chapter "Pilgrimage to Nonviolence."

D. [King] Not until I entered Crozer Theological Seminary in 1948 . . . did I begin a serious intellectual quest for a method to eliminate social evil. . . . I spent a great deal of time reading the works of the great social philosophers. . . . Walter Rauschenbusch's *Christianity and the Social Crisis* . . . left an indelible imprint . . . by giving me a theological basis for the

FIGURE 8.3 *Montgomery Bus Boycott*
Courtesy of Corbis Images.

social concern which had already grown up in me as a result of my early experiences. . . . I felt that he had fallen victim to the nineteenth century "cult of inevitable progress" which led him to a superficial optimism concerning man's nature. Moreover, he came perilously close to identifying the Kingdom of God with a particular social and economic system—a tendency which should never befall the Church. But . . . Rauschenbusch had done a great service for the Christian Church by insisting that the gospel deals with the whole man, not only his soul but his body; not only his spiritual well-being but his material well-being. . . .

I was also exposed for the first time to the pacifist position in a lecture by Dr. A. J. Muste. I was deeply moved by Dr. Muste's talk, but far from convinced of the practicability of his position. . . . I felt that while war could never be a positive or absolute good, it could serve as a negative good in the sense of preventing the spread and growth of an evil force. War, horrible as it is, might be preferable to surrender to a totalitarian system—Nazi, Fascist, or Communist. . . .

. . . one Sunday afternoon I traveled to Philadelphia to hear a sermon by Dr. Mordecai Johnson, president of Howard University. . . . Dr. Johnson had just returned from a trip to India, and . . . he spoke of the life and teachings of Mahatma Gandhi. . . . I left the meeting and bought a half-dozen books on Gandhi's life and works.

. . . As I read I became deeply fascinated by his campaigns of nonviolent resistance. . . . The whole concept of "Satyagraha" . . . was profoundly significant to me. . . . Prior to reading Gandhi, I had about concluded that the ethics of Jesus were only effective in individual relationships. The "turn the other cheek" philosophy and the "love your enemies" philosophy were only valid, I felt, when individuals were in conflict with other individuals; when racial groups and nations were in conflict a more realistic approach seemed necessary. But after reading Gandhi, I saw how utterly mistaken I was. . . . It was in this

Gandhian emphasis on love and nonviolence that I discovered the method for social reform that I had been seeking for so many months.

But my intellectual odyssey to nonviolence did not end here. During my last year in theological school, I began to read the works of Reinhold Niebuhr. The prophetic and realistic elements in Niebuhr's passionate style and profound thought were appealing to me, and I became so enamored of his social ethics that I almost fell into the trap of accepting uncritically everything he wrote.

. . . in *Moral Man and Immoral Society* . . . he argued that there was no intrinsic moral difference between violent and nonviolent resistance. The social consequences of the two methods were different, he contended, but the differences were all in degree rather than kind. Later Niebuhr began emphasizing the irresponsibility of relying on nonviolent resistance when there was no ground for believing that it would be successful in preventing the spread of totalitarian tyranny. It could only be successful, he argued, if the groups against whom the resistance was taking place had some degree of moral conscience, as was the case in Gandhi's struggle against the British. . . .

. . . As I continued to read . . . I came to see more and more the shortcomings of his position. For instance, many of his statements revealed that he interpreted pacifism as a sort of passive nonresistance to evil expressing naive trust in the power of love. But this was a serious distortion. My study of Gandhi convinced me that true pacifism is not non-resistance to evil, but nonviolent resistance to evil. Between the two positions, there is a world of difference. Gandhi resisted evil with as much vigor and power as the violent resister, but he resisted with love instead of hate. True pacifism is . . . a courageous confrontation of evil by the power of love, in the faith that it is better to be the recipient of violence than the inflicter of it, since the latter only multiplies the existence of violence and bitterness in the universe, while the former may develop a sense of shame in the opponent, and thereby bring about a transformation and change of heart.[14]

Complete the following multiple-choice questions by **circling** the appropriate answer.

1. According to King, Rauschenbusch's primary influence on him was in providing a theological basis for looking at human beings as
   a. individuals rather than as part of a group.
   b. possessing a material as well as a spiritual side to which the clergy must devote attention.
   c. essentially spiritual creatures.
   d. capable of producing a "Heaven on Earth."

2. King criticizes Rauschenbusch on which *two* of the following points? Rauschenbusch was
   a. too pessimistic about human nature.
   b. too optimistic about human nature.
   c. insensitive to the negative impact of capitalism on human society.
   d. too inclined to associate a specific social and economic system with the perfection of human society.

3. Why was King initially dubious about pacifism?
   a. It was impractical.
   b. It was too aggressive in outlook.
   c. He did not like the people espousing it.
   d. It was only useful against totalitarian systems.

4. According to King, Niebuhr distorted pacifism by equating it with
   a. hatred of one's enemies.
   b. violent nonresistance to evil.
   c. a naive acceptance of democracy.
   d. nonresistance to evil.

5. According to King, Gandhi's Satyagraha could be effective by
   a. forcing opponents to change because of economic pressures.
   b. forcing the state to intervene to protect civil rights.
   c. persuading opponents to change by making them feel ashamed.
   d. persuading opponents to change for fear of violence.

6. According to Niebuhr in passage C, which of the choices in question 5 would make nonviolent resistance potentially successful for African-Americans in the South?
   a.
   b.
   c.
   d.

   In the space following, **write a paragraph** summarizing the roots of King's nonviolent social activism. In developing your paragraph, you may use documents A through D as well as the background material provided on each selection. Be sure to begin your paragraph with an appropriate topic sentence.

_____

_____

_____

_____

_____

_____

_____

_____

_____

_____

_____

_____

_____

_____

Why Some Are Called

James Thomas Flexner, a biographer of George Washington, calls the first president "the indispensable man." No other person in America during the revolt against Great Britain and the first years of the republic, Flexner asserts, possessed the combination of qualities necessary to bring to a successful conclusion the struggle for independence and to hold the new nation together once that struggle had ended.[15]

Did Martin Luther King, Jr., play an indispensable role in the civil-rights movement for African-Americans between 1955 and his assassination in 1968? Or had the movement already achieved momentum by the time King was thrust upon the national scene in 1955–1956 through the Montgomery bus boycott, thus making his role significant but hardly indispensable? Were the efforts of the National Association for the Advancement of Colored People (NAACP) through the courts and in the U.S. Congress actually more central to the cause of African-Americans than the highly visible activities of King? How important were efforts at grassroots organization in the Deep South, often spurred by the Student Nonviolent Coordinating Committee (SNCC) and peopled by courageous if relatively obscure men and women, both white and black? And what about the significance of individuals whose actions provided the spark for a single event but who then retreated forever to the background? Such questions address the issue of an individual's place in history.

King clearly combined several qualities of leadership matched by no other African-American of his time. He was polished, well educated, and intellectual enough to appeal to wealthy northern liberals, but he was sufficiently down-to-earth, eloquent, and charismatic to reach poor African-Americans in the South as well. King was able to mobilize southern African-Americans behind a movement for desegregation in public facilities and politics as no one else had done before.

Yet, over time, King failed to unite African-Americans, North and South, behind his strategy of nonviolent resistance. In the mid-1960s, when he increasingly directed his activities toward cities above the Mason-Dixon Line and toward economic rather than civil-rights issues, he ran into considerable difficulty. By some estimates, King's stature was in decline at the time of his death, and only his martyrdom saved—or bolstered—his reputation as the preeminent leader of his people.

Furthermore, even King's role in the civil-rights movement is open to question. Although he led the Montgomery bus boycott, for example, the event grew out of the spontaneous refusal late one afternoon of a tired but dignified and determined seamstress, Rosa Parks, to give up her seat in the white section of a public bus. The boycott's success was very much in doubt until the U.S. Supreme Court ruled on November 13, 1956, in a case argued by NAACP lawyers, that segregation on public buses was unconstitutional. Two years earlier, lawyers for the same organization had persuaded the high court to declare racial segregation in public schools unconstitutional.

In the aftermath of the March on Washington of August 1963 and King's famous "I Have A Dream" speech (see Figure 8.4), *Time* magazine placed a portrait of the NAACP's executive secretary on its cover, declaring that "if there is one Negro who can lay claim to the position of spokesman and worker for a Negro consensus, it is a slender, stoop-shouldered, sickly, dedicated, rebellious man named Roy Wilkins"[16] (see Figure 8.5). Although King led demonstrations in Birmingham, Alabama, that proved crucial to President John F. Kennedy's submittal of a civil-rights bill to Congress during the summer of 1963, the lobbying efforts of the NAACP's Clarence Mitchell, Jr., arguably produced the bill's enactment early the following year and created the momentum necessary in the legislative branch for passage of the Voting Rights Act in 1965. SNCC's grassroots organizing and protests in the South over the previous three years were also critical.

Even King's detractors concede that, as former NAACP official Denton L. Watson has written, he was "a catalyst and will always remain a monumental figure in civil-rights history." "His greatest contributions," Watson asserts, "were his ability to arouse the human spirit to unparalleled heights and to burden the consciences of white liberals."[17] But Watson and others dispute the almost godlike stature that King attained in the first generation after his death.

FIGURE 8.4 *Martin Luther King at the March on Washington, August 1963*
Courtesy of AP/Wide World Photos.

How should we contend with this controversy over King's place in history? Certainly we have too little information before us here to render a judgment. In fact, a careful and comprehensive study of the matter would take years to complete, and even then our conclusions would be challenged by others. This is true partly because advocates of different positions on how best to advance the cause of African-Americans have an important stake in resolution of the issue. King espoused a distinct strategy that some rejected, both during his lifetime and later on. To these people, King's nonviolent tactics could never lead to full equality in America.

Another factor, however, rests in the inherently imprecise nature of the enterprise. To address the issue of King's place in history, we at some point must ask what America in the 1950s and 1960s would have been like without him, or at least without his leadership of the

FIGURE 8.5 *NAACP Executive Secretary Roy Wilkins*
Courtesy of Corbis Images.

civil-rights movement, and that involves asking what would have happened had a situation been different from what it was. Such questions often are interesting and even essential in grappling with important issues, but they can never be answered definitively. Nevertheless, we can frame precise questions to focus our research and to ensure a coherent addressing of the issue. Indeed, framing appropriate questions is an essential skill in doing history.

Exercise 4: King's Place in History (Part I)

In the space provided, write three specific questions you would want answered in addressing the role of King in the Montgomery bus boycott of 1955–1956. Think about the needs of the African-American community in Montgomery as it confronted a largely hostile white majority, about the organization of the African-American community in Montgomery before King's arrival in 1954, and about the significance of outside forces in influencing the outcome of the bus boycott. In preparing your questions, do not hesitate to refer to earlier sections of this chapter or to your textbook.

1. _____

_____

2. _____

_____

3. _____

_____

King—Warts and All

Other sources of controversy over King's place in history are his marital infidelities and his plagiarizing portions of his writings while in graduate school. After he became a national figure in the Montgomery bus boycott, King was away from home more often than not and was constantly the object of sexual overtures from attractive women. King often accepted their offers—a fact not made public until the mid-1980s. In his Pulitzer Prize–winning biography, David J. Garrow reports that some friends of King saw his behavior "as 'a natural concomitant' of the tense, fast-paced life" he led, while others viewed "it as standard ministerial practice in a context where intimate pastor-parishioner relationships long had been winked at." Still others regarded King's conduct as "typical of the overall movement"—that is, married men in the civil-rights movement frequently engaged in sexual relationships with women other than their wives. Garrow also notes that King insisted that his wife play the role of traditional housewife and mother, rather than taking on a highly visible role in the movement.[18]

King's plagiarism while at Crozer Theological Seminary (1948–1951) and at Boston University (1951–1954) became public knowledge in 1990 and was the subject the following year of a roundtable discussion in *the Journal of American History*. The publication offered a standard definition *of plagiarism* as "*any* unacknowledged appropriation of words or ideas," and it judged King guilty of the practice in a large number of "his academic papers, including the dissertation."[19] In commenting on the findings, King biographers Garrow and David L. Lewis agreed that King had to have been aware that he was engaging in behavior unacceptable in the academic world. But they and others also pointed out that, as David Thelen writes, King often "grounded his activities on the borders between cultures [, most notably] . . . between expectations bred of evangelical, southern, African American folk cultures [, where the borrowing of words and ideas without acknowledgment was widespread and acceptable,] and those bred of northern, white, university scholarship," where such borrowing in written work was generally forbidden.[20]

Cornish Rogers, a fellow African-American student with King at Boston University, suggested to David Thelen that King expected Professor L. Harold DeWolf, his adviser there, to examine his work "with a fine-tooth comb," and that when DeWolf passed it, King simply assumed it was all right.[21] David L. Lewis speculated that DeWolf and other professors applied a lower standard to King because he was African-American. DeWolf in particular among his professors was known as a stickler for detail, so it is hard to believe, according to Lewis, that he was unaware of King's practice.

Whatever the precise details, King's sexual conduct and his plagiarism have stirred a lively discussion among scholars and editorialists in the popular press. Historians generally regard discovering what happened and then explaining why it happened as their two primary tasks. In contrast, editorialists preoccupy themselves with assessing the meaning of what happened. Many historians engage in this enterprise as well, even if only as a secondary activity. The final exercise of this chapter asks you to examine the behavior of King in relation to the question of his position as a historic figure.

Exercise 5: King's Place in History (Part II)

On separate sheets of paper, write a short essay on King's place in history in the context of his overall record. In completing this assignment, ask yourself how important his illicit sexual relations and plagiarism are in comparison to his efforts to promote civil rights for African Americans. Think of what we now know of the philandering of former presidents John F. Kennedy and Bill Clinton. Think of the fact that much of Kennedy's Pulitzer Prize–winning book *Profiles of Courage* was ghostwritten. Should these embarrassing facts in the historical record influence the judgments we make of individuals who have held—or hold—positions of leadership in our society? If so, how? Do these facts diminish their accomplishments in other areas? For example, is King's record on civil rights for African-Americans diminished by his traditional conception of the role of women—at least of the woman he chose as his wife?

This chapter has concentrated on written evidence and on examining the individual in the context of history and society. In the next chapter, we shift the focus to two elements of the modern media—motion pictures and television—and to the ways in which they reflect popular tastes and attitudes.

Notes

[1] John A. Garraty, *The Nature of Biography* (New York: Knopf, 1957), 31.

[2] Alan Shelston, *Biography* (London: Methuen, 1977), 3.

[3] Ibid., 348.

[4] Stephen Oates, *Let the Trumpet Sound: The Life of Martin Luther King, Jr.* (New York: Harper & Row, 1982), 15–16.

[5] David L. Lewis, *King: A Critical Biography* (Baltimore: Penguin Books, 1970), 22.

[6] Reprinted from *Parting the Waters: America in the King Years, 1954–63* by Taylor Branch, published by Simon & Schuster. Copyright © 1988 by Taylor Branch.

[7] Ibid., 94–95.

[8] Ibid., 95.

[9] Ibid., 95–96.

[10] Walter Rauschenbusch, *Christianity and the Social Crisis* (New York: Macmillan, 1907), 406–407.

[11] Walter Rauschenbusch, *A Theology for the Social Gospel* (New York: Macmillan, 1918), 4–6.

[12] Excerpted from M. K. Gandhi, *Satyagraha* (Ahmedabad: Navajivan Publishing, 1951), pp. 6–7.

[13] Reprinted from *Moral Man and Immoral Society* by Reinhold Niebuhr. Copyright 1932 by Charles Scribner's Sons; copyright renewed © 1960 by Reinhold Niebuhr.

[14] Copyright © 1958 by Martin Luther King, Jr., copyright renewed 1986 by Coretta Scott King, Dexter King, Martin Luther King III, Yolanda King, and Bernice King.

[15] James Thomas Flexner, *Washington: The Indispensable Man* (Boston: Little, Brown, 1974).

[16] *Time*, August 30, 1963, 9.

[17] Denton L. Watson, "Scholars' Focus on Martin Luther King Has Skewed Our Understanding of the Civil-Rights Struggle," *Chronicle of Higher Education*, January 23, 1991, A44.

[18] David J. Garrow, *Bearing the Cross: Martin Luther King, Jr., and the Southern Christian Leadership Movement* (New York: Morrow, 1986), 374–376.

[19] Martin Luther King, Jr., Papers Project, "The Student Papers of Martin Luther King, Jr.: A Summary Statement on Research," *Journal of American History* (June 1991), 31.

[20] David Thelen, "Becoming Martin Luther King, Jr.: An Introduction," ibid., 11.

[21] "Conversation Between David Thelen and Cornish Rogers," ibid., 54.

9: Analyzing Visual Media: Movies and Television

Mass Culture in America, 1950 to the Present

In 1956 American culture critic Bernard Rosenberg sadly warned that "contemporary man . . . finds that his life has been emptied of meaning, that it has been trivialized. He is alienated from his past, from his work, from his community, and possibly from himself . . . [at a moment when] he has an unprecedented amount of time on his hands which . . . he must kill lest it kill him." Rosenberg accused television of vulgarizing art and literature. "Never before," he lamented, "have the sacred and the profane, the genuine and the specious, the exalted and the debased, been so thoroughly mixed that they are all but indistinguishable." "Mass culture" threatened simultaneously "to cretinize our taste," "brutalize our senses," and "pave the way to totalitarianism."[1]

Although many analysts of American culture agreed with Rosenberg, his view did not go unchallenged. Fellow critic David Manning White questioned Rosenberg's and his allies' view of contemporary American society, contending that the highbrow critics of mass culture lacked a true sense of history. As White suggested, those who worked themselves into "such a frenzy over the stereotyped activity of the Lone Ranger as he shoots a couple of bad hombres [on television] on a Sunday's afternoon" should consider that, for nearly seven hundred years leading up to the twentieth century, bearbaiting, in which crowds watched dogs rip apart a chained bear, had been among the most popular recreations in England. Furthermore, whatever the quality of most offerings of the modern mass media, White pointed out that it made available a substantial menu of high culture to a larger audience than ever before. In 1956, for example, network television presented William Shakespeare's *Richard III*, starring Sir Laurence Olivier, and more than 50 million people tuned in to at least some portion of it. White found the United States in the 1950s to be far from the "cultural wasteland" that its critics lamented.[2]

Commentators of the 1950s disputed the quality of mass culture in the United States, just as they do today, but no one denied that television was playing an ever-increasing role in the lives of Americans. In 1950 only 12 percent of American homes possessed this ultimate dispenser of mass culture; five years later the figure was up to 67 percent. By 1960 nearly 46 million American homes—88 percent of the total—included at least one television set. A decade later, nearly one in three households had *more* than one set. In 1956 the average

139

hours of daily television watching topped five hours. Fifteen years later, the average daily usage per household was up to six hours.

Television provided tough competition for its predecessor in the mass visual arts, the movies. Financing for television came from on-the-air advertising, a system that allowed viewers to watch programs for nothing more than a small addition to their monthly electricity bills. Going to the movies meant leaving home and paying an admission fee. On any given evening, the average American family could enjoy several hours of entertainment at home for a few pennies, whereas two hours of movie entertainment would cost several dollars and require miles of travel. More and more Americans chose home and television. Weekly attendance at cinemas in the United States stood at 90 million for the first three years after World War II; by the mid-1950s the figure was half that, and it continued to drop. In 1987 only 25 million people a week went to the cinema. Yet movies still played a significant role in American culture. The emergence of home videos in the 1980s ensured their popularity well into the future.

The Mass Media and Cultural Change

Because television and movies occupy a substantial portion of our leisure time, our skill in interpreting their offerings plays an important part in our effort to understand the world around us. This chapter seeks to develop that skill by introducing you to movies and television as representations of American culture and as instruments for comprehending change over time.

Movie and television companies operate to make a profit. Most of the time, major production companies present what they think at least a substantial portion of us want to hear and see. Thus their productions say a good deal about mainstream American values, tastes, and ways of doing things. Companies sometimes try to mold our tastes and attitudes as well, but if they do so with a heavy hand or without a sense of the boundaries of public tolerance, they risk financial disaster.

The following exercises take you through a series of the most successful television programs from the 1950s through the 1980s. Then you will compare two well-known movies, that were filmed at least 30 years apart. By analyzing these popular examples of the mass media, you should grasp some of the changes and continuities in American life during three generations after World War II and develop some skill in evaluating television and film offerings as historical evidence.

Exercise 1: Situation Comedy During the 1950s

This exercise focuses on a significant element of the emerging television culture of the 1950s, the situation comedy. During those years, six sitcoms made the top 25 in the Nielsen ratings for at least three years. (*The* number of television-equipped homes tuned to a particular program on an average evening determines these ratings.) Most popular of all was "I Love Lucy," which in its six years of original shows finished first four times and never ranked lower than third. No other situation comedy approached that record, yet many were staples of American viewers. Each of the following three paragraphs provides a brief description of one of the highest-rated situation comedies from the 1950s. Exercise 1 tests your skill in making connections among the shows and encourages you to examine the significance of these connections in the context of American society and culture of the period.[3]

FIGURE 9.1 *The Ricardos at Home*
Courtesy of Photofest.

A The lead characters in "I Love Lucy" were Lucy (Lucille Ball) and Ricky Ricardo (Desi Arnaz). Of Scottish ancestry, Lucy was a housewife. Her Cuban husband Ricky, the leader of a band that performed in a New York nightclub, wanted to keep her that way. Lucy had different ideas. She wanted to be in show business, just like her husband, and her plots to get on stage often produced hilarious situations for the audience, maddening and embarrassing ones for her husband. The Ricardos lived in a middle-class apartment building in Manhattan (see Figure 9.1). Their landlords, Ethel (Vivian Vance) and Fred Mertz (William Frawley), were the leading secondary characters. Ethel often joined Lucy in her misguided adventures, much to Fred's dismay. In the episode of January 19, 1953, after a considerable publicity campaign, Lucy gave birth to Little Ricky. During the program's last season of weekly production (1956–1957), Little Ricky (Richard Keith) became a regular character. In early 1957, the Ricardo family, blessed by Ricky's steady advancement in the entertainment business, moved into a country home in Connecticut.

B "Father Knows Best" has been described as "the classic wholesome family situation comedy." The series took four years to reach the top 25, but it then rose all the way to sixth place in the 1959–1960 season. The setting was Springfield, a typical midwestern town, where Jim Anderson (Robert Young) resided with his wife Margaret (Jane Wyatt) and their three children, Betty (Elinor Donahue), Bud (Billy Gray), and Kathy (Lauren Chapin) (see

142   •   *Analyzing Visual Media: Movies and Television*

FIGURE 9.2 *The Andersons of "Father Knows Best"*
Courtesy of Photofest.

Figure 9.2). After a day on the job with the General Insurance Company, Jim came home to face the problems of a suburban family. Margaret was a sensitive, concerned homemaker, but, in the midst of a crisis, it was usually father who, "with a warm smile and some sensible advice," resolved the issue. Conflicts occasionally arose among the three children, but they were always mild in nature and they rarely carried over to the next episode.

C "The Danny Thomas Show" was the top-ranked situation comedy for the last three seasons of the 1950s. The series began in 1953 as "Make Room for Daddy" and changed in the fall of 1956 to its better-known title after actress Jean Hagen quit her role as wife of Danny Williams. Danny was "a sometimes loud but ultimately soft-hearted lord of household," whose job as a nightclub entertainer frequently took him away from home. The show focused on problems created by his absence from his two children, Terry (Sherry Jackson) and Rusty (Rusty Thomas). When Hagen left the show, Mrs. Williams was written out as having died, and the next season featured Danny—with the determined assistance of his children—exploring his new options for matrimony. By the beginning of the fall 1957 season, Danny had married Kathy (Marjorie Lord), who also added Linda (Angela Cartwright), a child from a previous marriage, to the household. The series continued in original episodes until 1964, with occasional changes in the cast of young people.

Go back over the descriptions of the three sitcoms, looking for patterns that reflect the values and ways of doing things in America during the 1950s. (*Hint:* You may find your textbook and the first two exercises in Chapter 8 in this book helpful.) **Identify** three patterns that fit all three popular programs.

1. _____
2. _____
3. _____

Exercise 2: Identifying Changes in Cultural Values

A common technique for examining cultural change is to compare evidence from different time periods. This exercise turns to leading sitcoms of the 1970s and offers you a chance to further develop your skill in detecting patterns of change over time.

The 1970s were great years for sitcoms. Sixteen of the genre finished in the top 25 of the Nielsen ratings for at least three years. During eight of the ten years, a sitcom finished first in those ratings. Five times, sitcoms controlled the top two positions and, in the 1974–1975 season, sitcoms held eight of the first ten slots, including numbers one through seven.

We have singled out four top shows to provide you with a source for comparison with the earlier decade. When you compare these descriptions with those in Exercise 1, some differences should become readily apparent. In addition, as you contemplate these differences, you will readily recognize some of the changes that had occurred in the United States between the two decades.

Read the following descriptions and complete the writing exercises that follow.

A "All in the Family" finished at the top of the Nielsen ratings for five seasons. As two broadcast historians have remarked, the program "changed the course of television comedy" by injecting "a sense of harsh reality to a TV world . . . previously . . . populated largely by homogenized, inoffensive characters and stories that seemed to have been laundered before [reaching the airwaves]. . . ." Lead character Archie Bunker (Carroll O'Connor) certainly was offensive to large numbers of potential viewers. A foreman for a tool and die company in New York City, Archie possessed a variety of prejudices often associated with poorly educated, working-class Americans of white, Anglo-Saxon Protestant lineage. As a resident of a city with representatives of virtually every racial and ethnic group imaginable, Archie came into frequent contact with people not to his liking. To him, African-Americans were "jungle bunnies" or "spades"; Chinese "chinks"; Jews "hebes"; Poles "Polacks"; and Puerto Ricans "spics." In his own home in the borough of Queens, he had to put up with his Polish son-in-law Mike Stivic (Rob Reiner). Mike, or "Meat Head" as Archie called him, did not hold a job because he was studying for a degree in sociology, and he was every bit as liberal as his father-in-law was conservative. The family next door, the Jeffersons, was black. Its head, George (Sherman Hemsley), owned a cleaning business, and his own feelings toward whites rivaled Archie's prejudice toward blacks. Archie's wife, Edith (Jean Stapleton), a homemaker, was best friends with George's wife, Louise (Isabel Sanford), also a homemaker, and "Meat Head" was a buddy of the Jeffersons' son, Lionel (Mike Evans), which ensured that Archie constantly had to contend with people of different races and ethnicity. The more tolerant women—Louise, Edith, and Archie's daughter Gloria (Sally Struthers)—often played peacemakers when the men grew raucous.

When "All in the Family" first aired in early 1971, it stirred so much controversy that it was nearly canceled. After a few months, however, it hit the top of the ratings. Crucial to its appeal was the fact that different groups reacted to it in different ways. Liberals saw Archie's lines, which among other things were laced with incorrect word usages, as a satire on bigotry, whereas many others sympathized with his prejudices and applauded him as one of their own.

B "Sanford and Son" finished in the top five of the Nielsen ratings four times during the 1970s. The show starred Fred Sanford (Redd Foxx), a sixty-five-year-old African-American junkyard owner in Los Angeles, and his live-in son and business partner, Lamont (Demond Wilson). A widower, Fred was perfectly content with his small business but was always under pressure from his more ambitious son to pursue it more vigorously. Lamont, in turn, frequently threatened to leave the business for something more profitable. Invariably, the threats would lead Fred to feign a heart attack and declare, with his head turned skyward, "I'm comin', Elizabeth [his deceased wife], I'm comin' to join you." Secondary characters included Donna Harris (Lynn Hamilton), a nurse and Fred's girlfriend, and Aunt Esther Anderson (LaWanda Page), who operated a rooming house next to the Sanfords' junkyard and home. The setting for most of the episodes was the Sanfords' living room.

C "Happy Days" began slowly in the 1974–1975 season, but, as a result of a shift in billing among the main characters, it rose in its third year to the top of the ratings. The series

FIGURE 9.3 *"Three's Company"*
Courtesy of Photofest.

exploited nostalgia for the 1950s and its supposedly simpler, more wholesome lifestyle. The setting was Milwaukee, Wisconsin, and initially the two main characters were high school students Richie Cunningham (Ron Howard) and Potsie Weber (Anson Williams). Secondary characters included Richie's father Howard (Tom Bosley), owner of a hardware store; his mother Marion (Marion Ross), a housewife; and Arthur "Fonzie" Fonzarelli (Henry Winkler), a stereotypical "greasy-haired motorcycle kid." What pushed the show up the charts was its shift in emphasis from the relationship between the naive Richie and his more experienced pal Potsy to that between the "cool" dropout Fonz and the "straight" kids represented by Richie. Fonzie's mannerisms, especially his thumbs-up gesture, were often imitated by American teenagers. For the most part, scenes alternated among Richie's home, Arnold's malt shop—a teenage hangout—and Jefferson High School.

D "Three's Company," set in Santa Monica, California, centered on the relationship of three roommates (see Figure 9.3)—Jack Tripper (John Ritter), Janet Wood (Joyce DeWitt), and Chrissy Snow (Suzanne Somers)—and their persistent efforts to persuade their landlords and others that nothing inappropriate was going on among them. Given the obvious sex appeal of the two women, doing so was not easy. Jack sometimes implied that he was a homosexual, and his adeptness in the kitchen added plausibility to the idea in the minds of his traditional landlords, the Ropers (Audra Lindley and Norman Fell). Janet, who worked in a florist shop, and Chrissy, a typist, totally lacked culinary skills, while Jack was training to become a chef. The sexual innuendos that abounded in the script led to complaints from religious groups, but the show finished twice in the second slot in the Nielson ratings.

If you compare the preceding descriptions with those from the 1950s, you will find that there was much greater diversity in leading sitcoms during the 1970s. Indeed, for the later period, it is difficult to think of three patterns that fit all or almost all of the programs covered as Exercise 1 asked you to do for the 1950s. Instead, list five elements that you found in any of the sitcoms of the 1970s that you did *not* find in the series from the 1950s.

1. _____
_____
2. _____
_____
3. _____
_____
4. _____
_____
5. _____
_____

Exercise 3: Change and Continuity in American Culture from the 1950s to the 1980s

Now let us turn to an examination of a situation comedy that dominated the Nielsen ratings during the second half of the 1980s—"The Cosby Show," which began telecasting on September 20, 1984. The show featured the Huxtables, an upper-middle-class African-American family. Most of the episodes took place in their residence (see Figure 9.4), a New York City brownstone. The father, Cliff Huxtable (Bill Cosby), was an obstetrician whose office was

FIGURE 9.4 *"The Cosby Show"*
Courtesy of Photofest.

attached to his home. The mother, Claire (Phylicia Rashad), was a lawyer. The parents did their best to juggle their careers with the task of raising four children. "I just hope they get out of the house before we die," Cliff gasped as he collapsed into bed at the end of the first episode. Yet the parents constantly showed warmth and affection toward their children, and toward each other, even when disciplining them for a variety of infractions.

Bill Cosby, who controlled the scripts, used the show to promote "child-rearing theories he had developed while pursuing his doctorate in education in the 1970s," as well as to celebrate aspects of African-American culture. Some critics attacked his approach for portraying African-Americans unrealistically and for ignoring the issue of race relations, but the show touched a responsive chord for American viewers. In the 1986–1987 season, 35 percent of homes with televisions on during its time-slot tuned into "The Cosby Show," a remarkable figure when one considers the steady decline of network viewing during the 1980s with the expansion of cable TV. One would have to go all the way back to the 1964–1965 season to find a program, the western "Bonanza," with a higher rating.

Write a paragraph on a separate sheet of paper outlining *at least* one aspect of "The Cosby Show" that is different from the sitcoms from the 1950s and 1970s discussed above and *at least* one aspect that appears in two or more of those sitcoms. Do the similarities and differences suggest anything about change and continuity in American life between the 1950s and 1980s?

Exercise 4: Patterns in Sitcoms of the 1990s

In comparing sitcoms of the 1950s and 1970s, we saw that by the latter decade much greater diversity existed in the types of people featured and the issues addressed. That pattern has continued right to the present, and it reflects the access to a larger number of channels enjoyed by a growing portion of the population. In class, region, race, and ethnicity, the viewing audience has become increasingly diverse, and entrepreneurs, whether people seeking to expand their markets through television advertising or producers of television programs trying to attract advertising, must find ways to appeal to segments of that audience.

"Seinfeld" is the most successful sitcom of the mid-1990s. It first aired in May 1990, when "Cheers" was at the top of the Nielsen charts, followed closely by "Roseanne," "A Different World" (a spinoff of "The Cosby Show"), "The Cosby Show," and "Murphy Brown." "Seinfeld" did not make the top 25 in the Nielsen chart until the 1992–1993 season, but in the season after that it ranked third, and over the next two seasons it finished at the very top. Just as significant, it generated successful "clones," programs that use different characters but essentially the same formula. We describe "Seinfeld" and the most obvious clone, "Friends," below and then pose questions, first about what they have in common with each other, then about how they compare with other sitcoms discussed in this chapter.

Although significant generalizations are possible from examining two programs that are similar and popular at the same time, "Seinfeld" and "Friends" represent only a portion of the popular sitcoms of the 1990s. Successful sitcoms "Roseanne" and "Home Improvement," for example, employ very different formulas. Thus tastes vary, not just across time, but from group to group and even person to person, at the same time.

A "Seinfeld" is set on the Upper West Side of New York City and includes four main characters, all in their thirties, all white, and all single. Jerry Seinfeld (himself) is a standup comic "coping with dating, nutty friends, and the indignities of city life." His former lover, Elaine Benes (Julia Louis-Dreyfus), is now his close but platonic friend. George Costanza (Jason Alexander), balding, stocky, and short, is a classic "worrywart" and Jerry's best friend. Cosmo Kramer (Michael Richards), Jerry's "next-door neighbor," is an "eccentric entrepreneur" who, despite his clumsiness, tends to emerge upright from his many scrapes. Often referred to as the "show about nothing," "Seinfeld" displays its characters during leisure time, either in Jerry's apartment or in a nearby diner, dealing with "life's trivia," but also in romantic relationships. Treatment of issues of human sexuality are sometimes quite explicit.

B "Friends" began broadcasting in September 1994 and tied for eighth place on the Nielsen chart during its first season. The program is set in New York City and features six intelligent, attractive, white men and women in their twenties. All of them are single. They are shown "hanging out" either at the apartment of Monica Geller (Courteney Cox) or at a nearby coffeehouse discussing "love, sex, feelings, dates, lack of dates, the prospect of dates, and other matters of importance in their lives."

1. Identify six similarities between "Seinfeld" and "Friends."

   a. _____

   b. _____

   c. _____

   d. _____

   e. _____

   f. _____

2. How many of those similarities fit "The Cosby Show"? Which ones? _____

_____

_____

_____

3. Which program from the 1970s of those described in Exercise 2 has the most in common with "Seinfeld" and "Friends"? Explain. _____

_____

_____

_____

4. Identify at least four differences between "Seinfeld" and "Friends" on the one hand and the programs from the 1950s discussed in Exercise 1 on the other. _____

_____

_____

_____

_____

_____

_____

_____

_____

_____

_____

Exercise 5: Change and Continuity in American Culture from the 1950s to the Present

Some cultural values persist and others change. Now that you have examined some of the leading sitcoms of the last two generations, you are prepared to comment on change and continuity in American culture since 1950.

On a separate sheet of paper, **write** a short (500-word) essay comparing leading sitcoms from the 1950s to the 1990s (their settings, their characters, their characters' relationships and values, and so forth). The key question you should address is, What does your comparison tell you about change and continuity in America from the 1950s to the 1990s? Use your responses to Exercises 1 through 4, as well as your textbook, to complete this assignment. You may also want to consult the ninth edition of Tim Brooks and Earl Marsh's *The Complete Dictionary to Prime Time and Cable TV Shows 1946–Present* (New York: Ballantine Books, 2007). In thinking about continuities, or aspects that stay the same, do not ignore the obvious. Changes often stand out in comparisons over time simply because they represent differences. Similarities are taken for granted because they are so common.

Once you have collected your thoughts, follow the same procedures you used in preparing essays in Chapters 6 and 7: construct a thesis; develop an outline, including sections for an introduction, a body, and a conclusion; write a first draft; and then revise it to produce a final draft.

Exercise 6: Movies and Culture

Now that you have some experience evaluating television programs as reflections of American culture, let us move on to a more challenging exercise on movies. This time you will go to the sources themselves—two movies from different time periods—and use them to understand change and continuity in American life. This exercise will also ask you to find reviews or commentaries on these movies, which will reinforce the library skills you acquired in Chapter 4 and enhance your understanding of how each film fits into its time period.

You have three pairs of movies from which to choose. The first pair includes *The Man in the Gray Flannel Suit* (1956), the story of a man trying to juggle the demands of career and family, and *Working Girl* (1986), which depicts a young woman's struggle to succeed on Wall Street. The movies have some obvious differences: for example, the first is a drama, the second a romantic comedy. Yet they reveal much about the times in which they appeared, and some of the differences between them reflect changes in American culture over a thirty-year period. The same is true of the reviews and commentaries. What critics said, and who said it where can be every bit as important in identifying contemporary values and concerns as the movies themselves.

The second and third pairs include movies that possess obvious similarities. The second pair are about men who fought in foreign wars and then returned home to resume their earlier lives. The first, *The Best Years of Our Lives* (1946), was about three veterans of World War II; the second, *The Deer Hunter* (1978), is about veterans of the Vietnam War. The third pair are both murder mysteries—in fact, the second is based on the script of the first, which was a movie adapted from a play. Alfred Hitchcock directed *Dial M for Murder* (1954). Set in London, England, in the 1950s, the movie has all the suspense and twists of plot one would expect from a Hitchcock film. *A Perfect Crime* (1998) represents a takeoff on that classic, updated to the New York of the 1990s. Despite the differences between the three pairs of movies, all of them help us understand similarities and differences in American life between the decade following World War II and more recent eras.

Two reasons for selecting these pairs as your range of choices are (1) all the films should be readily available to you (either in your university film library or in a local video outlet) and (2) all of them were widely commented on at the time of their release. Your instructor may help you make arrangements to view the films as a group.

As your final assignment in this chapter, write a four-to-five page essay (typewritten, double-spaced) analyzing the movies and the reactions to them as reflections of change and continuity in recent American history. In preparing your essay, take the following steps:

1. Review your readings and lecture notes on the time periods in which the two movies were filmed. Then watch each movie. Take careful notes throughout, with particular attention to the following questions:

    a. How are gender roles portrayed in the films?

    b. How is success defined?

    c. What produces the main conflicts in the two movies?

    d. How does the use of language compare in the films?

    e. How is human sexuality treated?

    f. What is the pace of the action?

    g. To what degree do your answers to the above questions suggest change in American culture? continuity?

2. Look up the following commentaries on the movies you chose as your subjects and take extensive notes. Then try answer the questions that follow.

The Man in the Gray Flannel Suit: See the *New York Times*, April 13, 1956, p. 21, and April 22, 1956, section H, p. 1; and *The New Yorker* 32 (April 21, 1956), 75–76.

Working Girl: See the *New York Times*, December 21, 1988, p. C22; January 15, 1989, p. E27; and February 3, 1989, p. 30.

The Best Years of Our Lives: See the *New York Times*, November 22, 1946, p. 27, and *The New Yorker*, November 23, 1946, p. 75.

The Deer Hunter: See the *New York Times*, December 15, 1978, section 1E, p. 5, and *The New Yorker*, December 18, 1978, p. 66.

Dial M for Murder: See the *New York Times*, May 29, 1954, p. 13, and *Newsweek*, May 10, 1954, p. 100.

A Perfect Murder: See the *New York Times*, June 5, 1998, p. E12, and *Newsweek*, June 15, 1998, p. 70.

a. How do you think commentators might have reacted to each movie if the time frame of each release were reversed?

b. What do your conclusions tell you about change and continuity in America from the time span between the two movies?

3. Think back to what you learned in the exercises on television sitcoms about cultural change in America after World War II. Do the films confirm your conclusions?

4. Review the steps on essay writing in Exercise 5 of Chapter 7. Use them as guides in writing your essay.

This chapter has introduced you to the challenge of examining television programs and movies in different time periods. You should now have a greater understanding of change and continuity in American life, and of the attitudes and behavior of individuals or generations other than your own. Comparisons across time can also prove useful to people faced with important decisions in their personal lives or work. With this point in mind, we turn to the concept of historical analogy in Chapter 10.

Notes

[1] Bernard Rosenberg and David Manning White, eds., *Mass Culture* (Glencoe, Ill.: Free Press, 1957), 4, 5, 9.

[2] Ibid., 14, 16.

[3] The descriptions in Exercises 1, 2, and 3, with occasional direct quotations, are based on Tim Brooks and Earle Marsh, *The Complete Dictionary to Prime Time Network and Cable TV Shows, 1946–Present*, 6th ed. (New York: Ballantine Books, 1995), 26–28, 168–169, 184–185, 257–258, 322–324, 365–366, 377–378, 687–688, 792–793, 917.

10: *Historical Analogy: Using the Past in the Present*

Korea, Vietnam, and the Persian Gulf

In making decisions, people often compare a present situation to a past occurrence, using a similarity between two events for guidance. The course chosen in that past occurrence may have had negative consequences, for example, so the person in the present situation avoids a similar approach. Or, the earlier course may have had positive consequences, in which case the person in the present situation replicates the approach. However, such a procedure can sometimes prove costly. As discussed at the beginning of this volume, all human events possess unique qualities, thus making reasoning by historical analogy a precarious enterprise.

Yet as scholars Richard E. Neustadt and Ernest R. May observe, "The future has no place to come from but the past, hence the past has predictive value."[1] The challenge is not to resist using history to guide us; rather, it is to gauge *when* to use history and *how*. This chapter shows you how some American leaders have used the past to make important foreign policy decisions and offers you the opportunity to decide whether they used it well. In the process, you will develop insights about the limits that history holds for policymakers as well as its potential. These insights, in turn, should advance your skill in using historical analogy in your own life.

The Lessons of World War II

Since 1945 the lessons of World War II have served a fundamental purpose for the makers of U.S. foreign policy. The idea emerged during the war that if only the United States had acted differently between 1931 and 1939 the conflict could have been averted. The United States should have halted the aggressions of Japan, Italy, and Germany before those powers became so strong that only a major war could stop them. With the defeat of those nations, American leaders determined to thrust their country into the international arena as never before in peacetime. Only such involvement, they believed, could avert another global conflict. Thus the postwar era became one of expanding U.S. intervention abroad—politically, economically, and militarily.

Exercises 1 through 3 center on decisions leading to the three largest U.S. military interventions since 1945—Korea in 1950, Vietnam in 1965, and the Persian Gulf in 1990. In each case, American leaders used historical analogies to make their decisions. We ask you to examine those analogies and to reach your own conclusions about their applicability.

151

Exercise 1: Korea and the Lessons of the 1930s

In the wee hours of the morning of June 25, 1950 (Korean time), communist North Korea launched an all-out military attack on its American-sponsored neighbor to the south, the Republic of Korea (ROK). Over the next several days, North Korean forces advanced rapidly, capturing Seoul, the South Korean capital, and routing ROK troops all along the front. Only a quick movement of American troops to the peninsula from Japan could prevent the North Koreans from overrunning the entire country. See Figure 10.1.

U.S. President Harry S Truman received word of the North Korean attack late on a Saturday evening while relaxing at his home in Independence, Missouri. He rushed back to Washington the next day and convened a series of meetings of his top advisers to discuss the evolving crisis. On the three-hour flight to the nation's capital, Truman later wrote in his memoirs, he reflected on events of the last two days:

> I recalled some earlier instances: Manchuria, Ethiopia, Austria. I remembered how each time that the democracies failed to act it had encouraged the aggressors to keep going ahead. Communism was acting in Korea just as Hitler, Mussolini, and the Japanese had acted ten, fifteen, and twenty years earlier. I felt certain that if South Korea was allowed to fall, Communist leaders would be emboldened to override nations closer to our own shores. If the Communists were permitted to force their way into the Republic of Korea without opposition from the free world, no small nation would have the courage to resist threats and aggression by stronger Communist neighbors. If this was allowed to go unchallenged, it would mean a third world war, just as similar incidents had brought on the second world war.[2]

By the time Truman's plane landed in Washington, the United Nations Security Council had convened in New York at American behest and voted unanimously to call for a cease-fire in

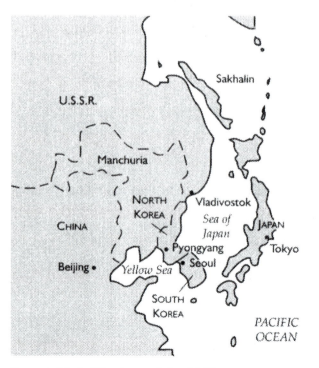

FIGURE 10.1 *Northeast Asia, 1950*

Korea and a withdrawal of North Korean forces from South Korea. (The Soviet Union was boycotting the United Nations at the time.) Two days later, again at American beckoning, the U.N. Security Council recommended that member nations "furnish such assistance to the Republic of Korea (South Korea) as may be necessary to repel the armed attack and to restore international security to the area."[3] Finally, on June 30, with a plea before him from field commander General Douglas MacArthur for the commitment of American troops to the fighting, Truman approved the dispatch of U.S. army units from Japan. The president's actions received widespread support in the United States and from America's allies in Europe, Asia, and Latin America. Even neutral India expressed approval.

Your task here is to evaluate the appropriateness of Truman's historical analogy. First we provide you with background on the three cases from the 1930s cited by Truman: Japan's attack on Manchuria, Italy's invasion of Ethiopia, and Germany's occupation of Austria. We also provide background on Korea. Then we ask you to examine Truman's use of history.

As you read the following material, keep comparing the cases to Korea.

Case Study I: Manchuria

Japan had been expanding its influence in Manchuria, the rich, northeastern region of China, since the turn of the century. During the 1920s, however, the rising tide of nationalism in China jeopardized Japan's position. The Nationalist government of China frequently encouraged boycotts of Japanese goods. With the onset of the worldwide depression in 1930, this policy increasingly threatened Japan's interests.

On September 18, 1931, Japanese troops, guarding a railway that Japan had controlled in Manchuria since 1906, used an explosion outside Mukden as a pretext to seize key cities and towns throughout the region. During the following months, Japan's Kwantung army occupied all of Manchuria and set up a puppet regime. Japan's action violated three treaties to which Japan was a signatory: the Kellogg-Briand Pact of 1928, which outlawed war, the Nine-Power Treaty of 1922, which recognized the territorial integrity of China, and the covenant of the League of Nations, which prohibited members from resorting to war before exhausting its mechanisms for the peaceful resolution of conflicts.

The League of Nations moved sluggishly in response to Japan's action. It gave little consideration to applying economic sanctions, which, in any event, would have been useless without cooperation from the United States (not a member of the League). In March 1932, the League finally voted not to recognize Japan's conquest of Manchuria, a stance that the United States had adopted two months earlier. Later in the year, the League assigned blame for the entire incident to Japan. Japan responded by withdrawing from the organization but not from Manchuria.

Japan's expansion in Asia did not end with Manchuria. In 1937 Japan moved southward along the China coast. Three years later, it occupied northern Indochina and during the following summer it advanced into the southern portion of that French colony. With the last action, the United States instituted an economic embargo on Japan, thus setting the two nations on a collision course that culminated at Pearl Harbor on December 7, 1941.

Case Study 2: Ethiopia

Italy's attack on Ethiopia was the first act of aggression by a European power during the 1930s. Italy had attempted to conquer that East African nation in the late nineteenth century, only to suffer a humiliating defeat. In October 1935, Benito Mussolini, Italy's fascist dictator, sought to avenge that defeat and expand his African empire. Although the weakest of Europe's great powers, Italy possessed a modern, mechanized army against which Ethiopia's troops, often armed with knives and spears, were clearly overmatched.

In this case, the League of Nations acted immediately. It condemned Italy for violating its covenant and called for economic sanctions against the aggressor. These sanctions did not include an embargo on petroleum, however, which was Italy's paramount need. Great Britain and France refused to support a petroleum embargo, fearing that Italy would retaliate in the Mediterranean and that the United States, which at the time was a major oil exporter, would refuse to comply. Many in Great Britain and France also feared that extreme action would lead Mussolini to turn to Germany, which, under the rule of Nazi Adolf Hitler, already was making noises about altering the European balance of power.

Because of these nations' fears, an effective system of collective security never emerged against Italy, and it conquered and annexed Ethiopia in May 1936. The League rescinded its economic sanctions two months later.

Emboldened by his Ethiopian success, Mussolini soon sent large quantities of men and materiel to Spain to support a fascist rebellion against the republic there. France and Great Britain sponsored a Non-Intervention Committee to discourage outside involvement in the Spanish civil war, but despite Italian and German membership in that group, Mussolini and Hitler openly flouted its purpose. The United States Congress passed a neutrality act prohibiting shipments to either side. Given the magnitude of assistance provided to the Spanish rebels by Italy and Germany, U.S. policy clearly helped the fascists to emerge victorious in Spain in the spring of 1939.

Meanwhile, Italy withdrew from the League of Nations, formed a close alliance with Germany, and swallowed Albania. In June 1940, Italy joined Germany in war against France and Great Britain.

Case Study 3: Austria

Germany's annexation of Austria in March 1938 was only the first step in Hitler's expansion in Europe. He already had flouted the terms of the Treaty of Versailles ending World War I by rearming and by reoccupying the Rhineland on Germany's western frontier. Now he turned to annexing new territory. See Figure 10.2.

Austria was a small, ethnically German nation, but the Treaty of Versailles forbade *Anschluss* (union) between Germany and Austria. In the early 1930s France moved to prevent even a customs union between the two nations. Yet Hitler acted with a boldness that kept both France and Great Britain off balance.

In February 1938, Hitler declared it Germany's responsibility to promote the rights of Germans no matter where they resided. Those rights included self-determination, he announced, and the 7 million Austrian Germans were being denied that right. In the face of this external pressure and considerable agitation by Nazis within his own realm, Austrian chancellor Kurt von Schuschnigg called a plebiscite for March 9 to determine whether the people desired union with Germany. Hitler mobilized his troops along Austria's border, insisting that the plebiscite be called off. Schuschnigg complied, but now Hitler demanded his resignation and replacement by Nazi leader Arthur Seyss-Inquart. Austrian president Wilhelm Miklas resisted this demand, however, and on March 11 troops from Germany crossed the border into Austria. Four days later, Hitler's armies seized Vienna. Great Britain and France did nothing beyond issuing verbal protests.

Soon Hitler began pressuring Czechoslovakia for the liberation of its Sudeten Germans. Czechoslovakia was a multiethnic nation carved out of the Habsburg empire after World War I. On its western border with Germany lay the Sudetenland, which possessed a German majority. When Hitler's harassment of Czechoslovakia reached a climax in September 1938, British and French leaders supported his demand for annexation of the Sudetenland rather than risk early war. Completely isolated politically, its country virtually

FIGURE 10.2 *Europe, 1935*

surrounded by German forces and its ethnic Germans agitating in the Sudetenland, the Czechoslovakian government complied. To cheering crowds in London, British prime minister Neville Chamberlain declared, "I believe that this is peace in our time." Hitler promised that the Sudetenland was his last territorial demand in Europe. In March 1939, however, he took the remainder of Czechoslovakia.

Great Britain and France finally balked, and when Hitler turned on Poland they guaranteed its borders. Poland had been divided among Russia, Prussia (later Germany), and Austria late in the eighteenth century only to be pieced back together in the aftermath of World War I. In the west, it received territory inhabited by a German-speaking majority, and this land—the Polish corridor—separated Germany proper from its easternmost province, East Prussia.

Poland's resistance to Hitler, unlike Czechoslovakia's, failed to collapse. Thus on September 1, 1939, Hitler moved his armies into Poland to take what he wanted by force. In response, Great Britain and France declared war on Germany.

By this time, Germany controlled central Europe, had fortified its western frontiers, and had protected its eastern flank through a nonaggression pact with the Soviet Union. With the United States adhering to a strict policy of neutrality regarding European conflicts, the British and French stood alone against Germany. The only recourse for Great Britain and France was to fight a long war, which eventually drew in the Soviet Union and the United States and became the most destructive conflict in human history.

Case Study 4: Korea

Annexed by Japan in 1910, Korea gained an opportunity for independence with its oppressor's defeat in World War II. During that conflict, the three major nations of the Allied camp—the Soviet Union, the United States, and Great Britain—agreed that Japan should lose its vast empire. "In due course," Korea should become "free and independent."[4] Detailed agreements were not made about Korea's postwar fate, however; the Allies merely committed themselves verbally to a four-power (the three Allies plus China) trusteeship over Korea as a means of guiding its people toward self-government. As World War II came to a close in August 1945, the United States proposed to the Soviet Union that Soviet and American troops alone occupy the Korean peninsula, with the thirty-eighth parallel providing the dividing line between them. The Soviets immediately accepted.

The Americans considered the division temporary, but the Soviets moved quickly to close off their zone to outside influence. Over the next two years, the two sides failed to agree on methods for reuniting the country. Finally, in September 1947, the Truman administration decided to present the Korean issue to the U.N. General Assembly.

In November, the General Assembly overwhelmingly passed a resolution sponsored by the United States recommending that the United Nations supervise elections throughout Korea as a first step toward creating a united, independent nation. The Soviet Union, which earlier had proposed a withdrawal of foreign forces from the peninsula to permit Koreans themselves to determine their own fate, refused to cooperate with the United Nations in conducting elections. Under U.S. urging, the international organization set up elections below the thirty-eighth parallel. In August 1948, again under joint sponsorship by the United States and United Nations, the Republic of Korea (ROK) was established under the right-wing leadership of President Syngman Rhee. The ROK claimed authority over the entire peninsula, but the United Nations recognized its sovereignty only over territory below the thirty-eighth parallel.

Meanwhile, the Soviet Union supervised elections in its own zone. This process led in September to the declaration of the Democratic People's Republic of Korea (DPRK) under the communist leadership of Kim Il-sung. Like its southern counterpart, the DPRK claimed authority over the whole country. Thus by the fall of 1948, the peninsula was divided between two hostile governments, each denying the legitimacy of its neighbor. Each received sponsorship from a superpower and occupier that, in turn, was engaged in a larger "cold war" with the other.

At the end of 1948, the Soviet Union announced the withdrawal of its troops from North Korea, but the United States kept some eight thousand soldiers in the south. Conditions below the thirty-eighth parallel had been extremely unsettled since the fall of 1946, as a civil war raged between leftist and rightist forces. Washington feared that removing its troops prematurely would lead to a collapse of the ROK and a severe blow to U.S. credibility. Yet in June 1949 the United States followed the Soviet lead, leaving behind only a group of several hundred military advisers.

South and North Korean military forces were of relatively equal strength in mid-1949, but that balance did not last. The North soon acquired a substantial body of heavy equipment from the Soviet Union, including tanks, artillery, and fighter planes. Then, in early 1950, thousands of Korean nationals who had fought with victorious communist armies in China during the civil war there returned home and joined the North Korean armed forces.

In the South, meanwhile, the ROK army virtually destroyed the guerrilla movement below the thirty-eighth parallel. Although the Rhee regime remained unpopular with many people—indeed, it was constantly at loggerheads with the National Assembly—it showed no sign of falling apart. If the North was to take over the entire peninsula in the near future, it clearly would have to resort to conventional military action.

On June 25, 1950, North Korea attacked South Korea. Soviet troops did not participate directly in the North Korean attack, but Soviet equipment and training had played a key role in the development of the DPRK army. American leaders assumed that Moscow was behind the offensive.

Identifying Likenesses and Differences

You are now prepared to evaluate Truman's use of history in the Korean case. Richard E. Neustadt and Ernest R. May, who have written a book on how policymakers can use history for guidance, advocate constructing lists of likenesses and differences to gauge the applicability of past cases to present conditions. The writing down of pertinent information, they argue, ensures a disciplined process of evaluation and guards against rushing into poorly thought-out courses of action based on inadequate or faulty data.[5] The following chart provides you with an instrument for following Neustadt and May's procedure. We have started to fill it out by listing one likeness and one difference between Manchuria and Korea. Complete the rest yourself, and then answer the questions that follow in the space provided.

Korea and Manchuria

Likenesses: A government uses force to take territory from an internationally recognized government. _____

_____

_____

Differences: No great power was directly involved in Korea, as was the case in Manchuria.

_____

_____

_____

Korea and Ethiopia

Likenesses: _____

_____

_____

Differences: _____

_____

_____

Korea and Austria

Likenesses: _____

_____

_____

Differences: _____

_____

_____

1. To President Truman, incidents of the 1930s such as the Japanese seizure of Manchuria, the Italian conquest of Ethiopia, and Hitler's annexation of Austria suggested the truth of what principle? _____

_____

2. Compare the ethnic makeup of the territory occupied by Germany in March and October 1938 and that of the territories occupied by Japan and Italy during the 1930s. What was the difference? _____

   _____

3. In ethnic makeup, was the territory that North Korea attempted to occupy in 1950 more like that occupied by Germany or by Japan and Italy? _____

   _____

4. In what way were the methods used by Germany, Italy, and Japan in the 1930s and North Korea in 1950 similar? _____

   _____

5. Which do you consider more important in evaluating Truman's analogy—your response to question 3 or to question 4? Explain. _____

   _____

6. Which nation would you say was a bigger threat to the United States: Germany, Japan, and Italy during the 1930s, or North Korea in 1950? Explain. _____

   _____

7. Did North Korea's relationship with the Soviet Union make its action on June 25, 1950, more or less significant to the United States? _____ Explain. _____

   _____

8. Overall, do you find Truman's analogy persuasive or not? Write a paragraph supporting your choice. _____

   _____

   _____

   _____

   _____

   _____

   _____

   _____

   _____

   _____

   _____

Exercise 2: Vietnam and the Lessons of World War II and Korea

In the minds of most Americans, the Vietnam War is the greatest tragedy in U.S. foreign policy since World War II. The United States failed to achieve its fundamental objective—the prevention of a communist victory in South Vietnam. During the secret policy deliberations of 1964 and 1965 leading up to the massive escalation of U.S. military action, American leaders frequently used historical analogies to make their cases, sometimes in favor of and sometimes against deeper involvement. The Korean War often entered the discussions. Once President Johnson had made the decision to escalate, he and Secretary of State Dean Rusk emphasized the lessons of the 1930s in their *public* justifications.

In this exercise, we provide a background section on Vietnam and then portions of two documents, one by Undersecretary of State George Ball, who opposed U.S. escalation in Vietnam, and one by President Johnson, who ultimately rejected Ball's advice. In the former document, Ball, using the analogy of Korea, argued for caution. In the latter document, Johnson defended U.S. escalation in Vietnam, using the older 1930s analogy. Read the material presented, and answer the questions that follow.

Vietnam

As in Korea, Japan's defeat in 1945 led to an end of its occupation of Vietnam.[6] Japan had taken control of that French colony in 1940 and 1941 following France's defeat at the hands of Germany. With Japan's surrender, France tried to regain control not only of Vietnam but also of its two other Indochinese colonies, Laos and Cambodia. Great Britain's assistance and America's acquiescence enabled French troops to return, only to face resistance from a communist-led, nationalist-inspired organization called the Vietminh. In December 1946, after the breakdown of lengthy negotiations between the French and the Vietminh, the first Indochinese war began.

As the Cold War with the Soviet Union intensified and American fears of Asian communism grew with Mao Zedong's victory in the Chinese civil war during 1949, U.S. policy moved decisively into the French camp. In May 1950 the United States began furnishing aid to the French war effort. In the crisis atmosphere fueled by the outbreak of fighting in Korea in June 1950, U.S. assistance to the French grew steadily until 1954. Communist Chinese aid to the Vietminh reinforced America's determination.

In 1954 the French decided to withdraw from Indochina. The Eisenhower administration in Washington flirted with direct intervention but resisted the temptation. The threat of U.S. intervention, however, persuaded the Soviet Union and Communist China to pressure the Vietminh to accept less-than-total victory. At the Geneva Conference during the

FIGURE 10.3 *Indochina After the Geneva Conference, 1954*

spring and summer of 1954, Vietnam, Laos, and Cambodia received independence, and Vietnam was divided at the seventeenth parallel into "regrouping" zones, with the communist-controlled Democratic Republic of Vietnam located north of the line and the anticommunist Republic of Vietnam holding territory to the south (see Figure 10.3). The country was to be reunited in 1956 through internationally supervised elections. Although the United States participated in the Geneva Conference, it refused to sign the agreements, saying only that it would not use military force to disrupt the elections.

With the French withdrawing from Vietnam, the United States quickly became the most influential outside force, at least below the seventeenth parallel. Washington strongly backed Ngo Dinh Diem, the prime minister of the Republic of Vietnam, and took the lead in creating the Southeast Asia Treaty Organization (SEATO), which included the United States, New Zealand, Australia, the Philippines, Thailand, Pakistan, Great Britain, and France. Under the Geneva Accords, the Indochinese states were not permitted to join a military alliance, but SEATO members signed a protocol that put Laos, Cambodia, and South Vietnam under their protection. SEATO members agreed to *consult* one another if subversion or insurrection threatened one of the governments, although in the event of external aggression any member *could* react immediately under its own authority. In the mid-1960s, American leaders claimed that SEATO obligations dictated U.S. military intervention to save South Vietnam from communism.

Despite U.S. support, the Republic of Vietnam never prospered. Aware that North Vietnam's Ho Chi Minh would win any national election, Diem and the United States refused to permit such an event in 1956. Thus, the United States adopted the position that South Vietnam was, in itself, a legitimate independent entity. Diem, however, proved a reclusive leader who made little effort to build popular support in the countryside, where the vast majority of Vietnamese resided. By early 1961, when John F. Kennedy became president of the United States, rebellion was spreading rapidly in rural South Vietnam. That rebellion originated in popular discontent below the seventeenth parallel. In late 1960, however, North Vietnam helped to found the National Liberation Front (NLF) below the seventeenth parallel. Though dominated by communists, the NLF (also known as the Vietcong) received backing from South Vietnamese of various ideological stripes.

President Kennedy deepened U.S. involvement by increasing American military advisers in South Vietnam from 692 in early 1961 to nearly 16,000 two years later. In the fall of 1963 Kennedy finally gave the green light to a group of South Vietnamese military officers to overthrow Diem. Three weeks after Diem's overthrow and assassination, Kennedy himself was assassinated and succeeded in the White House by Lyndon B. Johnson. Conditions in South Vietnam continued to deteriorate, presenting Johnson with the unenviable choice of an embarrassing retreat or a stepped-up effort.

The choice grew increasingly stark as Diem's successors proved even less capable than he. The Military Revolutionary Council that took over from Diem lasted merely three months before being replaced in a bloodless coup by General Nguyen Khanh. Weakened by corruption and intense internal factionalism, not to mention growing insurrection in the countryside, and increasing infiltration of military units from North Vietnam, the Khanh regime staggered along until February 1965, when Generals Nguyen Cao Ky and Nguyen Van Thieu seized power in Saigon.

Through all this, President Johnson refused to make a decisive commitment either to escalate U.S. involvement drastically or to pull out. He knew from his experience as a senator during the late 1940s and early 1950s that events abroad could have a disastrous effect on domestic programs, not to mention the political fate of a sitting president and his party. On the one hand, the communist victory in China, which the United States had tried to prevent without direct military intervention, had produced sharp criticism of the Truman administration at home. On the other hand, so did the U.S. intervention in Korea in the early 1950s, which in its initial stages received widespread public approval. Chinese intervention in response to the movement of U.S. ground forces into North Korea produced an eventual military stalemate near the thirty-eighth parallel, however, and prolonged and indecisive fighting left the American people disgruntled. The ongoing war in Korea was the key issue in the Republican electoral victory of 1952. With that lesson before him, Johnson postponed a decision until after the election in November 1964. Given the hawkish rhetoric of his Republican opponent, Barry Goldwater, Johnson appeared moderate and statesmanlike. He won a landslide victory.

By early 1965 the Republic of Vietnam's fortunes were in such decline that Johnson had to make a choice. In February, he ordered sustained bombing missions above the seventeenth parallel in retaliation for Vietcong (communist) attacks on American bases in the south. By spring the NLF controlled as much as 75 percent of the countryside; soldiers from the South Vietnamese army deserted by the thousands; and infiltration of troops from North Vietnam increased, in part perhaps in response to U.S. bombing. If the United States did not sharply increase its role in the war on the ground in South Vietnam, where some 56,000 American soldiers already had landed, that area soon would be in communist hands. In April, Johnson approved the dispatch of 40,000 additional troops to help protect American bases along the coast and to launch limited attacks against the enemy.

Events continued to conspire against Johnson. By mid-May, American escalation had stirred significant protests at home, on college campuses, in the press, and in Congress, as well as in allied capitals such as London and Ottawa and at the United Nations. To exacerbate LBJ's dilemma, the Vietcong launched a major offensive against the South Vietnamese army, inflicting the heaviest casualties to date. In late July the president decided to commence saturation bombing in South Vietnam and, despite fears of Chinese intervention, a gradual increase in air attacks on North Vietnam. He also dispatched 50,000 more U.S. troops. By the end of the year, he promised General William Westmoreland, the commander of American forces in Vietnam, an additional 50,000. The decision for open-ended escalation had been made, although Johnson's ongoing sensitivity to elements of the Korean analogy kept him from ordering U.S. ground forces to operate north of the seventeenth parallel.

The escalation continued for nearly three years. In the spring of 1966, the United States began using its heaviest bombers against North Vietnam and in late June commenced bombing in the Hanoi and Haiphong areas. Secret bombing of North Vietnamese infiltration routes in Laos had begun two years before, but Johnson continued to restrict U.S. ground operations to South Vietnam. His primary objective was to produce high enemy casualties rather than to occupy new territory. By early 1968 more than 520,000 troops were in South Vietnam.

Escalation ended after the enemy launched a major military operation, the Tet offensive, in early 1968. Although the action produced high casualties for North Vietnamese and Vietcong forces and no significant territorial gains, it catalyzed antiwar protests in the United States. Public support for the war had been declining for some time, and when the Tet offensive showed that no victory for the United States was on the horizon, organized opposition to the war heightened. Thus when American military leaders requested more U.S. troops at the end of February, President Johnson turned them down. At the end of March, he deescalated the bombing campaign in North Vietnam in an effort to begin peace talks. He also announced an end of his bid for reelection in November. The gradual withdrawal of American troops from South Vietnam commenced under President Richard Nixon in 1969 and was completed in 1973. South Vietnam fell to North Vietnam two years later.

Document A is an excerpt from President Johnson's news conference of July 28, 1965.

A. Why must young Americans, born into a land exultant with hope and with golden promise, toil and suffer and sometimes die in such a remote and distant place?

The answer, like the war itself, is not an easy one, but it echoes clearly from the painful lessons of half a century. Three times in my lifetime, in two World Wars and in Korea, Americans have gone to far lands to fight for freedom. We have learned at a terrible and a brutal cost that retreat does not bring safety and weakness does not bring peace.

It is this lesson that has brought us to Viet-Nam. This is a different kind of war. There are no marching armies or solemn declarations. Some citizens of South Viet-Nam at times, with understandable grievances, have joined in the attack on their own government.

But we must not let this mask the central fact that this is really war. It is guided by North Viet-Nam and it is spurred by Communist China. Its goal is to conquer the South, to defeat American power, and to extend the Asiatic dominion of communism.

There are great stakes in the balance.

Most of the non-Communist nations of Asia cannot, by themselves and alone, resist the growing might and the grasping ambition of Asian communism.

Our power, therefore, is a very vital shield. . . . Surrender in Viet-Nam [would not] bring peace, because we learned from Hitler . . . that success only feeds the appetite of aggression. The battle would be renewed in one country and then another country, bringing with it perhaps even larger and crueler conflict, as we have learned from the lessons of history.[7]

Document B is an excerpt from a memorandum that Undersecretary of State George Ball wrote to Secretary of State Dean Rusk, Secretary of Defense Robert McNamara, and White House Chief of Staff McGeorge Bundy on October 5, 1964.

B. . . . There are at least five principal differences between the present position of the United States in South Viet-Nam and our situation in South Korea in 1951:

    a. We were in South Korea under a clear UN mandate. Our presence in South Viet-Nam depends upon the continuing request of the GVN [Government of South Vietnam] plus the SEATO [Southeast Asia Treaty Organization] protocol.

    b. At their peak, UN forces in South Korea (other than ours and those of the ROK) included 53,000 infantrymen and 1000 other troops provided by fifty-three nations.*

In Viet-Nam we are going it alone with no substantial help from any other country.

    c. In 1950 the Korean Government under Syngman Rhee was stable. It had the general support of the principal elements in the country. There was little factional fighting and jockeying for power.

In South Viet-Nam we face governmental chaos.

    d. The Korean War started only two years after Korean independence. The Korean people were still excited by their newfound freedom, they were fresh for the war.

In contrast, the people of Indochina have been fighting for almost twenty years. . . . All evidence points to the fact that they are tired of conflict.

    e. Finally, the Korean War started with . . . a classical type of invasion across an established border. It was so reported within twelve hours by the UN Commission on the spot. It gave us an unassailable political and legal base for counteraction.

In South Vietnam there has been no invasion—only a slow infiltration. . . . The Viet Cong insurgency does have substantial indigenous support. Americans know that the insurgency is actively directed and supported by Hanoi [capital of North Vietnam], but the rest of the world is not so sure. . . . Many nations remain unpersuaded that Hanoi is the principal source

Author's Note: In fact, only seventeen nations contributed combat forces to Korea.

of the revolt. And, as the weakness of the Saigon government becomes more and more evident, an increasing number of governments will be inclined to believe that the Viet Cong insurgency is, in fact, an internal rebellion.[8]

Before answering the questions at the end of this exercise, fill in the chart of likenesses and differences. We have assisted you in getting started by including one likeness and one difference between the 1930s and Vietnam. In completing the chart or answering the questions that follow, do not hesitate to refer to the background material in Exercise 1.

1930s and Vietnam

Likenesses: Attempt by one government to overthrow another. _____

_____

_____

_____

Differences: Legitimacy of government of South Vietnam widely questioned, unlike China (Manchuria), Ethiopia, and Austria. _____

_____

_____

_____

Korea and Vietnam

Likenesses: _____

_____

_____

_____

Differences: _____

_____

_____

_____

1. Document A was a *public* statement immediately accessible to millions of people. Document B was a *private* statement available only to top government officials in the State Department and the White House. How does this fact influence the way you evaluate them? Explain. _____

_____

_____

_____

2. One assertion in George Ball's comparison of Korea and Vietnam clearly conflicts with information in the background material we provide. What is that statement? Does the conflicting background information undermine Ball's overall analysis? Explain. _____

_____

_____

_____

3. Compare Ball's characterization of the situation in Vietnam with Johnson's. _____
_____
_____
_____

4. What background information on Vietnam do you find most important in evaluating the arguments of Johnson and Ball? Explain. _____
_____
_____
_____

5. Although Johnson rejected Ball's comparison of Korea and Vietnam in his ultimate decision to escalate, there was another analogy involving Korea that the president did take into account in defining the limits of U.S. escalation in Vietnam. Identify that analogy.
_____
_____
_____

6. On the basis of the information you have, which man—Johnson or Ball—do you think drew more valid historical comparisons? Why? Write a well-constructed paragraph answering these questions. _____
_____
_____
_____
_____
_____
_____
_____
_____
_____
_____

Exercise 3: The Persian Gulf, Vietnam, and World War II

We move now to the Persian Gulf crisis and war of 1990–1991. We lack the kind of official documents for this series of events that we have for the 1930s, Korea, or Vietnam, but we do have a large body of public statements from leading U.S. decisionmakers, including President George H.W. Bush (the father of president George W. Bush) and Senator John Kerry (then and now a Democratic Senator from Massachusetts, in 2004 the Democratic nominee for president). Although such evidence must be used cautiously in explaining decisions, it at least gives us a sense of what American leaders thought would appeal to the public and the world at large, and it often gives real insight into official thinking. Following are some of the analogies that President Bush and Senator Kerry advanced in debating the case for a military response to Iraq's attack on Kuwait. This exercise asks you to evaluate the analogies by examining the background information provided here and in Exercises 1 and 2. Note whether or not this exercise undermines or reinforces the views you now hold on why Bush chose the course he did and whether he chose wisely.

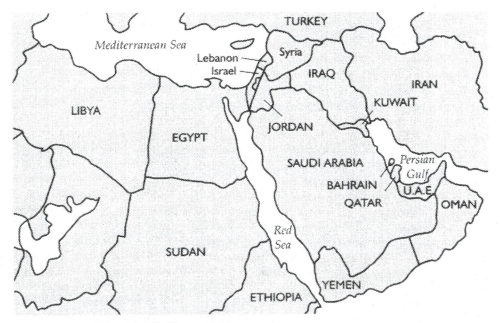

FIGURE 10.4 *The Middle East, 1990*

The Persian Gulf Crisis

After weeks of building tension, Iraq invaded Kuwait several hours before dawn on August 2, 1990 (see Figure 10.4). Kuwait's tiny army could not match the well-equipped Iraqi armed forces, which had spent the bulk of the previous decade fighting Iran. Iraq's troops met only brief and scattered resistance in Kuwait and within days occupied the entire country. Mechanized Iraqi units soon perched ominously on Kuwait's border with Saudi Arabia, possessor of the world's largest known oil reserves.

Iraq's action left Arabs deeply divided, but most of the world reacted with horror and outrage. President Bush immediately ordered economic sanctions against Iraq and froze Iraqi assets in the United States. "This [aggression against Kuwait] will not stand," he declared. The Soviet Union joined the United States in condemning the attack and suspended arms shipments to Iraq. The twelve-nation European Community, plus Japan and Canada, joined the United States in imposing trade sanctions. In Cairo, fourteen of the twenty-one members of the Arab League voted to condemn Iraqi aggression. On August 6 the United Nations Security Council passed a resolution by a 13-to-0 vote (Yemen and Cuba abstained) calling on U.N. members to end all economic dealings with Iraq and occupied Kuwait. Fearful of an Iraqi attack on Saudi Arabia, Bush received permission from the Saudi government to station U.S. air and ground forces on its territory. Deployment from the United States began early on August 7. On the same day, Turkey announced the closing of its oil pipeline out of Iraq.

Iraqi president Saddam Hussein responded by declaring Kuwait's annexation to Iraq. His government had announced on August 5 that Iraq's forces soon would begin withdrawing from Kuwait, but now Hussein claimed that his troops were needed to redraw boundaries established during an earlier era of Western colonialism. Those boundaries, he asserted, had enabled a corrupt Arab minority, the ruling class of Kuwait, to grasp a huge portion of Arab wealth. "Thank God that we are now one people, one state that will be the pride of the Arabs," he exulted.

Iraq had laid claim to Kuwait years before Hussein came to power. In 1961, when Great Britain granted full independence to the small sheikdom, the government in Baghdad asserted that Kuwait was part of Iraq, that it had been separated from Iraq by the British in the aftermath of World War I. Iraq's threat of military action led Great Britain to send troops to Kuwait, and tensions eventually subsided. The Arab League, as well as the United Nations, admitted Kuwait to membership, thus rejecting Iraq's claim. In October 1963 Iraq finally recognized Kuwait's independence. During the Iran-Iraq war from 1980 to 1988, Kuwait supported Iraq with generous loans. The United States did the same with arms aid. Both countries feared the expansion of an Iran governed by Muslim fundamentalists. But in 1990 repayment of the loans became an issue between Kuwait and a financially strapped Iraq, which, in part because of past U.S. assistance, had emerged as the strongest military power between Israel and Pakistan.

In mid-July 1990, Iraq's verbal attacks on Kuwait turned extreme, particularly over the smaller country's production of oil far in excess of OPEC quotas. Kuwait's production levels, along with those of Saudi Arabia and the United Arab Emirates, kept international prices low and impeded Iraq's effort to restore a healthy economy. Yet in late July, Hussein told Egypt and the United States that his intentions were peaceful.

Iraq's action on August 2 belied this claim. If Iraq's seizure of Kuwait held up, Hussein would control 20 percent of the world's known oil reserves. Even if he refrained from occupying all or part of Saudi Arabia, his armed forces of more than a million men would outclass any other in the region. His show of force against Kuwait would give him considerable power to intimidate his oil-rich neighbors. He would be able to push world oil prices steadily upward, which not only would help Iraq's economic recovery but allow him to build up his armed strength to even greater heights. Already he had a substantial arsenal of chemical weapons and was reportedly no more than five years away from possessing nuclear arms. Such concerns brought together a diverse coalition to oppose Iraq.

The United States led that coalition, but it was hardly the only contributor to the economic sanctions or the military buildup in the Saudi desert. The trade embargo was reinforced by U.N. Security Council resolutions authorizing the use of force to prevent the transport of goods by water to and from Iraq and then to extend the blockade to the air. By the end of September, the embargo seemed relatively leakproof, and twenty-one other nations had committed armed forces to the coalition. West Germany and Japan had promised other assistance.

Still, many people worried that if the sanctions, along with coalition military forces in the Saudi desert, stayed in place for an extended period the coalition would split apart. Despite the support of most Arab leaders, the coalition drew much opposition among Arab peoples, especially after Saddam hinted that he might withdraw from Kuwait if Israel were to withdraw from territories it occupied on its borders. Saddam also might divide his adversaries by offering to withdraw from Kuwait on the condition that Iraq receive the disputed Rumaila oil field in northern Kuwait and two strategic islands in the Persian Gulf. Evolving public opinion in the United States was an additional concern. By mid-October, polls showed Bush's favorable rating down to 56 percent from 79 percent at the beginning of the year, and antiwar demonstrators organized marches in twenty cities throughout the country.

Bush decided during the second half of October that the United States needed to build up its ground forces in Saudi Arabia to give him an offensive option. His military advisers believed that to push Iraq out of Kuwait quickly and at a low cost to friendly forces would require a virtual doubling of troops to more than 400,000. Over the next two months, an intense public debate developed over whether the United States should make an early military move to expel Iraq from Kuwait or wait longer to see if the economic sanctions would produce the desired result. The debate took on a real sense of urgency after the U.N. Security Council voted on November 29 to authorize the use of force against Iraq if it did not withdraw from Kuwait by January 15, 1991. Informed observers knew that the best time for military operations in the region would be during January, February, and early March, before the heat and windstorms or Muslim religious holidays. Some analysts in the United States suspected that President Bush wanted early military action to ensure resolution of the conflict prior to his reelection campaign in 1992. The debate culminated between January 10 and 12, 1991, when Congress took up the matter, finally voting by a narrow margin in the Senate and a larger one in the House to authorize the president to use force against Iraq.

Early on the evening of January 16, Eastern Standard Time, as coalition aircraft flooded the skies over Iraq, White House spokesman Marlin Fitzwater announced to the world that "the liberation of Kuwait has begun."

Historical Analogy in the Persian Gulf Crisis

We now turn to excerpts from two speeches by President Bush, the first given less than two weeks after Iraq invaded Kuwait, the second only hours after coalition forces launched Operation Desert Storm, the military campaign to liberate Kuwait. Following these excerpts is a speech by Senator John Kerry during the debate in Congress over whether or not to authorize early offensive action against Iraq. In his first speech (document A), Bush sought to justify his decision to deploy U.S. forces in the Persian Gulf and the Saudi desert; in the second (document B), he sought to justify the decision for war. In one instance, he used the experience of the 1930s to bolster his arguments; in the other, he used Vietnam. Kerry, a Vietnam veteran, centered his speech (document C) on that conflict in pleading for patience in the Persian Gulf.

Document A is excerpts from remarks that President Bush made to the Department of Defense on August 15, 1990.

A. . . . Our action in the Gulf is about fighting aggression and preserving the sovereignty of nations. It is about keeping our word . . . and standing by old friends. It is about our own national security interests and ensuring the peace and stability of the entire world. We are also talking about maintaining access to energy resources that are key, not just to the functioning of this country but to the entire world. Our jobs, our way of life, our own freedom [and that] of friendly countries around the world would all suffer if control of the world's great oil reserves fell into the hands of that one man, Saddam Hussein.

So, we've made our stand not simply to protect resources or real estate but to protect the freedom of nations. We're making good on long standing assurances to protect and defend our friends. . . . We are striking a blow for the principle that might does not make right. Kuwait is small. But one conquered nation is one too many.

A half century ago our nation and the world paid dearly for appeasing an aggressor who should and could have been stopped. We're not about to make that mistake twice.[9]

Document B is a portion of Bush's January 16, 1991, address to the nation announcing allied military action in the Persian Gulf.

B. Some may ask: Why act now? Why not wait? The answer is clear: . . .

The United States, together with the United Nations, exhausted every means at our disposal to bring this crisis to a peaceful end. However, Saddam clearly felt that by stalling and threatening and defying the United Nations, he could weaken the forces arrayed against him. . . .

Prior to ordering our forces into battle, I instructed our military commanders to take every necessary step to prevail as quickly as possible, and with the greatest degree of protection possible for American and allied service men and women. I've told the American people before that this will not be another Vietnam, and I repeat this here tonight. Our troops will have the possible support of the entire world, and they will not be asked to fight with one hand tied behind their back. I'm hopeful that this fighting will not go on for long and that casualties will be held to an absolute minimum.[10]

Document C is from Senator John Kerry's address to the U.S. Senate on January 11, 1991.

C. . . . I am willing to accept the horror that goes with war—when the interests or stakes warrant it. My belief is, though, that our impatience with sanctions and diplomacy does not yet warrant accepting that horror and my fear is that our beloved country is not yet ready for what it will witness and bear if we go to war.

The question of being ready and certain is important to many of us of the Vietnam generation. We come to this debate with . . . a searing commitment to ask honest questions and with a resolve to get satisfactory answers so that we are not misled again. . . .

Our VA hospitals are already full of several generations of veterans who carry or wear daily reminders of the costs of war. . . . In a country that still struggles with agent orange, outreach centers, post-traumatic stress disorder, homeless veterans—is this country ready for the next wave?

. . . Let me say right up front that the Iraqi crisis is in most ways not like Vietnam. It is very different indeed—different in international implications—different in purposes—different in risks—different in stakes—different in military strategy and opportunities. I am convinced also that it will be different in outcome.

But in one . . . critical facet, it demands that one of the central lessons of the Vietnam experience be applied—do not commit U.S. forces to combat in a potentially prolonged or bloody conflict unless Americans have reached a consensus on the need to do so. That consensus must be broad and openly arrived at with full respect for the constitutional role of the Congress—not by unilateral action by the president. . . . The memory of Vietnam says to all of us that it is far, far better that we risk . . . reining in this rush to war now, rather than trying to get the American people [to] support it at some time down the road after the shooting has started. Nothing, nothing could faster bring us a repetition of the divisions and the torment this nation faced during the 1960s and 1970s. . . .

Some . . . have suggested that sanctions alone cannot force Saddam Hussein to withdraw from Kuwait. They note that sanctions can be evaded; that the alliance could break up, with Iran agreeing to pipe Iraqi oil or the Soviet Union suddenly shifting its support for our policy to opposition. They say now is the time to strike, while the alliance is strong. They suggest that the failure of sanctions is an obvious truth that the rest of us are willfully ignoring. . . .

[Yet] with the sanctions, time is not on Saddam Hussein's side, but ours. Sanctions cost Iraq much, they cost us little. . . .

Some say look at how he survived a 7-year war with Iran. If he can do that, he will survive the sanctions. . . . However, there are major differences. During that war, it was Iran which was, for the most part, cut off from the outside world, not Iraq. And it was during that war that the Soviet Union, France, China, the United States, and other Western nations provided Saddam Hussein the guns and butter to wage the campaign against Iran. . . .

Today, Saddam Hussein does not enjoy any of that luxury.[11]

Rather than answering a series of specific questions about the materials you have read, **write a 1,000-word essay** on separate sheets of paper analyzing Bush's and Kerry's use of historical analogy in addressing the Persian Gulf crisis. The 1930s and Vietnam taught very different lessons. Identify those lessons and the method by which Bush applied them to the issues at hand. Also explain how Bush's lessons learned from Vietnam differed from those learned by Kerry. Finally, evaluate the persuasiveness with which the two men used history to justify their positions. In doing so, you may go beyond the analogies made by Bush and Kerry to outline analogies of your own. To complete this assignment, create your own likenesses/differences chart along the lines of those in Exercises 1 and 2. Also review the steps for essay writing in Chapter 5, Exercise 5.

Historical Analogy and the Wars of George W. Bush

The events of September 11, 2001 and its aftermath brought national security issues to the forefront in a way that had not occurred since early 1991. In response to Al Queda's successful attacks on the World Trade Center in New York City and the Pentagon outside Washington, D.C., President George W. Bush launched a "Global War on Terror" that embroiled the United States in major military engagements in Afghanistan and Iraq. This exercise asks you to examine the rationales, goals, and contexts of the decisions for war that the second President Bush made with particular attention to similarities and differences confronted by the three commanders-in-chief discussed earlier in this chapter.

9/11 And Its Aftermath, 2001–2003

American and British intelligence quickly identified Al Qaeda, an international terrorist organization led by Osama bin-Laden and based in eastern Afghanistan, as the instigator of the 9/11 attacks. Previously this organization had been determined complicit in attacks on American embassies in Africa in 1998 and on the U.S.S. Cole off the coast of Yemen in 2000.

In office for less than eight months, President Bush took little time to decide on a bold course of action. As historian Gary Hess observes,

> Bush . . . thought that the United States had to act quickly and decisively against Al Qaeda not just in retribution but to disabuse Osama bin-Laden and his followers of any notion that the United States lacked the will and the capacity to use its military power against them. The failure of the United States to act forthrightly . . . to earlier attacks . . . had encouraged Al Qaeda to strike again and again, culminating in the September 11 assault.[12]

From September 19 to 24, with broad international support as well as a congressional resolution authorizing the use of force against those responsible for the attacks, Bush ordered the deployment of U.S. military forces to bases in Central Asia, the Persian Gulf, and the Indian Ocean; demanded that the Taliban government that ruled most of Afghanistan turn over Osama bin-Laden and his Al Qaeda allies, close all terrorist training camps within the country, and release all "unjustly imprisoned" foreign nationals, including Americans; and froze assets in the United States held by organizations supporting terrorists. In a speech to the American people and the world, the president said of the enemy:

> We have seen their kind before. They're the heirs of all the murderous ideologies of the 20th century. By sacrificing human life to serve their radical visions, by abandoning every value except the will to power, they follow in the path of fascism, Nazism and totalitarianism.[13]

On October 7 the United States commenced air attacks on targets in Afghanistan. On the same day the president announced on national television that the attacks were targeted at "Al Qaeda terrorist training camps and military installations of the Taliban regime," that Canada, Australia, Germany, and France had "pledged forces as the operation unfolds," that over "forty countries in the Middle East, Africa, Europe and across Asia" had "granted air transit or landing rights" to American armed forces, and that "many more" nations had "shared intelligence." Taliban leaders had failed to meet American demands, Bush continued, and now they would "pay the price."[14] Precisely what that price would be was not clearly defined, but in a press conference four days later he seemed to indicate that one objective was to overthrow the Taliban government while another was to construct—perhaps with U.N. aid and certainly with international cooperation—a stable, responsible regime in its place.

In that same press conference, the president was asked by Reuters correspondent Steve Holland if the United States could "avoid being drawn into a Vietnam-like quagmire in Afghanistan." Given the bitter experience with Vietnam in the 1960s and 1970s, the quagmire into which the Soviet Union had fallen during the 1980s after invading Afghanistan, and Bush's warning to the American people on September 20 that "this war will not be like the war against Iraq a decade ago, with a decisive liberation of territory and a swift conclusion," the question was on many people's minds.[15] Afghanistan was a sizable country with much rugged terrain and since the mid 1970s a history of internal chaos. Bush had a ready response:

> We learned some very important lessons in Vietnam. Perhaps the most important lesson that I learned is that you cannot fight a guerrilla war with conventional forces. That's why I've explained to the American people that we're engaged in a different type of war, one obviously that will use conventional forces but one which we've got to fight on all fronts.
>
> . . . the first shot in the war was when we started cutting off their money, because an Al Qaeda organization can't function without money. And we're continuing our efforts to reach out to willing nations to disrupt and seize assets of the Al Qaeda organization.
>
> We are in the process of rounding up Al Qaeda members around the world. There are Al Qaeda organizations in, roughly, 68 countries. And over 200 [members of that organization] have now been apprehended. And every time I talk to a world leader, I urge them to continue finding the Al Qaeda representatives and bring them to justice.
>
> As far as the conventional forces, we've got a clear plan, and it's to say to the host [Taliban] government that you have been given your chance [to] . . . turn over the parasites that hide in their [sic] country. They obviously refused to do so and now . . . we are dismantling their military, disrupting their communications, severing their ability to defend themselves. And slowly but surely we're smoking Al Qaeda out of their caves so we can bring them to justice.
>
> . . . how long will this last? This particular battlefront will last as long as it takes to bring Al Qaeda to justice. It may happen tomorrow; it may happen a month from now; it may take a year or 2. . . . I am determined to stay the course.[16]

The United States and its allies took military action in Afghanistan without explicit approval from the U.N. Security Council, but on September 28 that body did pass a resolution calling on nations to prevent terrorist groups from organizing within their borders and suppressing them if they already existed. In these early days of what Bush called the Global War on Terror (GWOT), the president consistently solicited broad international support, including that of the United Nations. This effort led to passage of another U.N. Security Council resolution on November 14, which condemned the Taliban regime for permitting Afghanistan to become a base for the export of terrorism and supported the efforts of Afghans to replace it.

Bush also emphasized that U.S. action in Afghanistan was not against the people of that country, but only those who supported or harbored terrorists. Along with military action, the president initiated a massive relief program for Afghan civilians, an increasing number of whom were in desperate need of food and other supplies. This program reinforced the initial U.S. military effort on the ground in Afghanistan. This effort featured CIA and special forces operatives assisting anti-government militias, who for years had been fighting the Taliban.

Those groups were particularly strong in the north, where they had combined into what was known as the Northern Alliance. With U.S. and other assistance, especially from the United Kingdom, the Northern Alliance made rapid progress against government forces. By the middle of November, the Northern Alliance controlled most of the north, including the capital city Kabul. Taliban and Al Qaeda forces were on the run and concentrated in the east in the Tora Bora mountains and further south around the city of Kandahar.

Anti-Taliban forces, aided by U.S. Marines and U.K. special forces, captured Kandahar during the first week of December and by the 17th of the month they had suppressed organized resistance in the Tora Bora region. In less than 10 weeks and with under 10,000 American "boots on the ground," the Taliban government was destroyed and Al Qaeda's safe haven in Afghanistan eliminated. Nonetheless, hundreds of Taliban and Al Qaeda leaders and fighters, including Mullah Mohammed Omar of the former and Osama bin-Laden, had escaped, mostly into tribal areas of western Pakistan where they received support from the local population and elements of Pakistani army and intelligence organizations.

At Bonn, Germany, meanwhile, the United Nations sponsored a conference of representatives from Afghan opposition groups and neighboring and other interested countries. The purpose of the gathering was to devise a plan through which a new government for Afghanistan could be established that would achieve legitimacy throughout the country and in the international community. As a result an Afghan Interim Authority (AIA) was established on December 22 with 30 members and a six-month mandate, to be succeeded by a Transitional Authority for two years and then national elections under a new constitution. Hamid Karzai, an opposition leader from Kandahar, quickly emerged as chairman of the AIA.

Much remained to be done to quell the turmoil in Afghanistan. At the end of 2001, however, prospects for a successful venture looked promising. With a minimal American military presence–including advisers to assist in training an Afghan army–substantial international assistance, and a sizable U.S. investment in political and economic reconstruction and development, Afghanistan's recent history of instability and as a source of international terrorism might be overcome.

Yet Afghanistan was only a part of the GWOT that Bush was considering. Indeed, on November 21 the president had put Secretary of Defense Donald Rumsfeld to work evaluating the existing war plan for Iraq. The commander-in-chief had by no means decided on a war to overthrow Saddam Hussein, but even before 9/11 considerable sentiment had existed, both within and outside his administration, that the Iraqi dictator was a menace to the Middle East and perhaps even to the United States. In 1998, in defiance of agreements made at the end of the first Persian Gulf War, Saddam had expelled international inspectors from his country and it was widely suspected that he had resumed programs to develop weapons of mass destruction, including nuclear weapons. In the aftermath of 9/11 fears emerged that he was in cahoots with international terrorists, including Al Qaeda.

During the first half of 2002, Bush ramped up his rhetoric against so-called rogue states. In his state of the union address on January 29, while bragging about U.S. accomplishments and prospects in Afghanistan, he declared that "our war against terror is only beginning," that "the pursuit of two great objectives" continued:

> First, we will shut down terrorist camps, disrupt terrorist plans and bring terrorists to justice. And second, we must prevent the terrorists and regimes who seek chemical, biological or nuclear weapons from threatening the United States and the world.

Of particular concern, Bush continued, were North Korea, Iran, and Iraq, who with their terrorist allies constitute an axis of evil, arming to threaten the peace of the world. By seeking weapons of mass destruction, these regimes pose a grave and growing danger. They could provide these arms to terrorists, giving them the means to match their hatred. They could attack our allies or attempt to blackmail the United States. . . . We'll be deliberate, yet time is not on our side. I will not wait on events while dangers gather. . . . The United States . . . will not permit the world's most dangerous regimes to threaten us with the world's most destructive weapons.[17]

The president elaborated on this theme in his commencement address at West Point on June 1, in part by contrasting current realities with the Cold War:

> For much of the last century, America's defense relied on the Cold War doctrines of deterrence and containment. In some cases, those strategies still apply. But new threats also require new thinking. Deterrence—the promise of massive retaliation against nations—means nothing against shadowy terrorist networks with no nation or citizens to defend. Containment is not possible when unbalanced dictators with weapons of mass destruction can deliver those weapons on missiles or secretly provide them to terrorist allies.
>
> . . . the war on terror will not be won on the defensive. We must take the battle to the enemy, disrupt his plans, and confront the worst threats before they emerge.
>
> In the world we have entered, the only path to safety is the path of action.[18]

Bush and his allies referred to their strategy of initiating the use of military force as preemption, which had some legitimacy in international law, but the more widely accepted label for what they were about to propose regarding Iraq was preventive war, which had none.[19]

The rhetoric of the president and other high administration officials produced considerable dissent at home and even more abroad. Most notably at home, in August Brent Scowcroft, James Baker, and Lawrence Eagleburger, all top foreign policy officials during the first Bush presidency and the first Persian Gulf War, expressed strong reservations about a war to topple Saddam Hussein.[20] Within the current Bush administration, Secretary of State Colin Powell, the chairman of the joint chiefs of staff during the first Persian Gulf War and the most respected internationally of all the second Bush's advisers, also cautioned against war, especially without broad international support.[21]

Bush and his most trusted advisers, Vice President Dick Cheney, Secretary of Defense Donald Rumsfeld, and National Security Adviser Condoleeza Rice were not persuaded. Cheney took the lead in a speech on August 26 to the Veterans of Foreign Wars in making the case publicly for an aggressive approach to Saddam. He started by referring to the agreements made at the end of the war of 1991 that Saddam had broken over the last decade—to end his chemical, biological, and nuclear weapons programs and to accept intrusive international inspections. After conceding that "intelligence is an uncertain business," he asserted that "there is no doubt that Saddam Hussein now has weapons of mass destruction." Even if inspections were renewed, Cheney declared,

> Saddam has perfected the game of cheat and retreat, and is very skilled in the art of denial and deception. A return of inspectors would provide no assurance whatsoever of his compliance with U.N. resolutions. On the contrary, there is a great danger that it would provide false comfort that Saddam was somehow 'back in the his box.'
>
> Meanwhile, he would continue to plot. Nothing in the last dozen years has stopped him. . . . What he wants is . . . more time to husband his resources, to invest in his ongoing chemical and biological weapons programs, and to gain possession of nuclear arms. . . .
>
> We will profit . . . from a review of our own history. There are a lot of World War II veterans in the hall today. For the United States, that war began on December 7, 1941, with the attack on Pearl Harbor. . . . Only then did we recognize the magnitude of the danger to our country. Only then did the Axis powers full declare their intentions against us. By that point, many countries had fallen. And our nation was plunged into a two-front war resulting in more than a million American casualties. . . .
>
> Regime change in Iraq would bring about a number of benefits to the region. When the gravest of threats are eliminated, the freedom-loving peoples of the region will have a chance to promote the values that can bring lasting peace. As for the reaction of the Arab 'street,' the Middle East expert . . . Fouad Ajami predicts that after liberation, the streets of Basra and Baghdad are 'sure to erupt in joy in the same way the throngs in Kabul greeted the Americans.' Extremists in the region would have to rethink their strategy of Jihad. Moderates throughout the region would take heart. And our ability to advance the Israeli-Palestinian peace process would be enhanced, just as it followed the liberation of Kuwait in 1991.[22]

During the fall of 2002, the Bush administration turned its energies to mustering support for a war against Saddam in the U.S. Congress and the U.N. Security Council. Congressional elections were coming up in November and memories remained fresh of the first Bush's easy victory over Saddam in early 1991 in the face of widespread Democratic opposition to the rush to war. Thus most Democrats on Capitol Hill believed they held a weak hand to oppose the draft resolution before them to authorize the commander-in-chief's "use [of] all means that he determines to be appropriate, including force, in order to enforce the United Nations Security Council resolutions [of the 1990s], . . . defend the national security interests of the United States against the threat posed by Iraq, and restore international peace and security in the region."[23] On October 10 both the House of Representatives and the Senate passed such a resolution by better than two-to-one majorities.

Unlike his father the second Bush had more difficulty with the U.N. Security Council than with Congress. It took Secretary of State Powell until November 8 to persuade the former body to pass a resolution on Iraq. That resolution declared Iraq in "material breach" of previous Security Council resolutions, and demanded that Saddam provide "an accurate, full, final, and complete disclosure" of all efforts to develop ballistic missiles and weapons of mass destruction as well as subject his country to virtually unlimited inspections by designated U.N. bodies. But the resolution fell short of endorsing the use of "all necessary means" against Saddam if he failed to comply with tough inspections and disarmament demands. Rather, the Iraqi dictator was warned that he would face "serious consequences" for defiance.[24] With Saddam now claiming that he would comply with U.N. inspections, some if not all of the permanent members, each of whom possessed a veto, clearly expected the United States to return to the Security Council before launching a war.

U.N. inspectors quickly got to work in Iraq as the United States began a build-up of its armed forces in the area. On January 6, 2003 Hans Blix, the head of the inspection team, reported to the Security Council that the Iraqi government was cooperating with the inspectors and that weapons of mass destruction were yet to be found. Subsequent reports on January 27 and February 14 emphasized that inspections remained incomplete, that Saddam's cooperation was good but less than perfect, and that no significant stockpiles of weapons of mass destruction or an active nuclear weapons program had been discovered. Completion of the process of inspection would take not days or weeks but months, putting the completion date beyond the end of March and the best period for commencement of military operations.

Bush was determined to act soon. On January 28 he called for the reconvening of the Security Council on February 5 and asserted that the British recently had learned of an effort by Saddam to acquire weapons-grade uranium from Africa. In fact, the British report was unsubstantiated, but this did not stop Secretary Powell from going before the Security Council with claims that Iraq had a substantial stockpile of chemical weapons as well as active programs to develop nuclear weapons and medium range ballistic missiles. On the basis of these "all well documented" claims, he requested passage of a resolution approving the use of force against Iraq. With France in the lead and Russia and China not far behind, most members of the Security Council insisted that the intelligence was inconclusive and that more time should be given to complete the inspections. Blix's March 7 report that Iraqi cooperation had gotten even better since late January and now included destruction under his group's supervision of dozens of missiles reinforced this sentiment. The French already had announced that they would veto the U.S.-proposed resolution and, with the exception of the United Kingdom, the other permanent members might also vote in the negative. On March 17, therefore, Bush withdrew the resolution from consideration, announced that the resolution passed the previous November gave him sufficient authority to act, and issued an ultimatum that Saddam and his two sons must give up power in Iraq and leave the country within 48 hours. The Saddams held their ground and U.S. military operations against them commenced on March 19.

Bush went to war with a "coalition of the willing" of over 40 nations of whom only three—the United Kingdom, Poland, and Australia—were contributing ground troops. The coalition did not include key NATO allies France, Germany, and Turkey, which would not even permit use of its airspace for the transport of military forces into northern Iraq. The United States possessed slightly over 200,000 military personnel in the region from the eastern Mediterranean to the Persian Gulf and the British possessed 45,000 more. Although this was less than half the number of the forces mobilized in the region for the first Persian Gulf War, they were widely considered to be more than sufficient to defeat Saddam's military, which was much weakened since January 1991. Whether in the aftermath of such a defeat U.S. and allied forces were adequate to maintain order in a country characterized by sharp ethnic and religious divisions until a new indigenous authority could be established remained in doubt. With the exception of Powell, top U.S. officials appeared to believe that the vast majority of Iraqis would welcome the invaders as liberators and that a post-war occupation would be relatively short and modest in cost.

We know, of course, that what is often known as the Second Persian Gulf War proved to be anything but short or modest in cost. Despite the optimism of early 2002, neither did the war in Afghanistan. Indeed, of the five wars in which the United States has engaged since World War II, only the first Persian Gulf War was short, relatively cheap, and undeniably victorious.

Exercise 4: Class Discussion on the War on Terror

Rather than write another essay, we now ask you to prepare for a class discussion by doing three things. First, look up the sources cited in endnotes 20 and 21 below that provide the arguments of key dissenters on Bush's decision. (Those in endnote 20 are readily available on the internet through a Google search. Perhaps your instructor will provide you with the pertinent pages in the final source through your library's reserve system.) In reading the dissenters' arguments, think about how their use of historical analogy compares with that of Bush and Cheney provided above. Second, on separate sheets of paper, construct similarities and differences charts comparing the circumstances at the beginning of the First and Second Persian Gulf Wars and at the beginning of the Afghanistan and the Second Persian Gulf Wars. Think about what lessons might be learned from these cases that would be useful to future presidents. Third, expand your thoughts to include all the wars discussed in this chapter. What was different about the First Persian Gulf War than all the other wars that helps us understand why its course and outcome were so different than the other four? What do your conclusions suggest about preparations we should make for the future and the circumstances under which our leaders should determine that war is necessary and/or advisable?

We hope that these exercises have reinforced in your mind the importance of collecting facts and of carefully weighing them before you reach conclusions. We hope as well that this chapter has given you a better appreciation of both the utility of drawing analogies with the past to help reach conclusions in the present and the risks of doing so. Whether you are developing an opinion about what should be done by the U.S. government to protect the nation's interests or about what course you should pursue in your job, the past can be a useful guide, but only if employed with care and with an understanding that all events have a measure of uniqueness.

The next chapter will reinforce our point about the need to collect facts and weigh them carefully before making judgments. It also will show you how the past can be used to address some of the fundamental issues facing our nation as we more forward in the twenty-first century.

Notes

[1] Richard E. Neustadt and Ernest R. May, *Thinking in Time* (New York: Free Press, 1986), 251.

[2] Harry S Truman, *Memoirs*, vol. 2 (Garden City, N.Y.: Doubleday, 1956), 334. Li writing this exercise, we have made extensive use of "Korea and the Thirties," Case Project, John F. Kennedy School of Government, Harvard University.

[3] U.N. document S/1511.

[4] Truman, *Memoirs*, 2:316.

[5] May and Neustadt, *Thinking in Time*, chs. 3–6.

[6] In preparing this background section, we have made extensive use of "Americanizing the Vietnam War," Case Project, Kennedy School of Government, Harvard University.

[7] *Public Papers of the Presidents of the United States: Lyndon B. Johnson, 1965*, vol. 2, 794–795.

[8] "Top Secret The Prophecy of the President Rejected" by George W. Ball, © 1972, as originally printed in *The Atlantic*, 230, July 1972, p. 37.

[9] *Weekly Compilation of Presidential Documents* 26 (August 10, 1990), 1255–1257.

[10] Ibid., 27 (January 21, 1991), 50–52.

[11] *Congressional Record*, vol. 137, no. 7, 102nd Cong., 1stsess. (January 11, 1991), S249–S254.

[12] Gary R. Hess, *Presidential Decisions for War: Korea, Vietnam, the Persian Gulf, and Iraq*, second edition (Baltimore: Johns Hopkins University Press, 2009), 229.

[13] President Bush Addresses the Nation, September 20, 2001, http://www.washingtonpost.com/wp-srv/nation/specials/attacked/transcripts/bushaddress_0.

[14] President George W. Bush's Address to the Nation on 7 October 2001, http://www.johnstonarchive.net/terrorism/bush911d.html.

[15] For Bush's speech to the nation on September 20, 2001, see http://www.washingtonpost.com/wp-srv/nation/specials/attacked/transcripts/bushaddress_0 . . .

[16] The President's News Conference, October 11, 2001, http://www.presidency.ucsb.edu/ws/index. Php?pid=73426.

[17] Text of President Bush's 2002 State of the Union Address, http://www.washingtonpost.com/wp-srv/onpolitics/transcripts/sou012902.htm.

[18] President Bush Delivers Graduation Speech at West Point, June 1, 2002, http://georgewbush-whitehouse.archives.gov/news/releases/2002/06/20020601-3.html.

[19] In generally accepted academic usage, preemption involves initiating military action when such action by an enemy is imminent. Preventive war involves initiating military action against an enemy who is developing the capability to take such action at sometime in the future but not immediately.

[20] See Brent Scowcroft, "Don't Attack Saddam," *Wall Street Journal*, August 15, 2002; James A. Baker III, "The Right Way to Change a Regime," *New York Times*, August 25, 2002; "Eagleburger questions possible Iraq move," CNN.com, http://cnn.allpolitics.printthis.clickability.com/pt/cpt?expire=-l&title=CNN.com+-+Eagleb. . . .

[21] See Bob Woodward, *Plan of Attack* (New York: Simon & Schuster, 2004), 149–52.

[22] Full text of Dick Cheney's speech," http://www.guardian.co.uk/world/2002/aug/27/usa.iraq/print.

[23] See http://www.mtholyoke.edu/acad/intrel/bush/resolution.htm.

[24] For a full text of Resolution 1441, see http://www.un.org/News/Press/docs/2002/SC7564.doc.htm.

11: *Hidden History and the Law*

Rights, Abortion, Sexuality, and the War on Crime, 1965–1980

———◆—•—◆———

As we have learned over the preceding pages, historians depend on primary sources. However, much of human history does not get recorded by neutral recording devices. This is especially true when it comes to activities, ideas, and institutions that the society of the time dislikes or disapproves. Often, but not always, governments will respond to calls for greater morality by passing laws that criminalize previously legal actions. Depending on the enforcement of these laws, these activities and the people who engage in them are said to go "underground" where it becomes difficult for historians to find sources.

Law enforcement agencies, public health groups, religious organizations, and even private do-gooders do provide the historian with material on this underground world. The problem then becomes how to use these sources, for they require special handling. Because too often they were not created by individuals or groups well disposed toward the activities they observe, the sources have a greater degree of bias than the historian would wish. Other sources, created by the individuals at risk for prosecution, may hide facts or dissemble. The sources may not reflect the whole of the story. Law enforcement agencies may only be arresting the easy targets. The law cases the prosecution of crimes creates are written in a language of their own. In statistical terms, the sample may be unrepresentative. The most notorious example is of a wealthy person who is able to "buy" his or her way out of even a charge of illegal behavior, much less prosecution. A good lawyer can make all the difference, but so can a well-placed "contribution." For these reasons alone, a good historian has to be careful when writing about these "hidden histories."

It takes a specially trained eye to see what is hidden. It takes a special skill to ferret out the facts from the fluff. It takes good judgment to be able to write about subjects one finds abhorrent, but needs to be told. In this chapter we will help you to develop these skills. You will also learn about what some have called the underside of American life, but may now be looked upon as just another part of American history – its legal history.

Tools of Legal History

The tools of a good legal historian are the same as any other type of historian, but the legal historian must combine their use with a knowledge of how law works in the United States. The U.S. system of adjudication is known as a common law system, derived from its English inheritance before the American Revolution. Common law is a shorthand description of a legal system that uses several elements: legal proceedings involve adversarial trials, the losing side may appeal a decision of law as opposed to fact to a superior or appellate court, and those appellate court judges must usually justify their ruling in a written opinion. Those appellate opinions, if considered worthy, become what are known as precedents – interpretations of the law that are accepted as law themselves.

The United States adds another complication to this already complex system with a national or federal constitution – the U.S. Constitution – that declares itself to be the supreme law of the land, but only within its self-defined realm. Local matters are left to the states and their subdivisions. The U.S. Constitution additionally divides the national or federal government into three distinct branches: the legislature or Congress, the executive or President, and the judiciary headed by the justices of the U.S. Supreme Court. According to the terms of the Constitution as it has been interpreted, the Congress makes the laws also known as statutes or acts, the President enforces those enactments, and the courts of the judiciary interpret the works of the other two branches according to the dictates of the Constitution.

Legal historians combine an analysis of the work product of all of these different types of government actors to form an understanding of this part of America's past. In the exercises that follow, you will try your hand at analyzing these kinds of sources: legislative, executive, and judicial. Keep in mind though that good legal history is not just about legal sources, but the other types of histories and sources this volume introduces as well.

Morality and Religion

In the U.S. Supreme Court case of <u>Church of the Holy Trinity v. United States</u> (1892), Justice David Brewer wrote one of the most misinterpreted sentences in the history of the court: "These and many other matters which might be noticed, add a volume of unofficial declarations to the mass of organic utterances that this is a Christian nation." While Brewer was not declaring that Christianity was the official religion of the United States, it was certainly a valid description of the religious beliefs of the vast majority of the U.S. population. Although the United States was founded on largely non-religious, that is secular, grounds, religion has been a major part of American life, including its laws, from its beginnings down to the present day. As such, religion – the belief in the supernatural and certain rules that come from that supernatural power – has provided a great deal, if not all, of the morality behind the nation's laws.

Morality – the rules for conduct that define what is good and what is bad – makes societies function in the way that they do. Therefore, good history must take it into account when describing legal history. But, because moral systems have changed over time, historians must understand these changes before analyzing the sources before him or her. The first step is to look at religion and comprehend the many different kinds of religious faiths in America during its long history.

Exercise 1: The Good, the Bad, and the Historical

List below four of the major religions and denominations present in the United States from 1865 to the present.

_____

_____

While you have made a start at understanding morality in the United States, it is only a start. Now, you have to look at those religious groups you have just listed and determine whether they agree on any particular items. **List** below at least two or three of the activities you think most of the adherents of these religions would agree are bad, and, therefore, should be prohibited.

_____

_____

Many historians of religion agree with social scientists and some researchers into human psychology and biology that religions usually serve an important societal function by prohibiting certain things and promoting others. For the list of prohibited activities you made, **write** the reasons you think religious people might have prohibited them.

_____

_____

_____

_____

Abortion

One of the most controversial topics in America today is the issue of abortion – technically, the termination of a woman's pregnancy before it has come to term. Even this phrasing of the issue is subject to criticism because the terms one uses to describe the issue are contested by the people who feel strongly about the subject. Some writers have even made the argument that the issue of abortion is **the** dividing point in American political, social, and cultural life. Like many things in the post-World War II era, people often call the debate over abortion a war: the abortion wars. Unsurprisingly, the debate is not a recent one. Even the early American colonies had laws about abortion. As we warned you at the start of this chapter, it is not a pleasant subject to even think about, but it is important.

As with most activities that law forbids and morality frowns upon, the termination of pregnancies in the United States happened, but these activities did not get reported on a regular basis. Anti-abortion law advocates like Planned Parenthood founder Margaret Sanger had reason to dramatize the problem including to over-report the incidence of abortions as well as their often gruesome consequences. Prohibition was not the only reason abortion was underground. Religious organizations almost invariably condemned even the dissemination of contraception, also known as birth control, literature.

However, whether from the effects of post-World War II society and culture or the arrival of contraceptive prescription drugs like "the pill", attitudes toward sexual behavior changed, particularly among the baby boom generation going to colleges and universities in record numbers. The behaviors of adolescents combined with the liberation many felt being away from home for the first time to sponsor both a resistance to the supposed conformity of the 1950s and experimentation with different lifestyles. Historians often refer to this overall youth revolt as the "counter-culture" with its change in sexual behavior as the "sexual revolution." Though not all young people engaged in these acts of rebellion, Americans' attitudes toward sex did change.

This greater consciousness towards sexual matters gave fuel to the demand for a "reform" of the abortion laws, and constitutes the opening of a hidden history in American law.

Exercise 2: Abortion Law

In the passages below are excerpts from primary sources concerning abortion. Though they may be unpleasant to read about, you should use your skills as a historian to look at them objectively with a trained eye for the hidden meanings as well as the outward import of these documents. **Answer** the questions that follow the passage to hone your historian's skill set.

In 1873 the United States Congress passed a law entitled "An Act for the Suppression of Trade in, and Circulation of, Obscene Literature and Articles of Immoral Use" (42nd Congress, 3d Session, chapter 258). This law exercised a considerable influence, not only on federal law, but at the state level as well as they passed their own versions. Though overturned in the landmark law case of Griswold v. Connecticut (1965), these acts were foundational pieces of legislation. The impetus behind them came from a moral reformer named Anthony Comstock. For that reason, even though he never held public office, the federal act became known as the Comstock Act, and its approach to morality derisively referred to as "Comstockery." Comstock was born in Connecticut in 1844 and became a devout Protestant. He dedicated his life to fighting what he believed to be immorality. Below is the first section of the Comstock Act.

> **A** Be it enacted by the Senate and House of Representatives of the United States of America in Congress assembled, That whoever, within the District of Columbia or any of the Territories of the United States, or other place within the exclusive jurisdiction of the United States, shall sell, or lend, or give away, or in any manner exhibit, or shall offer to sell, or to lend, or to give away, or in any manner to exhibit, or shall otherwise publish or offer to publish in any manner, or shall have in his possession, for any such purpose or purposes, any obscene book, pamphlet, paper, writing, advertisement, circular, print, picture, drawing or other representation, figure, or image on or of paper or other material, or any cast, instrument, or other article of an immoral nature, or any drug or medicine, or any article whatever, for the prevention of conception, or for causing unlawful abortion, or shall advertise the same for sale, or shall write or print, or cause to be written or printed, any card, circular, book pamphlet, advertisement, or notice of any kind, stating when, where, how, or of whom, or by what means, any of the articles in this section hereinbefore mentioned, can be purchased or obtained, or shall manufacture, draw, or print, or in any wise make any of such articles, shall be deemed guilty of a misdemeanor, and on conviction thereof in any court of the United States having criminal jurisdiction . . . where such misdemeanor shall have been committed; and on conviction thereof, he shall be imprisoned at hard labor in the penitentiary for not less than six months nor more than five years for each offense, or fined not less than one hundred dollars nor more than two thousand dollars, with costs of court.[1]

1. What kinds of items are prohibited under the act? _____
   _____

2. What are the punishments upon conviction of violating the act? _____
   _____

3. In your opinion, is the law comprehensive or limited in scope? Why do you think so?
   _____
   _____

4. Given that laws are passed in order to prohibit an activity the law-giver believes is a problem, why do you think the Congress was concerned with people doing the things the act proscribes? _____

_____

_____

Because federal officials did not enforce the Comstock Act themselves, Comstock had to rely on a technique known today as the private attorney general action. Comstock would pretend to be a woman in need of information or a publication and write to his target whether it be a publisher, a magazine, or a bookseller. Once the target had sent the material through the U.S. mail, Comstock had proof that they had violated the act. He could then present the evidence to his local U.S. Attorney, who could then prosecute the offender. Combined with the passage of local ordinances and state law governing "obscene" material, Comstock and other religious advocates succeeded in suppressing most of this literature, which became generally known as pornography whether or not it was scientific in nature. Thus, even medical textbooks had to omit material that might fall afoul of these laws. Like other prohibited activities, these items did not vanish. They went underground.

During the 1960s an increasing number of Americans took issue with parts of the Comstock Law, and some of them established lobbying organizations. The National Association for the Repeal of Abortion Laws (NARAL) was one such group and by 1970 it had gained the attention of New York Congresswoman Shirley Chisholm, who described her thinking on the abortion issue in a speech to other African-Americans. What occasioned the remarks was the nationwide efforts of groups like the National Association for the Repeal of Abortion Laws (NARAL) to lobby state governments on behalf of their cause. Even then, the issue was highly contested.

B In August of 1969 I began to get calls from NARAL, . . . a new organization . . . looking for a national president. In the New York State Assembly, I had supported abortion reform bills . . . and this had apparently led NARAL to believe I would sympathize with its goal: complete repeal of all laws restricting abortion. As a matter of fact, when I was in the assembly, I had not been in favor of repealing all abortion laws. . . . But since that time I had been compelled to do some heavy thinking on the subject, mainly because of the experiences of several young women I knew. All had suffered permanent injuries at the hands of illegal abortionists. . . . It had begun to seem to me that the question was not whether the law should allow abortions. Experience shows that pregnant women who feel they have compelling reasons . . . will break the law, and even worse, risk injury and death, if they must get one.

For me to take the lead in abortion repeal would be an even more serious step than for a white politician to do so, because there is a deep and angry suspicion among many blacks that even birth control clinics are a plot by the white power structure to keep down the numbers of blacks, and this opinion is even more strongly held by some in regard to legalizing abortions. But I do not know any black or Puerto Rican women who feel that way.[2]

1. What do you conclude was Chisholm's position on whether abortion should be legal or not? _____

2. What evidence does Chisholm support for her position? _____

_____

3. What phrases, terms, and phrasing does Chisholm use that lead you to make your conclusions? _____

4. What about Chisholm or the venue for her remarks might lead you to be skeptical about her arguments? _____

_____

In the passage that follows, a young attorney named Roy Lucas wrote about how a lawsuit in federal court could overturn state abortion laws as a violation of the U.S. Constitution in a law review article entitled, "Federal Constitutional Limitations on the Enforcement and Administration of State Abortion Statutes" (North Carolina Law Review 46 (1968): 730–78 [footnotes omitted]).

C Until recently, mishandled criminal abortions claimed the lives of an estimated ten thousand American women each year. The vast majority of these individuals were married – wives and mothers. Legal hospital abortions, on the other hand, presently account for the termination of only eight to nine thousand pregnancies yearly. This figure contrasts sharply with the probable one-quarter to two million annual illegal abortions performed within the United States. Such persistent flouting by citizens of laws written and enacted in the last century is the subject of increasing public controversy and discussion. It brings into focus sensitive issues of family planning and marital autonomy, church-state relations, subjective sexual taboos, and the mysteries of human procreation, life and death.

To date efforts at promoting or stifling abortion reform have focused legislative action both in the United States and abroad. This article, however, examines the possibility of federal constitutional bases for invalidating state abortion restrictions. . . .

Increased public interest in the liberalization of abortion laws is evident in the currents of modern thought. In the sphere of family planning, many citizens today do not believe that a particular moral norm ought to be forced on all of a society unless the sacrifice in individual liberty of choice is offset by a significant societal benefit. This view, as applied to the abortion reform setting, necessarily further assumes that the value to be accorded to developing fetal tissue is a subjective moral choice that ought not to be dictated by the state. It is a premise widely shared, especially by those individuals whom rigid abortion laws most directly affect.[3]

1. What do you conclude about the morality of the author? _____

   _____

2. What evidence does he use to support his argument? _____

   _____

3. What terms does he use that might lead you to believe he has taken a side in the abortion debate? Why do you think so? _____

   _____

   _____

The national debate over abortion became even more heated with the U.S. Supreme Court case of Roe v. Wade (1973). Roe was a class action law suit – a legal case in which the plaintiff is a group of people classified together for the purposes of representation in a court – brought against the state of Texas challenging its anti-abortion law. In addition to hearing oral arguments both the plaintiffs and defendants made before the justices and reading their written arguments or briefs, the Court also allowed other interested parties to submit briefs for the justices' consideration. One of these briefs was by the pro-abortion law group Americans United for Life. It is excerpted below.

D The child in the womb is a person within the meaning of the Equal Protection Clause of the Fourteenth Amendment [of the U.S. Constitution]. The Equal Protection Clause forbids classifications of law that are arbitrary, capricious or unreasonable. To allow the child in the womb to be killed by abortion, where it is not necessary to save the life of his mother, would be to subject him to arbitrary, capricious and unreasonable classification. This is so because he is in fact a living human being and his young age and his situation do not provide a sufficient basis for a legal determination that he be subject to death were older human beings are not so subject. . . . .

The child in the womb meets these criteria of personhood under the Equal Protection Clause. He is human, he lives and he has his being. That is, he is a living human being. As the highest court of New Jersey [in 1960] summarized the state of scientific knowledge, "Medical authorities have long recognized that child is in existence from the moment of conception.". . . .

Even if one somehow does not concede that the child in the womb is a living human being, one ought to at least give him the benefit of the doubt. Our law does not permit the execution, or imprisonment under sentence, of a criminal unless his guilt of the crime charged is proven beyond a reasonable doubt. The Innocent child in the womb is entitled to have us resolve in his favor any doubts we may feel as to his living humanity and his personhood.[4]

1. What terms are different from the previous selections and how does their use affect the argument? _____

_____

2. How do you think the venue, a legal brief for the U.S. Supreme Court, has affected the writing of this argument? _____

_____

_____

3. What do you believe is the key piece of evidence for this argument and why? _____

_____

_____

4. Is the morality of this argument different or the same as the previous passages? Why do you think so? _____

_____

_____

As you may have noticed from performing the previous exercise on abortion, it is very difficult for a historian to check his or her judgments at the door and view a piece of historical evidence objectively. Some theorists argue that this is an impossible task and that all history reflects the views of its author. Others argue that the historical writing has an existence apart from its author. Therefore, any interpretation by a reader has a legitimacy of its own. Unfortunately, historians must deal with material that challenges their dedication to their craft. Do take heart. These kinds of challenges can also make us better observers and writers of history.

Sexuality

Keeping in mind exercise one on morality and the law, it should come as no surprise that the United States has a long history of attempting to regulate, prohibit, and otherwise influence

Americans' sexual behavior. While Americans have dedicated a great amount of political energy to guaranteeing personal liberty, they have also called upon government to address so-called social ills in ways that invade personal privacy. Some of these restrictions, like the laws prohibiting sex between humans and sheep for example, may seem odd to our present-day way of thinking; but, the laws governing sexual relations have always presented this conflict between individual liberty and the society's right to set rules governing all of its members.

As we noted above, the 1960s constituted an important turning point in this legal history as many Americans began to adopt less restrictive attitudes towards issues like premarital sex, marriage, sexual identity, and cultural representations of these activities in movies, the theater, and literature. While most of the challenges were in the form of attitudes and simple behavior, some of them were more openly confrontational. Although the communal, free-love, and mind-altering drug culture of the "hippies" gained the most notice, there were other groups that also began to question what they perceived as America's culture of conformity.

One of these groups was America's homosexual community. Because engaging in homosexual sex was a crime throughout most of the United States, they considered themselves a discriminated against minority group just like African-Americans. Subjected to FBI and U.S. Post Office surveillance as well as police raids on their hangouts and bars, homosexuals had few places to turn for support. Even the American Psychiatric Association classified homosexuality as a mental disorder and recommended shock therapy and other interventions to "cure" the disease. Although the gay and lesbian rights' movement began well before 1969, the modern movement marks its start with the symbolic Stonewall Riot on June 28, 1969, in a section of New York City, Greenwich Village, in the borough of Manhattan. The incident began as a reaction to a police raid on the Stonewall Inn. The Gay Pride March that followed the riot marked the beginning of a civil rights movement with major ramifications for American social, cultural, and political history.

Exercise 3: Life in the Closet

As noted above in the introduction to this chapter, the American legal system involves appellate court judges' opinions as well as statutes to determine the exact contours of the law. Although U.S. Supreme Court nominees have taken to analogizing what they do to "calling balls and strikes" as if they were impartial baseball umpires, the activity is actually much more complicated. It includes the need to look at prior decisions, read into the context of the particular wording in question, and place the case within the framework of the U.S. Constitution. The laws concerning homosexuals have been no different. **Read** the court opinions excerpted below in the case of Clive Michael Boutilier v. Immigration and Naturalization Service (387 U.S. 188[1967]) and **answer** the questions that follow.

Excerpts A and B below represent the majority and minority views respectively of the U.S. Supreme Court in the case of Clive Michael Boutilier v. Immigration and Naturalization Service (387 U.S. 118[1967]). In excerpt A Justice Tom Clark offers the court majority's reasons for upholding the deportation of Clive Michael Boutilier, a Canadian immigrant to the U.S. and is an admitted homosexual. The Immigration and Naturalization Service instituted deportation proceedings against Boutilier when he was charged with violating local "morals" laws by having intercourse with other men. The Immigration and Nationality Act of 1952 prohibited people "afflicted with psychopathic personality" from immigrating to the U.S. The INS asserted that "homosexuals and sex perverts" fell under this prohibition.

A The legislative history of the Act [Immigration and Nationality Act of 1952] indicates beyond a shadow of a doubt that the Congress intended the phrase 'psychopathic personality' to include homosexuals such as petitioner.

Prior to the 1952 Act the immigration law excluded 'persons of constitutional psychopathic inferiority.' 39 Stat. 875, as amended, 8 U.S.C. § 136(a) (1946 ed.). Beginning in 1950, a subcommittee of the Senate Committee on the Judiciary conducted a comprehensive study of the immigration laws and in its report found 'that the purpose of the provision against 'persons with constitutional psychopathic inferiority' will be more adequately served by changing that term to 'persons afflicted with psychopathic personality,' and that the classes of mentally defectives should be enlarged to include homosexuals and other sex perverts.' S.Rep. No. 1515, 81st Cong., 2d Sess., p. 345. The resulting legislation was first introduced as S. 3455 and used the new phrase 'psychopathic personality.' The bill, however, contained an additional clause providing for the exclusion of aliens 'who are homosexuals or sex perverts.' As the legislation progressed (now S. 2550 in the 82d Congress), however, it omitted the latter clause 'who are homosexuals or sex perverts' and used only the phrase 'psychopathic personality.' The omission is explained by the Judiciary Committee Report on the bill. . . .

Likewise a House bill, H.R. 5678, adopted the position of the Public Health Service that the phrase 'psychopathic personality' excluded from entry homosexuals and sex perverts. The report that accompanied the bill shows clearly that the House Judiciary Committee adopted the recommendation of the Public Health Service that 'psychopathic personality' should be used in the Act as a phrase that would exclude from admission homosexuals and sex perverts. H.R. Rep. No. 1365, 82d Cong., 2d Sess., U.S.Code Cong. & Admin. News 1952, p. 1653. It quoted at length, and specifically adopted, the Public Health Service report which recommended that the term 'psychopathic personality' be used to 'specify such types of pathologic behavior as homosexuality or sexual perversion.' We, therefore, conclude that the Congress used the phrase 'psychopathic personality' not in the clinical sense, but to effectuate its purpose to exclude from entry all homosexuals and other sex perverts.[5]

1. What is the finding of the majority of the Court as per Justice Clark's opinion in <u>Boutilier v. INS</u> (1967)? _____

2. What evidence does Justice Clark use to support his conclusion? _____

_____

3. List the terms and concepts you would find out of place in today's society. _____

_____

_____

_____

4. If you were writing the history of law's treatment of homosexuals, what conclusions would you draw from this Supreme Court opinion? _____

_____

_____

_____

B Justice William O. Douglas wrote a dissent and Justice Abe Fortas signed onto it. It is excerpted below:

Mr. Justice DOUGLAS, with whom Mr. Justice FORTAS concurs, dissenting.

The term 'psychopathic personality' is a treacherous one like 'communist' or in an earlier day 'Bolshevik.' A label of this kind when freely used may mean only an unpopular person. It is much too vague by constitutional standards for the imposition of penalties or punishment. . . .

It is common knowledge that in this century homosexuals have risen high in our own public service—both in Congress and in the Executive Branch—and have served with distinction. It is therefore not credible that Congress wanted to deport everyone and anyone who was a sexual deviate, no matter how blameless his social conduct had been nor how creative his work nor how valuable his contribution to society. I agree with Judge Moore, dissenting below, that the legislative history should not be read as imputing to Congress a purpose to classify under the heading 'psychopathic personality' every person who had ever had a homosexual experience. . . .

If we are to hold, as the Court apparently does, that any acts of homosexuality suffice to deport the alien, whether or not they are part of a fabric of antisocial behavior, then we face a serious question of due process. By that construction a person is judged by a standard that is almost incapable of definition. I have already quoted from clinical experts to show what a wide range the term 'psychopathic personality' has. . . .

We held in Jordan v. DeGeorge, 341 U.S. 223, 71 S.Ct. 703, 95 L.Ed. 886, that the crime of a conspiracy to defraud the United States of taxes involved 'moral turpitude' and made the person subject to deportation. That, however, was a term that has 'deep roots in the law.' Id., at 227, 71 S.Ct. at 705. But the grab bag 'psychopathic personality'—has no 'deep roots' whatsoever.5 Caprice of judgment is almost certain under this broad definition. Anyone can be caught who is unpopular, who is off-beat, who is nonconformist. . . .

In light of these statements, I cannot say that it has been determined that petitioner was 'afflicted' in the statutory sense either at the time of entry or at present. 'Afflicted' means possessed or dominated by. Occasional acts would not seem sufficient. 'Afflicted' means a way of life, an accustomed pattern of conduct. Whatever disagreement there is as to the meaning of 'psychopathic personality,' it has generally been understood to refer to a consistent, lifelong pattern of behavior conflicting with social norms without accompanying guilt. Cleckley, supra, at 29.6 Nothing of that character was shown to exist at the time of entry. The fact that he presently has a problem, as one psychiatrist said, does not mean that he is or was necessarily 'afflicted' with homosexuality. His conduct is, of course, evidence material to the issue. But the informed judgment of experts is needed to make the required finding. We cruelly mutilate the Act when we hold otherwise. For we make the word of the bureaucrat supreme, when it was the expertise of the doctors and psychiatrists on which Congress wanted the administrative action to be dependent.6

1. Why does Justice Douglas disagree with Clark? _____

_____

_____

2. What is Justice Douglas' view of homosexuals and how does it compare with Clark's? ___

_____

_____

_____

3. How does Justice Douglas' take on the Constitution's requirements differ from Clark's?

_____

_____

_____

4. If you had to classify Justice Douglas' political views, where would you place him and why?

_____

_____

As you may have noticed from recent headlines, this was not the end of litigation concerning homosexuals and the law. In 1986 in the case of <u>Bowers v. Hardwick et al</u> (478 U.S. 186), Justice Byron White wrote for a five to four majority to uphold Georgia's anti-sodomy law. However, in 2003, in an opinion by Justice Anthony Kennedy, the Court reversed itself in the case of <u>Lawrence v. Texas</u> (539 U.S. 558). In another five to four decision, the Court declared that sodomy laws violated the due process clause of the Fourteenth Amendment to the U.S. Constitution. While sodomy laws are no longer an issue, the debate over homosexuals and the law continues most notably as to whether homosexual couples are entitled to marry – a status that only government can confer under law.

The War on Crime

In 1973, President Richard Nixon announced that the United States government was involved in a war, in this case a "war on drugs." Nixon had won the presidential elections of 1968 and 1972 at least in part based on his pledge to serve what he termed "the silent majority." He was contrasting his political program with that of the Democrats whom he was attempting to associate with anti-war protesters, civil rights marchers, and the U.S. Supreme Court under its liberal and active Chief Justice Earl Warren.

The Warren Court had become notable, not just for its decisions in <u>Brown v. Board of Education</u> (1954) holding that segregating public schools was unconstitutional, but also for its criminal law procedure decisions. Arguably the most famous, or infamous depending on your point of view, was the decision in <u>Miranda v. Arizona</u> (1966) commanding all law enforcement officers to inform criminal suspects of their Constitutional rights or face any resulting evidence getting excluded from the case. A firestorm of controversy greeted this decision with opponents declaring that the Warren Court was hamstringing law enforcement or, even worse, coddling criminals.

Accompanying these decisions was a sharp rise in the incidence of criminal activity during the late 1960s and early 1970s. Many social scientists attributed this phenomenon to social dislocation brought about by the decay of urban areas and/or the entering into adulthood of a large number of males from the Baby Boom generation. Whatever the reason(s), the increasing crime rate became a hot button political issue with important cultural and social dimensions. The Nixon administration's "war on crime" was a natural fit with Nixon's general antipathy for the "counterculture" and everything that went along with it. The "war on drugs" came as the next logical step.

As with sex and abortion, the drug culture in America had long been present and, by the start of the twentieth century, become seen as a social ill. Like the campaign against alcohol during Prohibition, the illegalization of drugs drove the practice underground making it another hidden history. Unlike Prohibition, the war on drugs has continued to this day. The Nixon administration saw drug use and the counter-culture as part of the same social phenomenon. The war on crime is thus both a hidden history and a legal history.

Exercise 4: Case v. Statutory v. Administrative Law

The law takes several forms: case law, statute, and administrative. Legal history involves the analysis of all three among other sources. The law for the War on Crime was no different. Below are selections from all three sources. You should treat them as you would any primary source. **Read** the following excerpts and **answer** the questions that follow.

A As noted above, Chief Justice Earl Warren wrote for the majority of the Supreme Court in <u>Miranda</u> that arresting officers needed to advise the alleged criminals of their constitutional rights. Here is an excerpt from that opinion justifying the decision.

In announcing these principles, we are not unmindful of the burdens which law enforcement officials must bear, often under trying circumstances. We also fully recognize the obligation of all citizens to aid in enforcing the criminal laws. This Court, while protecting individual rights, has always given ample latitude to law enforcement agencies in the legitimate exercise of their duties. The limits we have placed on the interrogation process should not constitute an undue interference with a proper system of law enforcement. As we have noted, our decision does not in any way preclude police from carrying out their traditional investigatory functions. Although confessions may play an important role in some convictions, the cases before us present graphic examples of the overstatement of the "need" for confessions. In each case, authorities conducted interrogations ranging up to five days in duration despite the presence, through standard investigating practices, of considerable evidence against each defendant. [n51] Further examples are chronicled in our prior cases. See, e.g., Haynes v. Washington, 373 U.S. 503, 518–519 (1963); Rogers v. Richmond, 365 U.S. 534, 541 (1961); Malinski v. New York, 324 U.S. 401,402 (1945). [n52] [p482].

It is also urged that an unfettered right to detention for interrogation should be allowed because it will often redound to the benefit of the person questioned. When police inquiry determines that there is no reason to believe that the person has committed any crime, it is said, he will be released without need for further formal procedures. The person who has committed no offense, however, will be better able to clear himself after warnings with counsel present than without. It can be assumed that, in such circumstances, a lawyer would advise his client to talk freely to police in order to clear himself.

Custodial interrogation, by contrast, does not necessarily afford the innocent an opportunity to clear themselves. A serious consequence of the present practice of the interrogation alleged to be beneficial for the innocent is that many arrests "for investigation" subject large numbers of innocent persons to detention and interrogation.[7]

1. What does Warren argue he is trying to protect with this decision? _____
   _____

2. What does Warren think will be the effect on law enforcement? _____
   _____

3. Look at the first ten amendments to the U.S. Constitution, known as the Bill of Rights. Which passages are relevant to Warren's opinion in <u>Miranda</u>? _____
   _____

4. Given the surrounding context of this case, what other area of the law and society do you think may be influencing the Court in <u>Miranda</u> and why? _____
   _____
   _____
   _____

B On July 10, 1973, President Richard Nixon issued the following executive order:

[Executive Order] No. 11727

July 10, 1973, 38 F.R. 18357

DRUG LAW ENFORCEMENT

Reorganization Plan No. 2 of 1973, which becomes effective on July 1, 1973, among other things establishes a Drug Enforcement Administration in the Department of Justice. In my message to the Congress transmitting that plan, I stated that all functions of the Office for Drug Abuse Law Enforcement (established pursuant to Executive Order No. 11641 of January 28, 1972) and the Office of National Narcotics Intelligence (established pursuant to Executive Order No. 16676 of July 27, 1972) would, together with other related functions be merged in the new Drug Enforcement Administration.

NOW, THEREFORE, by virtue of the authority vested in me by the Constitution and laws of the United States, including section 5317 of title 5 of the United States Code, as amended, it is hereby ordered as follows:

Section 1. The Attorney General, to the extent permitted by law, is authorized to coordinate all activities of executive branch departments and agencies which are directly related to the enforcement of laws respecting narcotics and dangerous drugs. Each department and agency of the Federal Government shall, upon request and to the extent permitted by law, assist the Attorney General in the performance of functions assigned to him pursuant to this order, and the Attorney General may, in carrying out those functions, utilize the services of any other agencies, federal and state, as may be available and appropriate.

Sec. 2. Executive Order No. 11641 of January 28, 1972, is hereby revoked and the Attorney General shall provide for the reassignment of the functions of the Office for Drug Abuse Law Enforcement and for the abolishment of that Office.

Sec. 3. Executive Order No. 11676 of July 27, 1972, is hereby revoked and the Attorney General shall provide for the reassignment of the functions of the Office of Narcotics Intelligence and for the abolishment of that Office.

Sec. 4. Section 1 of Executive Order No. 11708 of March 23, 1973, as amended, placing certain positions in level IV of the Executive Schedule is hereby further amended by deleting— (1) "(6) Director, Office for Drug Abuse Law Enforcement, Department of Justice"; and (2) "(7) Director, Office of Narcotics Intelligence, Department of Justice."

Sec. 5. The Attorney General shall provide for the winding up of the affairs of the two offices and for the reassignment of their functions.

Sec 6. This order shall be effective as of July 1, 1973.

Richard Nixon

THE WHITE HOUSE,

July 6, 1973"[8]

1. Look at the United States Constitution, in particular Article II. What provisions support President Nixon's issuance of this executive order? _____

   _____

2. What is the effect of this executive order? _____

   _____

3. What kind of law is this (statutory or judicial) and why do you think so? _____

   _____

   _____

4. What is the historical significance of this document? _____

   _____

   _____

   _____

C By the 1990s, the Drug Enforcement Agency (DEA) had been active for over two decades. America's war on drugs entered its third decade with an impressive set of numbers including tens of thousands of arrests, billions of dollars spent, and drug enforcement efforts that had spread to several foreign countries. Under a statute encouraging federal agencies to educate the public as to their activities and histories, the DEA set up a museum and posted its version of the history of the drug war. Part of that history appears below:

By 1971, the drug problem in America had reached what then-President Nixon described as a national emergency afflicting both the body and soul of America. Federal efforts were made on both the supply side of illegal drugs with amendments to the Controlled Substances Act as well as the demand side of illegal drugs with new programs for treatment, rehabilitation, education and research. All of these new efforts to thwart the growing drug problem in the U.S. served to fragment the federal approach with multiple authorities, competing priorities and a lack of communication. President Nixon set out to solve that problem in 1973 with Reorganization Plan Number Two which created the Drug Enforcement Administration, today the government's lead agency in fighting illegal drug trafficking. "With this new agency," Nixon said, "we will wage an all-out war on drugs."

Nixon and the federal government had reason to pay close attention to the drug problem in the mid-1970s. Drug use in America reached its peak in 1979, when one in nine Americans used drugs on a regular basis. During the 1970s, cocaine reappeared, touted as the champagne of drugs because it was expensive, high-status, and said to have no serious consequences. Notice the cocaine paraphernalia in front of you, ranging from cocaine kits to McDonald's coffee stirrers which cocaine addicts used to snort the drug. In South America, Colombian traffickers expanded beyond marijuana, linking up with enterprising American baby boomers to smuggle and distribute their new high-end product: cocaine. They established a beachhead in South Florida where gun battles on the streets of Miami were common through the early and mid-1980s. The Medellin Cartel, lead by Pablo Escobar, became the most wealthy, violent, and notorious drug trafficking organization to date. When that organization was brought down by American and Colombian forces in the early 1990s, it was replaced by the savvy Cali Cartel. Traffickers' weaponry and smuggling methods, many examples of which are shown in front of you, became more sophisticated. Smugglers loaded everything from hollowed-out surf boards to their own shoes with illegal drugs.[9]

1. From reading this history, what conclusions can you draw about the course of the war on drugs in the 1970s? _____

    _____

2. What flaws do you see in the DEA's account? _____

    _____

3. What possible motives would the DEA have in telling a particular kind of history about its activities? _____

    _____

4. Examine your own perspective on the war on drugs. What is that perspective and how do you think it impacts your view of the DEA's history? _____

    _____

    _____

    _____

This concludes our chapter on legal history and hidden history. The former is a valuable set of skills and the latter is an increasingly promising area of research for historians. Whatever one's views of lawyers and the law, there is no denying its impact on U.S. history. Statutes, judicial opinions, and regulations may be the stuff of the law, but one should not ignore the political, cultural, and social context of what lawyers' refer to as "black letter law." Do continue to ponder these contradictions in American law so important to understanding America and its history: religion, morality, and a supposedly secular government; the contest between democratic law-making and individual liberties; and the ever-elusive goal of justice in a system influenced by wealth and power.

You should also consider the question of whether or not these hidden histories are in point of fact a large majority of the story of American life. After all, the law only prohibits a certain amount of human activity while morality covers a great deal more. Additionally, even though some of us try to achieve celebrity and give up our private lives in the process, most of us attempt to keep much of our lives private. Hidden history is not just the immoral and the illegal. It is much of our history.

Notes

[1] N.E.H. Hull, Williamjames Hull Hoffer, and Peter Charles Hoffer, *The Abortion Rights Controversy in America: A Legal Reader* (Chapel Hill: University of North Carolina Press, 2004), 29–30.

[2] Hull, Hoffer, and Hoffer, *Abortion*, 89.

[3] Hull, Hoffer, and Hoffer, *Abortion*, 94.

[4] Hull, Hoffer, and Hoffer, *Abortion*, 121–122.

[5] William N. Eskridge, Jr. and Nan D. Hunter, eds., *Sexuality, Gender, and the Law* (New York: Foundation Press, 2004), 219–220.

[6] Eskridge and Hunter, 221–222.

[7] *Miranda v. Arizona* 384 U.S. 436 (1966), Cornell University Law School, "Miranda v. Arizona," Majority Opinion by Warren, C.J., http://www.law.cornell.edu/supct/html/historics/USSC_CR_0384_0436_ZO.html, Internet, accessed 8/18/2011.

[8] "Drug Enforcement Administration", History, 1970–1975, http://www.justice.gov/dea/history.htm; Internet, accessed 8/16/2011, 13.

[9] Drug Enforcement Agency, Museum, "Illegal Drugs in America: *A Modern History*", Stop Eleven: The Return of Cocaine and the Rise of the Cartels, http://www.deamuseum.org/ida/11.html, Internet, accessed 8/16/2011.

12: Comparisons: Seeking Patterns in Numbers

Is America in Decline?

A strange thing happened during the early months of 1988. A historical work of almost 700 pages of small print, 83 pages of notes, 38 pages of bibliography, and 52 tables and charts climbed onto the bestseller list. Its author was featured in a cover article in the *New York Times Magazine*, was interviewed on network talk shows, and testified before congressional committees. The book provided the focal point for lead editorials in top newspapers and magazines throughout the country. The writer was Yale historian Paul Kennedy. The book was *The Rise and Fall of the Great Powers* (New York: Random House, 1987). The commotion was over Kennedy's thesis that America was in decline.

Forecasts of decline are nothing new in American history. They trace back at least as far as the late seventeenth century, when Puritan ministers in Massachusetts Bay Colony warned that the declining piety of the people would bring God's wrath down upon them. A century later, in the aftermath of the successful struggle for independence from Great Britain but faced with social unrest and immobilized by a weak central government, many American leaders feared that the nation would split apart before it even got going. During the last decade of the nineteenth century, numerous observers worried that the growing materialism of Americans, combined with the rising divisions between business and labor and the economic instability that had accompanied urbanization and industrialization, boded ill for the nation's future. The United States was supposedly on the verge of losing much of the dynamism and vitality that had distinguished it from the older, decaying countries of Europe. In the twentieth century, the 1970s were years of widespread pessimism, "a crisis of confidence" in the minds of many observers, including President Jimmy Carter. The U.S. experience in Vietnam, the energy crisis, the Watergate scandal, growing evidence of Soviet military superiority, and the Iran hostage crisis produced deep anxiety about America's future.

President Ronald Reagan openly challenged the idea of national decline. His upbeat rhetoric upon entering the White House in 1981, combined with an economic boom that prevailed during most of his eight years in office, produced a shift in national mood. Polling data showed that most U.S. citizens were more optimistic about their future than at any time in a quarter century. *Time* magazine declared "a rebirth of the American spirit."[1]

Still, the huge federal budget and trade deficits that characterized the Reagan years generated much concern, which Kennedy's book suggested was well founded. The greatest single source of the budget deficit was a massive increase in spending for defense, a course that Reagan insisted was essential to protect U.S. interests abroad and security at home. Although Kennedy devoted only a small portion of his treatise to the United States in the 1980s, his account of the decline of great powers throughout history indicated that Reagan was tragically mistaken, that by putting so much of the country's resources into military and foreign ventures, he—and his predecessors from Harry S Truman onward—had committed the error of "imperial overstretch." The overcommitment of national resources to ventures abroad, Kennedy argued, had contributed to the relative decline of other leading powers and was having the same impact on the United States.

Kennedy had his critics. Joseph Nye of Harvard University, for example, challenged Kennedy's use of the years immediately following World War II as the starting point for an analysis of America's present and future stature. World War II, Nye argued, left the United States in a unique position of dominance. The war rendered tremendous destruction to the industrial plants of Germany and Japan and temporarily eliminated them as independent actors in international politics. The Soviet Union emerged victorious from the war, but it lost 20 million people and suffered devastating blows to its productive capacity. Japan occupied and ravaged much of China, and in the war's aftermath civil conflict delayed China's development. The United States, in contrast, was never occupied or its mainland attacked, and its gross national product virtually doubled between 1940 and 1945.

The United States emerged from the war with an economic strength unprecedented in modern history, but it could hardly maintain that position indefinitely. As World War II's effects on the other great powers gradually diminished, Nye pointed out, so too did America's lead over them. Yet that lead had begun to shrink more and more slowly since the 1970s and, if we take into account a broad range of power sources—basic resources, military forces, economic strength, scientific and technological development, national cohesion, culture and ideology, international institutions—the United States seemed overall to be firmly entrenched at the top.[2]

Numbers over Time: Economic Indicators

Kennedy and his allies helped to fuel a debate that has continued to the present day. Some analysts follow in Kennedy's path, comparing data over time about all the great powers to reveal how the United States is doing compared with its prime competitors—Japan, Germany, China, and the Soviet Union (now Russia). Although these scholars argue over what data is accurate and pertinent to the issue, they agree that comparing the United States to other nations is the proper approach. Other analysts use an absolute rather than a relative standard to evaluate America's position. They examine data from different time periods but pertinent to the United States alone. Their emphasis centers on how the quality of life for Americans has changed over time and on what recent trends bode for the future.

Whatever the data addressed, there is little doubt that analysts need to approach the issue of America's decline through historical methods, especially quantitative ones: compiling data, putting it in numerical form, and comparing it across time and place. It is to this last step that we devote this chapter. Because analyzing quantitative data is ever more common in a world passing through an "information revolution," this skill will prove of considerable use to you outside the classroom.

The exercises presented in this chapter ask you to make comparisons with numbers as well as to consider the question of America's decline. We begin by looking at a common analogy: the United Kingdom's position in the late nineteenth century and the United

States' position a century later. We move on to comparative statistics for nations in the 1980s and 1990s alone to give you a sense of how the United States has fared in recent years. These numbers should also provide a starting point for evaluating Joseph Nye's assertion that America's position relative to other great powers was fairly steady during the last decades of the twentieth century. Then we provide comparative data on education, ranging from the 1960s, when sophisticated multinational testing efforts began, to the 1990s. Finally, by looking at life in the United States during recent decades, we address the question, Is America in absolute decline?

Exercise 1: The British-American Analogy

One of the favorite exercises of forecasters of American decline is to compare the United States today with the United Kingdom in the late nineteenth century. These analysts see the recent trend of American development in relation to other great powers as similar to that of the United Kingdom a century ago, when it was the single most influential nation on earth but clearly was losing ground to others. Here we ask you to examine that analogy.

Unfortunately, it is not possible to provide comprehensive data on the relative positions of the two countries. Even if we could do so, the rapidly changing conditions over the last hundred years make comparisons inherently difficult and imprecise. Scholars are far from unanimous on the criteria for evaluating the positions of nations, so we begin by advising you to take care in drawing conclusions from the information presented here. Although these numbers may look precise, they represent approximations that, in some cases, are still open to dispute. Nonetheless, the information in Figures 12.1 and 12.2 and Tables 12.1, 12.2, and 12.3 provide some key comparisons. Study these tables and graphs carefully.

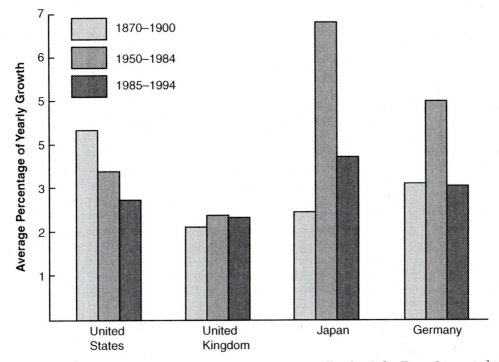

FIGURE 12.1 *Average Yearly Growth Rates in Gross Domestic Product* for Four Countries*[3]
*Gross domestic product is "the market value of all goods and services that have been bought for final use during a year. . . . GDP covers workers and capital employed within the nation's borders. GNP [in contrast] covers production by American residents, regardless of where it takes place."[4]

Questions about each table and graph will help focus your thinking. Questions relating to the whole series of tables and graphs will help you reach some tentative conclusions. Finally, we ask you to write a paragraph on the pros and cons of the analogy based on the information at hand.

Figure 12.1 is a bar graph showing the average percentage of yearly growth of four leading countries over three different periods. An **average** is computed by adding together all the individual numbers in a series (in this case, individual years over a span of years) and then dividing the sum by the total number in the series (in the case of 1985 to 1994, 10). A bar graph displays quantities. The extent, amount, or number of each category (in this case an individual country) is represented by a rectangle whose base is the *x*-axis of a graph. The *y*-axis depicts the quantity (in this case, the average percentage of annual change).

Questions on Figure 12.1

1. What two countries' rates were highest in the late nineteenth century? _____

   Do the rates help explain events between 1914 and 1918? Explain. _____

   _____

2. How do the rates for the 1950–1984 and the 1985–1994 periods differ from those for the earlier period? _____

   _____

   _____

   Can you see any long-term significance to these rates? _____

   If so, what? _____

   _____

Figure 12.2 shows three series of pie graphs. Frequently a pie graph is used to display the total evidence divided into its parts. Wedges represent the percentages that each group or category contributes to the whole. In Figure 12.2, each graph in an individual series, running horizontally, represents one aspect of a country's economy over a specific range of time. We could have presented the same information more concisely in a table, but instead we chose pie graphs to make the display more visually dramatic.

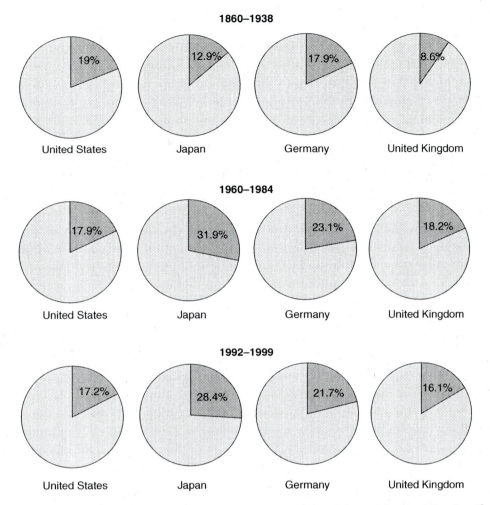

FIGURE 12.2 *Gross Fixed Capital Formation* as a Percentage of Gross National Product?*[5]
*Capital formation is the acquisition of materials—such as machinery, ships, and airplanes—that may be used for future production or in the rendering of services.

Questions on Figure 12.2

1. How are the rankings of the four countries for the first period different from the ranking for the last two periods? _____

_____

2. Do you think there is any connection between levels of capital formation in a country and the overall growth of the economy? _____ Explain. _____

_____

_____

Tables summarize and tabulate the characteristics of variables. Tables are always comparative in nature—that is, they compare one variable with another or show how a single variable changes over time or place. Table 12.1 provides comparisons over time (five different years over a century and a half), place (the United Kingdom and the United States), and economic/financial categories (gross national product, military spending, and manufacturing).

Table 12.1 A Comparison of British and American Global Rankings[6]

| Category | United Kingdom | | | United States | |
	1830	1870	1913	1950	2000
Gross national product	3rd	3rd	4th	1st	1st
Military spending	2nd	3rd	3rd	2nd	1st
Manufacturing	3rd	1st	3rd	1st	1st

Questions on Table 12.1

1. How do British rankings during the late nineteenth and early twentieth centuries compare to U.S. rankings during the second half of the twentieth century?_____

2. What, if anything, does that comparison suggest about British-American analogy? ___

Table 12.2 Population (in millions)[7]

Country	1880	1910	1950	1990	2000
United States	50.2	92.0	151.7	249.2	275.6
United Kingdom	35.1	45.0	50.6	57.6	59.5
Japan	37.0	49.6	82.9	123.5	126.6
Germany	45.2	64.9	69.0	79.4	82.8
China	412.0 (est.)	509.1 (est)	556.7	1,138.9	1,261.8

Question on Table 12.2

1. How do the patterns of the United States and the United Kingdom compare in relation to each other and to the other two countries? _____

Table 12.3 Defense Spending as Percentage of Gross National Product[8]

Year	U.K	U.S.	Japan	Germany	China
1870	2.0	0.9	—	—	—
1890	2.2	0.5	2.1	3.3	—
1910	2.8	0.9	5.8	2.9	—
1950	6.4	3.5	0	4.5	—
1960	6.4	8.7	1.1	3.4	—
1978	4.5	4.9	0.9	3.3	—
1984	5.2	6.3	1.0	3.2	—
1989	4.1	6.3	1.0	2.8	3.4
1993	3.6	4.5	1.0	1.9	2.5
1999	2.5	3.0	1.0	1.6	2.3

Questions on Table 12.3

1. How did patterns change among the four nations between the late nineteenth and early twentieth centuries and the late twentieth century? _____

   _____

2. Are the patterns of the United Kingdom and the United States similar or different? ____

   _____

   _____

Questions on Figures 12.1 and 12.2 and Tables 12.1, 12.2, and 12.3

1. Look again at Figures 12.1 and 12.2 and Table 12.1 and 12.2. What conclusions can you draw about the economy of the United Kingdom in the late nineteenth century and about the economy of the United States in the late twentieth century? _____

   _____

   _____

   _____

   _____

   _____

   _____

   _____

2. Does anything that happened in the world in general during the first fifty years of the twentieth century help to explain the rapidity of the United Kingdom's decline and the speed of America's rise? (*Hint:* You might find some of the material in the introduction to this chapter helpful.) Explain. _____

   _____

   _____

3. Do you see any connection between the population statistics in Table 12.2 and the relative rise or decline of the nations listed? (*Hint:* Consider rates of increase in population and size of population of the countries included.) Explain. _____

   _____

4. Look again at the data in Table 12.3. What explanation does it suggest for the patterns you found in Figures 12.1 and 12.2? (*Hint:* Ask yourself whether the data supports Paul Kennedy's thesis outlined at the beginning of the chapter.) _____

   _____

   _____

5. Write a paragraph on a separate sheet of paper evaluating the pros and cons of the British analogy based on the information given above.

Exercise 2: The 1980s and 1990s—Comparing Real Gross National Products

Following are three bar graphs on the real gross domestic products of several great powers. *Real gross domestic product* is the total monetary value of all the goods and services produced within a country over a specified period with inflation or deflation taken into account. For example, in

1923 Babe Ruth became the first baseball player with an annual salary of $50,000. In 1992 dollars, that salary would be worth $390,405. In comparing the salaries of major league baseball players in the 1920s to those of today, it would be important to take into account the declining value of the dollar between those two times. To do so, we would take the value of the dollar at one point in time, probably the present, and factor in its decline in value since the 1920s. Then we would adjust the earlier salaries accordingly. This method would give us a far more accurate idea of the magnitude of the change in salaries than if we used the raw numbers from both periods.

In Figures 12.3, 12.4, and 12.5, search for patterns in the numbers and think about what they suggest about nations' standing in relation to each other. Then answer the questions that follow.

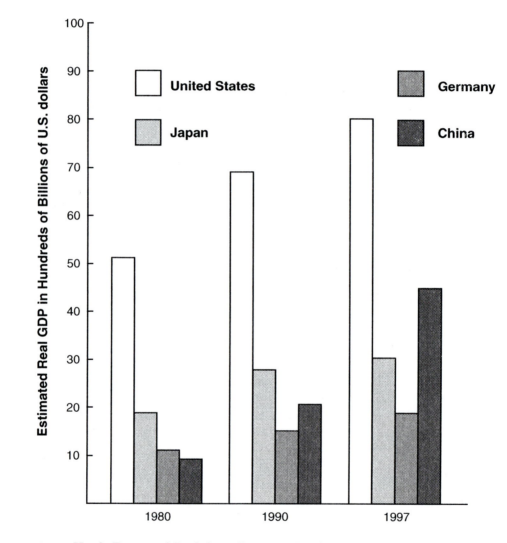

FIGURE 12.3 *Yearly Estimated Real Gross Domestic Product—in hundreds of billions of 1997 U.S. dollars*[9]

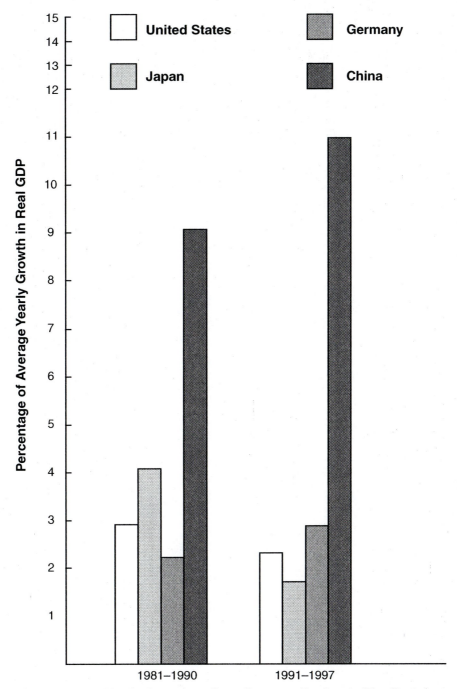

FIGURE 12.4 *Average Yearly Growth in Gross Domestic Product in Two Periods*

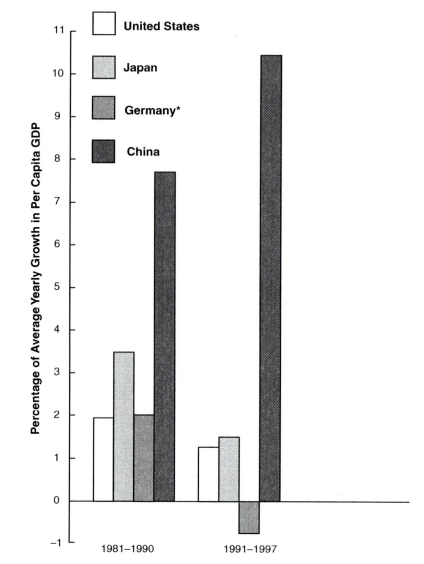

FIGURE 12.5 *Growth in Per Capita (Individual) Real GDP, 1981–1990 and 1991–1997 (Average Yearly Rate of Growth in Percentages)*
**Figures for 1981–1990 are for West Germany, for 1991–1997 a united Germany.*

Questions on Figures 12.3, 12.4, and 12.5

1. Which of the three graphs (Figures 12.3, 12.4, or 12.5) puts the United States in the best light? _____ Explain. _____
   _____

2. After reviewing Figures 12.3 through 12.5, explain why China's showing in Figures 12.4 and 12.5, if considered alone, could be misleading. (*Hint:* What are the starting points in 1981 for gross domestic product and per capital real gross domestic product?)
   _____
   _____

3. In determining the military potential of a nation, which of the three graphs would you consider the most important? _____ Explain. _____

_____

_____

_____

_____

4. China is the least advanced economically of the four countries listed in Figures 12.3, 12.4, and 12.5. Given that fact, if we had given figures on per capita gross domestic product rather than the growth of per capita gross domestic product, how do you think China would have fared in comparison with the other three countries? _____

Explain._____

_____

_____

_____

Which category, per capita gross domestic product or growth of per capita gross domestic product, would you regard as most important in determining countries' overall economic competitiveness in international markets? _____

Explain._____

_____

_____

_____

_____

Your answers to those questions illustrate the fact that numbers reflecting different aspects of the same general topic—in this case, national productivity—can have very different implications. Thus we constantly must ask ourselves what the numbers before us mean. Numbers—like literary sources—need to be interpreted.

Exercise 3: Education

Education greatly concerned Americans during the 1980s. This concern gained concrete expression in 1984 in a presidential commission's report entitled *A Nation at Risk*, which argued that the country's long-term well-being was threatened by the inferior education its children were receiving. Following are two series of tables comparing American education with that of several other nations. Read Tables 12.4 through 12.7 in Series A and Tables 12.8 through 12.10 and Figure 12.6 in Series B, and answer the questions that follow each series. Keep in mind that testing students is exceedingly difficult and expensive and that these comparisons include only representative samples from participating nations. The comparative testing of students of several different nations goes back only to the mid-1960s and remains limited even today.

Series A

Table 12.4 Public Expenditures for Education as a Percentage of Gross National Product, 1987[10]

United States	5.7
U.S.S.R.	7.3
Japan	5.0
West Germany	4.4
United Kingdom	5.0
Canada	7.2

Table 12.5 Number of Pupils per Teacher, Elementary Education, 1991[11]

United States	15.5
France	22.7
Japan	20.3
West Germany	21.4
United Kingdom	22.2

Table 12.6 Average Length of School Year for Elementary and Secondary Education (in days)[12]

United States	180
Japan	243
United Kingdom	196
Italy	210–215
West Germany	160–170

Table 12.7 Percentage of Population Aged 18 to 25 Engaged in Postsecondary Education, 1991[13]

United States	53.1
Sweden	21.1
United Kingdom	23.8
Canada	41.9
West Germany	25.4

Questions on Series A Tables

1. Which two of the four Series A tables put the United States in the most favorable light?

   _____

   Which one puts the United States in the least favorable light? _____ Explain.

   _____

   _____

   _____

   _____

2. Other than test results, what kind of information in addition to that provided in Tables 12.4 through 12.7 might help you evaluate American competitiveness in the area of education?

   a._____

   _____

   b._____

   _____

Series B

Table 12.8 Mathematics Achievement Test Scores for 13- and 17-Year-Olds, 1982 (numbers show the mean of questions answered correctly converted into percentages of total questions in the test)[14]

	13-Year-Olds	17-Year-Olds
United States	46.2	39.8
Japan	63.6	70.2
Sweden	43.4	57.5
United Kingdom	48.8	51.3
Canada	50.9	44.5

Table 12.9 Achievement in Math and Science for Eighth-Grade Students, 1995 and 1999 (average scores on standardized tests by country)[15]

Country	Science		Math	
	1995	1999	1995	1999
United States	513	515	492	502
Russia	523	529	524	526
England	533	538	498	496
South Korea	546	549	581	587
Japan	554	550	581	579

Table 12.10 Percentage of Undergraduate Degrees Awarded in Science in Selected Countries, 1991[16]

	All Science Degrees	Engineering Degrees
Austria	20.1	9.5
Canada	15.5	6.1
West Germany	31.5	20.2
Japan	23.5	21.1
United States	15.9	7.2

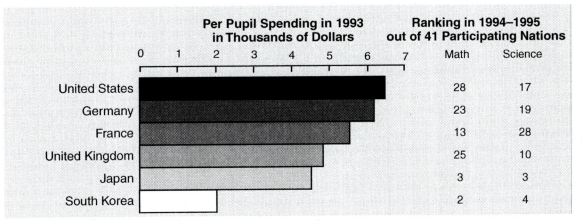

FIGURE 12.6 *Public Spending per Pupil (Bar Graph) and Ranking in Performance of 13-Year-Olds in Mathematics and Science Tests (Table)*[17]

Questions on Series B Tables and Figure 12.6

1. Would you say that the test scores reflected in Tables 12.8 through 12.10 and Figure 12.6 put the U.S. educational system in (a) a consistently favorable light, (b) a mostly favorable light, (c) a consistently unfavorable light, or (d) a mostly unfavorable light? __ Explain. _____

_____

2. The tests included in these tables and Figure 12.6 cover a chronological range from 1982 to 1999. Would you say the competitive position of the United States over that time (a) improved, (b) stayed the same, or (c) got worse? Circle one.

3. In the case in which tests were administered to more than one age group, did the mean scores of U.S. students get more or less competitive with increasing age? _____

4. What group of students that is *not* measured in Tables 12.8, 12.9, and 12.10 or in Figure 12.6 might put the United States in a better light? (*Hint:* Consider the information provided in Table 12.7.) Explain. _____

_____

_____

_____

How might the information on Table 12.10 qualify this hopeful perspective for the United States?_____

_____

_____

_____

5. Does the information provided in Figure 12.6 suggest a relationship between spending per pupil and performance in math and science? _____ Explain. _____

_____

_____

6. Does the information provided in the table portion of Figure 12.6 and in Table 12.6 suggest a relationship between the length of the school year in different countries and the performance of their students in math and science? _____ Explain. _____

_____

The United States and Absolute Decline

We move from comparative statistics to ones on the United States alone. The broad question we seek to address is, How has the quality of American life evolved during recent decades, and where is it likely to go in the near future? Has life become better for most people, stayed pretty much the same, or gotten worse—and is the recent trend likely to continue? Again, we make no attempt to provide data for a comprehensive assessment. Rather, we focus on the life expectancy and income. As you examine the following data, think through the implications of the information presented and consider areas not represented that would assist you in grappling with this question.

Exercise 4: Life Expectancy

Tables 12.11 and 12.12 provide information on life expectancy. Read each table and answer the questions that follow.

Table 12.11 Expected Length of Life at Birth, 1970–1985, and Projections, 1990–2010[18]

	Total			White			Black		
Year	Total	Male	Female	Total	Male	Female	Total	Male	Female
1970	70.8	67.1	74.7	71.7	68.0	75.6	64.1	60.0	68.3
1990	75.6	72.1	79.0	76.2	72.7	79.6	71.4	67.7	75.0
2010	77.9	74.4	81.3	78.3	74.9	81.7	75.0	71.4	78.5

Table 12.12 Infant Deaths in Total Population, 1960–1988*[19]

Year	Total Number	Rate per 1,000 Population
1960	111,000	26.0
1970	75,000	20.0
1980	46,000	12.6
1988	39,000	

*Infants are defined as babies less than 1 year old.

Questions on Tables 12.11 and 12.12

1. According to projections, will the change in life expectancy for those born between 1990 and 2010 be higher or lower than the change for those born between 1970 and 1990?

   _____

2. Is this true for both sexes and races? _____

3. Is the trend in Table 12.12 regarding the rate of change similar to the trend you detected in Table 12.11? _____ Is there a linkage between the *rate* of change in life expectancy and in infant mortality? Explain. _____

   _____

   _____

   _____

Exercise 5: Income and Poverty

Statistics on income provide one method to assess whether life is becoming better for Americans. When we break the numbers into specific income groups and by race and sex, however, we find that the picture is complex, a fact that Figures 12.7 and 12.8 and Table 12.13 through 12.16 make clear.

Figure 12.7 is a line graph, which shows change in data over time or compares the change in quantities against each other. Figure 12.7 displays changes in poverty rates from 1959 to 2001 by race and Hispanic origin. The x-axis represents years in five- or six-year intervals. The y-axis represents the percentage of people in the individual group represented that fall below the poverty line. The gray bars rising from the x-axis represent time periods in which the U.S. economy was in recession.

Table 12.13 Persons Below Poverty Level, 1960–2001 (by race and Hispanic origin)[20]

Year	Total Number in Millions				As Percentage of Entire Population			
	All Races	White Non-Hispanic	Black	Hispanic	All Races	White Non-Hispanic	Black	Hispanic
1960	39.9	28.3	na	na	22.2	17.8	na	na
1975	25.9	14.9	7.5	3.0	12.3	8.6	31.3	26.9
1980	29.3	16.4	8.6	3.5	13.0	9.1	32.5	25.7
1985	33.1	17.8	8.9	5.2	14.0	9.7	31.3	29.0
1990	33.6	16.6	9.8	6.0	13.5	8.8	31.9	26.2
1994	38.1	18.1	10.2	8.4	14.5	9.4	30.6	30.7
2001	32.9	22.7	8.1	8.0	11.7	7.8	22.7	21.4

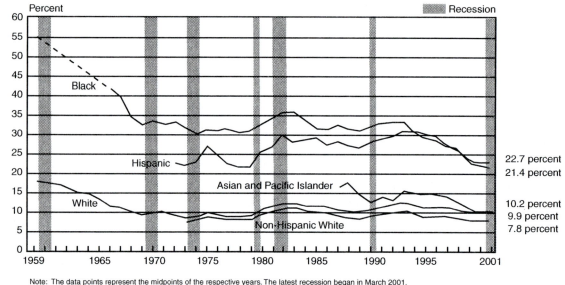

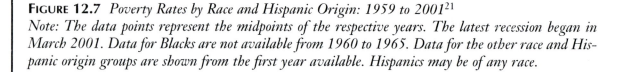

Note: The data points represent the midpoints of the respective years. The latest recession began in March 2001.
Data for Blacks are not available from 1960 to 1965. Data for the other race and Hispanic origin groups are shown from the first year available.
Hispanics may be of any race.
Source: U.S. Census Bureau, Current Population Survey, 196—2002, Annual Demographic Supplements.

FIGURE 12.7 *Poverty Rates by Race and Hispanic Origin: 1959 to 2001*[21]
Note: The data points represent the midpoints of the respective years. The latest recession began in March 2001. Data for Blacks are not available from 1960 to 1965. Data for the other race and Hispanic origin groups are shown from the first year available. Hispanics may be of any race.

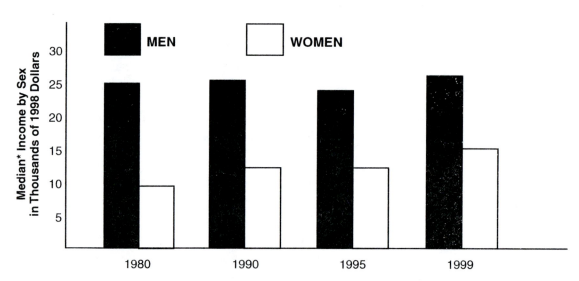

FIGURE 12.8 *Median Income of Men and Women (in constant 1998 dollars)*[22]
*Median is the point in a series of numbers that divides the series into two groups with equal numbers of entries. In the series 3, 4, 7, 9, 11, 14, and 16, for example, 9 is the median because there are 3 numbers on each side of it.

Table 12.14 Persons 65 Years Old and Over Below Poverty Level, 1974–2001 (by selected characteristics)[23]

Characteristic	Number Below Poverty Level (in thousands)			Percentage Below Poverty Level		
	1974	1990	2001	1974	1990	2001
Persons 65 and over	3085	3658	3414	14.6	12.2	10.1
Non-Hispanic White	2346	2471	2266	12.5	9.6	8.1
Black	591	860	626	47.7	33.8	21.9
Hispanic	117	245	413	28.9	22.5	21.8

Table 12.15 Children Below Poverty Level by Race and Hispanic Origin, 1970–1999[24]

Year	Number Below Poverty Level (in thousands)				Percentage Below Poverty Level			
	All Races	White	Black	Hispanic	All Races	White	Black	Hispanic
1970	10,235	6,138	3,922	na	14.9	10.5	41.5	na
1980	11,114	6,817	3,906	1,718	17.9	13.4	42.1	33.0
1990	12,715	7,696	4,412	2,750	19.9	15.1	44.2	37.7
1999	11,510	7,123	3,644	3,382	16.3	12.9	32.7	29.9

Table 12.16 Household Shares of Aggregate Income by Fifths of Total U.S. Households (in %)[25]

Year	Percent Distribution of Total Income					
	Lowest 5th	Second 5th	Third 5th	Fourth 5th	Highest 5th	Top 5%
1970	4.1	10.8	17.4	24.5	43.3	16.6
1980	4.3	10.3	16.9	24.9	43.7	15.8
1990	3.9	9.6	15.9	24.0	46.6	18.6
2001	3.5	8.7	14.6	23.0	50.1	22.4

Questions on Figures 12.7 and 12.8 and Tables 12.13 through 12.16

1. In evaluating how Americans did financially from 1980 through the 1990s, which item, Figure 12.7 or Figure 12.8, is the more useful? (*Hint:* Read the headings of both graphs.) Explain. _____

_____

2. *Overall,* how would you say Americans fared financially between 1980 and 2000? Explain.

_____

3. Add Table 12.16 and the factors of race, class, and sex to your analysis. Now how would you say Americans did financially from 1980 to 2000? _____

_____

4. Figure 12.8 shows that women still lag well behind men in income. Identify two reasons why you think this is so.

a. _____

_____

b. _____

_____

5. Do the figures in Figure 12.7 indicate that the 1980s or the 1990s were a better decade for Americans? _____

6. If you add Table 12.13 to your analysis, how does it affect your answer to question 5? Explain. _____

_____

7. Do the trends revealed in Tables 12.14 and 12.15 show similar patterns regarding the elderly and children? _____ Explain. _____

_____

8. Which of the trends revealed in Tables 12.14 and 12.15 would you consider most significant in influencing the direction of our country during the next generation or two? Explain. _____

_____

_____

9. In a single **paragraph on a separate sheet of paper**, analyze American life from 1970 to 2000 from the trends revealed in Figures 12.7 and 12.8 and Tables 12.13 through 12.16. Include in your paragraph an assessment of what these trends bode for the future. Organize your thoughts first by writing down on a piece of scrap paper all the age, gender, income, and ethnic or racial groups covered in these figures and tables. Also, write down the main point of your paragraph. Make sure the paragraph sticks to that point.

Questions to Ponder for the New Millenium

You probably asked yourself while writing the above assignment: How would statistics for the early years of the twenty-first century impact my analysis? How would Paul Kennedy and Joseph Nye assess the evolving position of the United States were they writing today? We will not burden you with another assignment to contend with these questions, but do not be surprised if your instructor presents some more recent statistics in class that suggest answers. Should the urge to do a bit more research on these matters become irresistible, you may find the next chapter on the internet extremely useful.

Meanwhile, to whet your appetite we present you with some additional bits of information and some questions to ponder.

(1) In 2009 U.S. defense spending was 4.7 percent of its gross national product; Japan's was 1 percent, China's 2.2 percent, and Germany's 1.4 percent.

Questions to ponder: How do these figures compare to those of the late twentieth century? Why has the percentage for the United States changed so much since 1999? How would Kennedy interpret the significance of the change?

(2) For the fiscal years 1998–2001, the U.S. federal government had a total budget SURPLUS of over 693 billion inflation-adjusted dollars. Since then, there has been a DEFICIT every year, with the lowest in 2007 (165 billion inflation-adjusted dollars) and the highest in 2011 (1650 billion inflation-adjusted dollars).

Questions to ponder: Why has there been a dramatic turnaround since 2001? Was the period 1998 to 2001 exceptional in U.S. history since 1945? If so, why?

(3) In 2011 China surpassed the United States as the world leader in manufacturing.

Between 2000 and 2011, growth in the Gross Domestic Product of the United States never exceeded 6 percent on an annual basis while China's never dropped below 6 percent and on occasion exceeded 10 percent.

Questions to ponder: What is the significance of China's becoming number one in manufacturing? Does a higher percentage of growth for China mean automatically that its absolute growth is higher than that of the United States? Is it easier or harder for the nation with the highest GDP to achieve a high percentage growth rate in a given year?

(4) As the public debt of the United States has increased, so too has the percentage of that debt held by foreign governments (from 13 percent in 1988 to 25 percent in 2007). In mid 2011 China was the largest foreign holder of U.S. government securities (36 percent).

Questions to ponder: Is it better to have Americans or foreigners hold the U.S. public debt? What are the implications of China, which has emerged as the leading competitor of the Unites States in a number of areas, holding the largest portion of the U.S. debt?

(5) The median income for American households (in inflation-adjusted dollars) dropped from 53,252 in 1999 to 49,445 in 2010. During the same period, the percent of all households with under 15,000 in annual income increased from 10.1 to 11.8. Among blacks the latter figures were 21.5 in 1999 and 25.8 in 2010; among Hispanics 14.8 in 1999 and 17.4 in 2010. During the first decade of the twenty-first century, the percent of the total U.S. population that was black or Hispanic grew from 24.8 to 28.9. The income of the top 20 percent of all households increased from 49.8 to 50.2 while the share of the bottom 20 percent of households declined from 3.6 to 3.3.

Questions to ponder: Do the above figures reinforce or counter trends since the 1970s? Do they have implications regarding any of the categories for measuring national power identified by Nye? Do they contribute to an understanding of the polarization of the nation's politics over the last decade?

Notes

[1] *Time*, September 24, 1984, 10.

[2] Joseph S. Nye, Jr., *Bound to Lead: The Changing Nature of American Power* (New York: Basic Books, 1990).

[3] The information in this figure is taken from Robert E. Lipsey and Irving B. Kravis, *Saving and Economic Growth: Is the United States Really Falling Behind?* American Council of Life Insurance and The Conference Board, Report No. 901, 9; and U.S. Department of Commerce, *Statistical Abstract of the United States, 1993, 1994*, and *1996* (Washington, D.C.: Government Printing Office, 1993, 1994, 1996 respectively), 853, 854–855, and 836 respectively.

[4] *The World Almanac and Book of Facts 1997* (Mahwah, N.J.: World Almanac Books, 1996), 154.

[5] Lipsey and Kravis, *Saving and Economic Growth*, 26; U.S. Department of Commerce, *Statistical Abstract of the United States, 1996*, 837, and *2001*, 833.

[6] Nye, *Bound to Lead*, 64.

[7] W. S. Woytinsky and E. S. Woytinsky, *World Population and Production: Trends and Outlook* (New York: Twentieth Century Fund, 1953), 44; United Nations, Department of International Economic and Social Affairs, *World Population Prospects, 1990* (New York: United Nations, 1991);

U.S. Department of Commerce, *Statistical Abstract of the United States 2001*, 822–24; and http://www.library.uu.nl/wesp/populstat/Asia/chinac.htm.

[8] Karen Rasler and William R. Thompson, "Defense Burdens, Capital Formation, and Economic Growth," *Journal of Conflict Resolution* 32 (March 1988): 71 (for figures before 1978); U.S. Arms Control and Disarmament Agency, *World Military Expenditures and Arms Transfers, 1989* and *1999–2000* (Washington, D.C.: Government Printing Office, 1990 and 2000), 1978 onward; CIA, Directorate of Intelligence, *Handbook of International Economic Statistics, 1996* (Washington, D.C.: Government Printing Office, 1996), 26.

[9] The date in the figures for Exercise 2 are taken from U.S. Central Intelligence Agency, *Handbook of Economic Statistics, 1990, 1995, 1996, 1997* (Washington, D.C.: Government Printing Office, 1990, 1995, 1996, 1997).

[10] National Center for Education Statistics, *Digest of Education Statistics 1996* (Washington, D.C.: Government Printing Office, 1991), 375.

[11] National Center for Education Statistics, *Digest of Education Statistics 1996* (Washington, D.C.: Congressional Research Printing Office, 1996), 437.

[12] Kenneth Redd and Wayne Riddle, "Comparative Education: Statistics on Education in the United States and Selected Foreign Nations" (Washington, D.C.: Congressional Research Service, 1989), 31.

[13] National Center for Education Statistics, *Digest of Education Statistics 1996*, 447.

[14] Redd and Riddle, "Comparative Education," 27.

[15] TIMSS, *International Science Report, 1999* and *International Mathematics Report, 1999* (http://timss.bc.edu/timss1999.html).

[16] National Center for Education Statistics, *Digest of Education Statistics 1996*, 447.

[17] *The Economist*, March 29–April 4, 1997, 23.

[18] U.S. Department of Commerce, *Statistical Abstract of the United States, 1996*, 88.

[19] Ibid., 92.

[20] U.S. Department of Commerce, Census Bureau, *Poverty in the United States: 2001* (Washington, D.C.: Government Printing Office, 2002), 21, 23–24.

[21] U.S. Census Bureau, Poverty in the United States: 2001 (Washington, D.C.: Government Printing Office, 2002), 6.

[22] U.S. Department of Commerce, *Statistical Abstract of the United States 2001*, 441.

[23] Ibid., 26–29.

[24] U.S. Census Bureau, *Statistical Abstract of the United States 2001* (*http://www.census.gov/prod/2002pubs/01statab/stat-ab01.html*), 442.

[25] U.S. Census Bureau (http://www.census.gov/hhes/income/histinc/ie3.html).

13: *Using the Internet*

Elections, Scandals, Dot Coms, and Y2K
in the 1990s

Internet Tales

"January 1, 1983 is considered the official birthday of the Internet. Prior to this, the various computer networks did not have a standard way to communicate with each other. A new communications protocol was established called Transfer Control Protocol/Internetwork Protocol (TCP/IP). This allowed different kinds of computers on different networks to "talk" to each other. ARPANET and the Defense Data Network officially changed to the TCP/IP standard on January 1, 1983, hence the birth of the Internet. All networks could now be connected by a universal language."[1]

Stop, think, and write. It is a rare student today who does not use the internet. Assignments are on Blackboard or some other provider. Communications through Facebook, Twitter or an instant messaging service are free (at least as we write). Students in the back of the room may be using their laptops to open these, or simply surf the web. What do you most often do with your laptop?

Regardless of how you use your computer, there are some general rules for using Internet sources and some specific rules for history students. The first regard the issue of safety. They second concern reliability. The following paragraphs are a kind of "read me" document of the sort that should always be opened and read before you begin to use any kind of software or download anything from the web.

The Internet is a wonderful source, rich, varied, and often trustworthy. It is also a minefield of dangers. Knowing how to access the former while avoiding the latter is a matter of simple judgment, taking precautions and following the rules. The gateway to the internet is the ISP or internet service provider. These are free but you will find them, to some degree, cluttered with advertising, pop-ups, spam, and other distractions. Your ISP will have a menu selection at the top of the page including "tools." Use these to limit pop-ups, spam, and "cookies" (bits of text left on your computer when you open certain websites that enable the website to share information with you).

Generally, do not open or download anything that has a disputed origin. How do you know what is safe? Buy programs from the publisher on line, not from a pop-up. Look at the web address. Is it the exact address of the seller? (Often viruses or spyware have addresses that look like a legitimate seller's address, but one word is spelled differently or a letter has been replaced by a typographical character or a number.) If you think a site is infected, leave it. (A good clue that a site is infected is that you cannot leave it or leave your web access software–the internet service provider or internet browser.) Turn off the computer! Sometimes this will erase the website from your browser's memory. If not, get IT help. Never follow the instructions on the screen–they were placed there by the hacker.

There are a number of commercial anti-virus and anti-spyware software you can purchase. Buy only from the seller's web site, never from a pop up or a non-authorized site. You may be buying damaged goods or actually buying a virus. The most popular of the legitimate anti-virus programs are Norton (from Symatec), McAfee, or Trend Micro PC-cillin. There are some safe "freeware" providers, like Malwarebyte and CCleaner. Some viruses (called "malware" or "rogue" programs) actually masquerade as anti-virus software. The most infamous of these are Antivirus Live, Advanced Virus Remover, Spyware Defender and Antivirus 2010. Instead of protecting you against a virus, they race through all your files, hide everywhere, and send information to hackers. They slow your machine. "Spyware" unlike viruses, does not cripple your machine. Instead, it sends messages from your files to an outside source. It infects some perfectly legitimate websites. Some websites advertise anti-spyware programs that are actually spyware. To combat it, you need anti-spyware, but again, only get anti-spyware from the website of a legitimate vendor.

In general, but not always, websites with the suffixes .org (a reputable organization, like the Public Broadcasting System), .gov (a government site like the Library of Congress), or .edu (an educational site like the University of Georgia) are safe. These suffixes (also known as URLs or uniform resource locators) should have "home" links. Look at the menu bar on the top or the left hand margin of the web page. Click on those to find out more about the site. The rules above still apply, as any site can be infected. Sites ending in .com may also be safe (for example the History Channel website ends in .com and so does CNN).

There are also suffixes that appear when you are in a site. For example, /html (hyper-text markup language) usually means that you can block and copy directly from the web page. A .jpeg or .jif means that the page is a scanned image and may not be copied directly to your word-processing page. You cannot copy directly from the pages on Google.books, even if the page is a limited or full view, or with Amazon book pages, even when it lets you "search inside this book." Remember–never just paste in anything from the web without putting the pasted material in quotation marks and citing the exact web source. Failing to do this amounts to plagiarism and has serious consequences.

Apart from a site that is safe from infection, history students using the web have to concern themselves with the reliability of the site. Is the information on it trustworthy? Up to date? Presented in an objective, unbiased fashion? If the site has an author (for example it is a blog), check the biography or the home of the site to find out more about the blogger. If the web page you have found is a contribution to a legitimate web site, for example a posting on one of the H-List sources, find out more about the contributor before you adopt his or her opinion as your own. Some web sites like the H-List have moderators who screen the entries, but in general, there is no Big Brother controlling who posts what on the Web. Posts can be satire, lies, or twisted mixtures of truth and lie. Use the same criteria to judge trustworthiness of a site as you would the trustworthiness of a book or article (as discussed in Chapter Four above). Look for the citations in the site–does the author substantiate his or her facts or have references to books and articles on the subject. (For example, some Wikipedia sites tell us that the entry lacks citations or is a 'stub' without a lot of documentation.)

Some information on history sites on the web is obsolete almost as soon as they are published–even when they are e-books! Some websites simply vanish, gone the next day. Whenever you use a website you need to cite the title of the entry along with the full website address, but some of these (for example from newspapers) are two or three lines long. Best is to print off everything you plan to cite, so that if the site disappeared from the internet, you still have evidence that you saw it. Of course, some of the sites are filled with images, and these may take up a lot of space in your printer's memory. A huge pdf with graphs and images, or jpeg or other images on a site, may require gigabytes of memory. Print these in stages, a few pages at a time. If your printer gasps and shuts down, turn it off for a few minutes (to clear the memory) and then try printing one page at a time. Always back up everything you have written, including images, to a CD or a memory stick (travel memory) as well as to your hard disk.

For the rest of this chapter, we will ask you to do some research using the Internet. **Keep in mind the following as you do the exercises:** 1) Verify the accuracy of your web source; 2) Keep track of your search path including your search terms and which search engine you used; 3) Provide proof of the Internet source by saving the page to your computer; 4) Never copy and paste something from the Internet into a document without enclosing the content in quotation marks and noting the source.

Presidential Elections: 1992, 1996, 2000

There were three elections at the start of the Internet era. All three had an Internet presence. All three indicate the complexities of using the web for historical research. The first problem you must solve is how to find resources. The search engines available use different algorithms to browse the various web pages looking for your search terms. But beware: every search engine has its own agenda and this agenda can affect your search.

You might also want to keep in mind the following tips for doing searches: 1) experiment with your search terms; 2) start with the more general, then narrow it down; 3) use the appropriate database for the information you are trying to find (news for reporting, websites for advocacy or university based information, government sites for government info).

Exercise 1: Search Engines

In 1992, President George Herbert Walker Bush ran for reelection against Democratic nominee Governor Bill Clinton of Arkansas and businessman Ross Perot of Texas, who ran as an independent on his own party's ticket. This three-way race had a critical impact on the outcome of the election, as Perot took votes from both Bush and Clinton. Your task is to find a consensus opinion on who suffered more from Perot's candidacy: Bush or Clinton. Keep in mind the software devise you used to scour the internet – the search engine – affects the results. At the time of publication, these are some of the most popular search engines: Google, a version of Google called Google Chrome, Bing from Microsoft, and Yahoo. **List** the search engines you used, your search terms, and the list, in order, of each search engine generated.

1. Search Engine: _____ Search Terms: _____

   Web Sites and Title: _____

   _____

2. Search Engine: _____ Search Terms: _____

   Web Sites and Title: _____

   _____

3. Search Engine: _____ Search Terms: _____
   Web Sites and Title: _____
   _____

4. What differences do you see in the results each search engine generated? _____
   _____

5. What is your conclusion about the different qualities of these search engines?
   _____

6. Whom do you conclude lost more votes to Perot: Bush or Clinton?
   _____
   _____

Exercise 2: Presidential Polling and the Media On-Line

In 1996 President Bill Clinton ran for reelection against the senior Republican Senator from Kansas, Robert Dole. Ross Perot also ran again, this time with less impact on the outcome of the election. Although in retrospect Clinton was the odds-on favorite with a strong economy and an eventually solid reputation in his handling of foreign affairs, his advantages were not always reflected in the polls. In this exercise you need to **locate** presidential polls over the course of the 1996 presidential election and **report** their monthly results from August to November. Remember to apply the rules for checking the reliability of web sites.

As with all Internet based research, you may not be able to locate all the information you wish to find. Remember that it is the effort that counts, and that the more searches you do the better you will get at the task. You should also keep in mind books and articles on the topic that you can access through the Internet. A lot of material is just not available on a website. Sometimes, you have to dig deeper.

1. Poll Name: _____ Margin of Error: _____
   Results: Aug. _____ Sept. _____ Oct. _____ Nov. _____
2. Poll Name: _____ Margin of Error: _____
   Results: Aug. _____ Sept. _____ Oct. _____ Nov. _____
3. Poll Name: _____ Margin of Error: _____
   Results: Aug. _____ Sept. _____ Oct. _____ Nov. _____
4. Do the polls vary? In what way(s)? _____
   _____
5. Why do you think the polls might vary? _____
   _____

Exercise 3: Government Documents on the Internet

The election of 2000 became one of the most controversial presidential elections in the country's history. The result of the election is no longer in dispute. After the U.S. Supreme Court intervened in the case of <u>Bush v. Gore</u> (2000), stopping the Florida Supreme Court's ordered recount of ballots, the state of Florida certified that George W. Bush, the Republican governor of Texas and the son of former president George Herbert Walker Bush, had won Florida's vote over Democratic Vice-President Al Gore of Tennessee. Despite the embarrassment of one of the world's most advanced countries having difficulty determining how people had voted, the United States could be proud that the dispute did not erupt into widespread violence. It also created a huge amount of material on the Internet, which had come into its own over the second half of the 1990s.

In order properly to understand why the vote in those Florida counties was so important, you need to do some research on the Electoral College.

1. Using the web find the U.S. Supreme Court case of <u>Bush v. Gore</u> (2000). Read the opinions. List the provisions of the U.S. Constitution involved in deciding the case according to the opinions. _____

   _____

2. Find maps of the Electoral College for the 2000 presidential election. Not counting Florida, what are the respective electoral counts for Bush and Gore? _____

3. Again, examining your Electoral College maps, do you find a geographic pattern to the states Gore won versus the ones Bush won? What are those patterns? _____

   _____

4. Some of the major newspapers in the United States, including <u>The New York Times</u>, examined the disputed ballots from Florida under the differing standards for deciding a disputed presidential election contended in <u>Bush v. Gore</u>. Locate that report in the newspaper and summarize its findings. _____

   _____

5. Evaluate the ease with which you found all of these sources. Was it difficult? Why or why not? _____

   _____

6. Many people argue that the United States government and the state governments should be as open as possible and make a concerted effort to educate the public through various venues like the Internet. Compare the efforts on the web to explain how the following offices of government work: The President of the United States, the Congress of the United States, your home state's governor, and your home state's legislature. Who has the most informative website? Why do you think so? _____

   _____

   _____

The OJ Simpson Murder Trial[2]

In the upscale Brentwood section of Los Angeles, California, on the evening of June 12th 1994, a "horrific yet routine domestic-violence homicide" became "a national drama, one that exposed deep fissures in American society." The "race card" played by counsel for the defense turned a straight-forward question of circumstantial and scientific evidence into a test of a nation's nerves. The defendant was former professional football star and sometime movie actor O.J. Simpson. After a televised trial that pitted a famous defense team against two assistant district attorneys, the jury brought in a verdict of not guilty. In the course of the trial and the months of soul searching and book contract signing afterward, another discursive space opened. The trial seemed a perfect mirror of the contradictions in a nation of laws. Was the apparatus of law enforcement so prejudiced that no police investigation could be trusted? Was the law that governed the trial so misshapen that an obviously guilty man could beat the rap with the aid of high-priced lawyers? Had a racially biased jury had found a verdict contrary to the evidence? Had a publicity loving judge turned the trial into a circus and all the participants into clowns? Or was the system itself broken? After all, 134 days in court might have been too long for any trial.[3]

Whatever one concludes about the quality of justice for the defendant or the two victims in the case, the subsequent debate was immensely valuable insofar as it opened up the criminal justice system to public observation. In the days after the trial, two veteran litigators explored the meaning of the criminal law. One was Vincent Bugliosi; the other was Alan Dershowitz. Both were controversial figures in their own right–Bugliosi one of the most effective prosecutors in the country and Dershowitz a successful criminal appeals lawyer. Both had achieved a measure of fame in the courtroom, Bugliosi for prosecuting Charles Mansion and his "family," Dershowitz for gaining a retrial of Claus von Bulow in the attempted murder of his wife. As a former LA prosecutor, Bugliosi thought that Simpson could have been convicted. Dershowitz, after months on the defense team, disagreed.

Bugliosi was outraged at the incompetence of all the legal people, but his conclusion rested on legal history, not courtroom histrionics. "It is my firm belief that the not-guilty verdict in the Simpson case has historical origins, conscious or otherwise, in the maltreatment, most physical, of blacks by white police officers throughout the years." It was a verdict on history, not present fact, he insisted. In fact, the police did not frame or conspire to frame Simpson, and despite some discrepancies in times and eyewitness testimony, did a fairly credible job gathering evidence. The District Attorney's office made the most egregious mistakes in failing to present incriminating evidence and fumbling the opportunities it had. The judge as well allowed too much latitude to the defense. But all of these missteps were understandable in light of the situation in Los Angeles at the time. No one wanted more race riots, and LA had suffered more than its share.[4]

But Bugliosi was worried about a more pervasive problem. In an America whose cable television stations clamored for more coverage of the trial, the media gave the case "a disproportionate amount of publicity." What is due proportion may be in the eye of the beholder, but a trial waged in the fickle eye of so many beholders (viewers by the millions followed the case on Trial TV) put immense pressure on the criminal justice system. While trials must be public and speedy, the nearly yearlong media event violated the spirit of the Fourth Amendment.[5]

Finally, Bugliosi stated that he would not have agreed to defend Simpson had he been asked, because he thought Simpson guilty. By implication, he was saying that the Simpson defense team, including Dershowitz, surely knew that Simpson was guilty and agreed to defend him anyway. Everyone is entitled to a defense, but everyone cannot afford, as Simpson could, a blue ribbon defense team. Bugliosi knew that the fate of any defendant depended as much on the quality of legal representation as the fact of innocence or guilt. In an adversarial system, how far can a lawyer go to represent a client? Bugliosi was certain that members of the Simpson defense team engaged "in a concerted, unprofessional, and unethical effort" to "deny the people their right to a fair trial."[6]

Dershowitz's defense of the defense was just as practical and detailed as Bugliosi's, but it did not matter to Dershowitz whether Simpson was guilty. What mattered was the fairness of the trial to the defendant, and to all others similarly situated. Dershowitz is a brilliant lawyer and student of the law. He is also a fierce advocate for his position in whatever setting he might find himself. He knew that much legal opinion targeted the trial and the defense team for abusing the system, and so had a personal stake in the debate that Bugliosi lacked.

Dershowitz had his own list of problems with the trial, but the list only partially overlapped Bugliosi's. The "less than exemplary" conduct of all the legal people undermined public faith in the outcome of the trial, he conceded. It took too long and the expert witnesses reveled in obscurity. The lawyers "placed their own agendas" before their sworn interests, and the Judge was not always there. But the real problem, in his estimation, was that a criminal trial was not "a quest for the truth," and should not be, as it was in colonial times; rather, it was a demonstration of the authority of the government. A trial could and should not be collapsed into its verdict. It would be easy to convict defendants on a lower standard of proof, but the result would be that innocent people, in particular people the government wanted to put away, would disappear. Trial would become part of a regime of tyranny. When Dershowitz wrote these words, in 1995 and 1996, the detention of suspected terrorists was nearly a decade in the future, but his warning was prescient.[7]

Exercise 4: Finding Sources

The O.J. Simpson Trial, and all other notable controversies in the public eye, has an Internet presence. Can you find, and then evaluate, Internet sources on the O.J. Simpson trial?

1. List three websites that have primary source materials relating to the O.J. Simpson trial. (Remember the definition of primary sources from Chapter Two)

   _____

   _____

2. List their authors/creators or the organizations that sponsor the website.

   _____

   _____

3. Rank these authors in terms of credibility from most reliable to least reliable. _____

   _____

   _____

4. Why did you rank them in this order? _____

   _____

   _____

   _____

5. Do you believe that this is sufficient research to write a good historical research paper on the O.J. Simpson trial? Why or why not? _____

   _____

   _____

   _____

The Clinton-Lewinsky Scandal

Below is the introduction from the Wikipedia entry for what it entitles, "The Lewinsky Scandal." **Read** it so you can proceed with Exercise 5.

Lewinsky scandal From Wikipedia, the free encyclopedia Jump to: navigation, search

The Lewinsky scandal was a political sex scandal emerging from a sexual relationship between United States President Bill Clinton and a 22-year-old White House intern, Monica Lewinsky. The news of this extra-marital affair and the resulting investigation eventually led to the impeachment of President Clinton in 1998 by the U.S. House of Representatives and his subsequent acquittal on all impeachment charges of perjury and obstruction of justice in a 21-day Senate trial.[1]

In 1995, Monica Lewinsky, a graduate of Lewis & Clark College, was hired to work as an intern at the White House during Clinton's first term, and began a personal relationship with him, the details of which she later confided to her friend and Defense department co-worker Linda Tripp, who secretly recorded their telephone conversations.[2] When Tripp discovered in January 1998 that Lewinsky had signed an affidavit in the Paula Jones case denying a relationship with Clinton, she delivered the tapes to Kenneth Starr, the Independent Counsel who was investigating Clinton on other matters, including the Whitewater scandal, the White House FBI files controversy, and the White House travel office controversy. During the grand jury testimony Clinton's responses were guarded, and he argued, "It depends on what the meaning of the word is is."[3]

The wide reporting of the scandal led to criticism of the press for over-coverage.[4][5][6] The scandal is sometimes referred to as "Monicagate,"[7] "Lewinskygate,"[8] "Tailgate,"[9] "Sexgate,"[10] and "Zippergate,"[10] following the "gate" nickname construction that has been popular since the Watergate scandal.[8]

The numbers in brackets are the endnote numbers. In order to complete the questions below, you need to find this article and examine the endnotes. Please do so now.

Exercise 5: The Credibility of On-Line Sources

1. What are the sources for this opening part of the article and are they primary or secondary or tertiary (from reference works for example)? _____
   _____
   _____

2. What is the reliability of these sources? _____
   _____

3. Try to find the "Starr Report," the report by independent counsel Kenneth Starr detailing what Starr believed amounted to impeachable offenses by President Bill Clinton. Put the website or source of the report here: _____
   _____
   _____

4. Editorial cartoonists, as you might imagine, had a field day with this scandal involving "sex" in the White House and other unsavory activities. Find them and describe them below. _____
   _____
   _____

5. President Bill Clinton tried to deal with the issue in a press conference. Arguably, he made the situation worse by denying that he had had "sex with that woman." Try to find the footage of President Clinton uttering those words. Where did you find it and how?
   _____

6. President Clinton also faced a lawsuit from a former Arkansas state employee who alleged then-Governor Clinton sexually harassed her. Find the U.S. Supreme Court case that allowed the lawsuit to proceed on the grounds that it would do little harm to the country to allow a civil lawsuit against a sitting president and give the full citation. _____
   _____

7. When the Republican-controlled Congress impeached and then acquitted Clinton based on his alleged behavior in the Lewinsky affair, they created a substantial number of records. Find them and report where you found them. _____

_____

_____

8. You have now done a great deal of research on the Clinton-Lewinsky affair. Do you now feel able to write a good historical research paper on it? Why or why not? __

_____

_____

The Dot Com Bubble

Read the excerpt below and **answer** the questions that follow.

The dot-com bubble was a stock market bubble which popped to near-devastating effect in 2001. It was powered by the rise of Internet sites and the tech industry in general, and many of these companies went under or learned some valuable lessons when the bubble finally burst. Many investors lost substantial sums of money on the dot-com bubble, helping to trigger a mild economic recession in the early 2000s. Analysts noted that some companies did not seem to be sobered by the burst of the bubble when web 2.0 sparked a fresh round of investing and speculation around 2004.

Several factors combined to cause the dot-com bubble, which is usually defined as the period of investment and speculation in Internet firms which occurred between 1995 and 2001. 1995 marked the beginning of a major jump in growth of Internet users, who were seen by companies as potential consumers. As a result, numerous Internet start-ups were birthed in the mid to late 1990s. These companies came to be referred to as "dot-coms," after the .com in many web addresses.

Many of these companies engaged in unusual and daring business practices with the hopes of dominating the market. Most engaged in a policy of growth over profit, assuming that if they built up their customer base, their profits would rise as well. Many dot-coms also expended a great deal of energy in market domination, attempting to corner the bulk of customers for a particular need.[9]

Exercise 6: The Variety of Web Sources

1. What is this article's answer to why there was a dot com bubble? _____

2. Find three other websites explaining the dot com bubble of the 1990s and list them below:

   a. _____

   b. _____

   c. _____

3. Do they agree with the one excerpted above, and if not, how do they differ? _____

   _____

   _____

4. What were the names of these now extinct dot com companies and what service or goods did they provide? _____

   _____

5. Do some internet based research on "bubbles" in the financial markets. How old a phenomenon is it? What is the most recent one? Is there another one forming? What is it in?

   _____

   _____

   _____

Y2K

As the 1990s came to its end, most people were planning premature parties to celebrate the arrival of the new millennium. (Because the calendar started with the year 1, the year 2000 was, thus, the last year of the old millennium. But there were others who were concerned that the change over to a new millennial date would wreck havoc with electronic equipment and software that used calendars. A basic confusion as to whether it was 1900 or 2000 might cause a catastrophic result, or so it was feared. The issue was "Y2K," the abbreviation for Year Two Thousand. Thanks to some scrambling by government and private industry, only a few people were charged tens of thousands of dollars in late fees on their overdue books and videos. (You really should not have checked that out since 1900 without returning it!) But, it did give rise to some amusing takes on what would have happened if the U.S. and the rest of the industrialized world had not spent all that time updating its calendars.

Exercise 7: Finding Visual Media

Animated television shows have been around since television and animation, but the 1990s saw the proliferation of these forms of entertainment. With the advent of the Internet and sites like YouTube, fans could record these shows and post them on the Internet free of charge. Once the popularity of these on-line videos became known, media and entertainment companies began scouring the web for what they called their intellectual property. Many forms of media are copyrighted, that is protected by federal law. Let us test your skill finding these sources even if you cannot successfully view these restricted materials.

1. Find the "Family Guy" episode devoted to the Y2K issue. Hint: It is a post-apocalyptic search for a Twinkie factory. List the number of the episode and its original airing date here: _____

   _____

2. Where can a viewer find a copy and how did you find out the information above?

   _____

3. "The Simpsons" television show also did a Y2K themed episode. Find it and list the same information you had to find for the "Family Guy" episode here: _____

   _____

4. Scott Adams, a former cubicle-dweller himself, created a popular cartoon strip called "Dilbert." It was made into a short-lived, animated series. Find its Y2K episode and find out its data and list it here: _____

   _____

5. In the "Dilbert" episode, our hero Dilbert gets assigned to a team to perform the Y2K rectification effort for their company. Who gets assigned to the team? _____

   _____

Extra Credit: Watch Some TV

If you would like some extra credit for this chapter, **watch** the aforementioned episodes of "Family Guy," "The Simpsons," and "Dilbert," then, **write** an essay summarizing the plots, examining the variations, and draw some conclusions about what these cartoon shows have to tell us about the 1990s.

Notes

[1] "A Brief History of the Internet" www.usg.edu/galileo/skills/unit07/internet07_02.phtml.

[2] This introduction is taken with permission from the author from Peter Charles Hoffer, <u>A Nation of Law: America's Imperfect Pursuit of Justice</u> (Lawrence: University Press of Kansas, 2010), 158–161.

[3] Jeffrey Toobin, <u>The Run of His Life: The People v. O.J. Simpson</u> (New York: Random House, 1996), 12.

[4] Vincent Bugliosi, <u>Outrage: The Five Reasons Why O.J. Simpson Got Away with Murder</u> (New York: Norton, 1996), 262.

[5] Ibid., 270.

[6] Ibid., 276, 277.

[7] Alan M. Dershowitz, <u>Reasonable Doubts: The O.J. Simpson Case and the Criminal Justice System</u> (New York: Simon and Schuster, 1996), 196–199.

[8] "The Lewinsky Scandal," Wikipedia, http://en.wikipedia.org/wiki/Lewinsky_scandal, Internet, accessed 8/20/2011.

[9] wiseGeek, clear answers for common questions, "What was the Dot Com Bubble?" http://www.wisegeek.com/what-was-the-dot-com-bubble.htm, Internet, accessed 8/20/11.

14: History and Professional Ethics

Testifying, Plagiarism, and Citing the Source, the 1990s and 2000s

The period from 1990 to 2010 was a time when cable television, the spread of personal computers and the multiplication of web sites, and visual recording devices like the video cam, Skype, and digital cameras brought the media into every home, school, and workplace. Newspapers, once the source of most news, had already given way to television, and in the 1990s cable stations like CNN covered the news 24/7. Stations also turned to "talking heads," leading figures in the fields of law, finance, and politics, to explain current and past events, and predict the future. Now many web sites and downloadable on-line course packages bring these into the classroom.

Historians entered the mainstream of the media in the 1990s and the 2000s. The History Channel, the documentaries that Ken Burns made, the American Experience series on the Public Broadcasting Service were just the tip of the iceberg. Familiar faces like biographers Doris Kearns Goodwin and Michael Beschloss, Civil War Era experts like James McPherson and Eric Foner were staples on Cable television and National Public Radio feature programs. Historians performed as expert witnesses in courtrooms in tobacco, lead paint, Indian rights, and state boundary lawsuits.

But the so called "culture wars" of the period painted academic historians in a different light. The expression reappeared in James Hunter's book length essay, <u>Culture Wars: The Struggle to Define America</u> (1991). Hunter, a sociologist at the University of Virginia, depicted a deeply divided America, no longer along racial lines, but in its politics and culture. Based on interviews with (presumably typical) Americans, Hunter concluded "America is in the midst of a culture war that has had and will continue to have reverberations." The differences of opinion were so sharp and the gulf so great that they did not seem to him bridgeable. The issues that divided Americans into progressives and traditionalists–abortion rights, gay rights, privacy, whether America was a Christian nation–had a political and an educational side. The political side gave conservatives like Pat Buchanan a platform for his 1992 presidential campaign. As he told the Republican National convention that year in a keynote address, if America was "God's country," it had no place for abortion, homosexuality, and secular humanism. The educational side showed itself in a campaign against "political correctness" on campuses, a supposedly liberal attempt to curb freedom of speech in the name of liberal causes like gay rights.[1]

These were decades of tumult for American historians and American history. The new media exposure had lured academic historians into a public quarrel and induced them to boast of their expertise. In the controversy over the National History Standards (NHS) from 1992 to 1996, the tumultuous career of the planned <u>Enola Gay</u> exhibit at the Smithsonian Air and Space Museum, from 1987 to 1995, and the impeachment and trial of President Bill Clinton, historians played a featured role from the start, sharing the stage with politicians, educators, veterans, and public intellectuals of all political inclinations. A series of damaging revelations about plagiarism involving some of the most famous historians, followed by the discovery a young star in the profession had fabricated key data for his prize winning book, and then the revelation that another prize winning historian was inventing his own history, cost public confidence in the reputation of the profession. All of the historians involved in these scandals were familiar faces in the new media. Had the lure of public exposure somehow blunted scholars' professional ethics?

The historians were quick to defend themselves, but at the same time, they took a long hard look at their own conduct. Were they policing themselves, or was that very idea inappropriate to academic freedom? Over the course of three years, the American Historical Association's professional division rewrote the association's <u>Statement on Standards of Professional Conduct</u> to reflect these concerns. In part it reads: "This Statement on Standards of Professional Conduct addresses dilemmas and concerns about the practice of history that historians have regularly brought to the American Historical Association seeking guidance and counsel . . . to identify a core set of shared values that professional historians strive to honor in the course of their work . . . Historians strive constantly to improve our collective understanding of the past through a complex process of critical dialogue-with each other, with the wider public, and with the historical record . . . Historians cannot successfully do this work without mutual trust and respect. By practicing their craft with integrity, historians acquire a reputation for trustworthiness that is arguably their single most precious professional asset. The trust and respect both of one's peers and of the public at large are among the greatest and most hard-won achievements that any historian can attain. It is foolish indeed to put them at risk." But as the very project of redoing the <u>Statement</u> hints, during this period, the professional ethics of the historians was repeatedly put to the test.[2]

Students in history classes were not immune to these controversies, for the availability of historical sources in the new media seemed to erode students' ethics. In scandal after scandal, some involving entire classes, students found themselves accused of violating honor codes. Every college or university has such a code. In part, the University of Georgia's reads: " "Academic Honesty" means performing all academic work without plagiarism, cheating, lying, tampering, stealing, giving or receiving unauthorized assistance from any other person, or using any source of information that is not common knowledge without properly acknowledging the source." But students assigned research papers in history courses were simply cutting and pasting passages from web sites, buying papers from on-line purveyors, and otherwise presenting others' work as their own. Plagiarism grew to epic proportions as the new media made improper copying almost too easy.[3]

In the following pages, linked to events in the 1990s and 2000s, you will be given the opportunity to spot and analyze ethical lapses, questionable practices, and improper conduct by historians and students of history. This is not a chapter for the faint-hearted. For in history courses as in the rest of your college career, you should hold yourselves to the highest standards of academic conduct. To do anything less is to begin to slide down the slippery slope toward criminal culpability, and no one wants to end up there.

Historians as Expert Witnesses

Historians are often signed up by a law firm to prepare materials supporting their side in a lawsuit. They do research and report in writing (affidavits) or in pre-trial hearings (depositions). They may testify in court. More and more historians are joining this queue. The rewards are considerable–the hourly rate is mid-three figures, and the hours can pile up. At first, historians provided these services without pay. Southern historians John Hope Franklin and C. Vann Woodward and constitutional historian Alfred Kelly helped the NAACP deal with historical questions in <u>Brown v. Board of Education</u> (1954). In the 1960s and 1970s, historians worked for lawyers representing Indian tribes in the effort to regain ancestral lands and for states quarreling with one another over boundary lines and water rights. More recently, they have provided research and testified in voting rights (reapportionment) cases, and suits involving the dangers of tobacco products, lead paint, and asbestos. There is a corporation that recruits and trains historians for this occupation and supplies their names to law firms. Some historians called into service as expert witnesses truly believed in their cause. J. Morgan Kousser, who has spent the past two decades testifying for racial minorities in voting rights cases, regards the experience as "affording opportunities to tell the truth and do good at the same time." Other historians were not so pleased with their experience. Alfred Kelly, whose expert witnessing helped the Legal Defense Fund of the NAACP win <u>Brown v. Board of Education</u> later recalled "here I was, caught between my own ideals as a historian and what these people [the LDF] in New York wanted and needed." Historian David Rothman explained his own dilemma: "To enter the courtroom is to do many things, but it is not to do history. The essential attributes that we treasure most about historical inquiry must be left outside the courtroom door."[4]

Exercise 1: Write a Paragraph on Expert Witnesses

The key problem faced by historians serving as expert witnesses derives from the fact that the American legal system is inherently adversarial. Lawyers are trained to be advocates, as unless they become judges they are hired by one side or the other in cases. Expert witnesses are hired in the same fashion, but historians are not trained to be advocates. Thus historians pursuing "that noble dream" of objectivity—that is, of researching a topic with an open mind and assessing the results in an unbiased and comprehensive fashion—face inherent difficulty when they are hired to testify on one side of a case. This is so partly because most historians serving as expert witnesses get paid a substantial sum of money for their services. If their conclusions and testimony do not satisfy the lawyers who are paying them, the historians will be dropped as expert witnesses. As a result the temptation is ever-present to give the lawyers what they want, regardless of whether or not the evidence justifies it. A second difficulty is that, when a historian testifies, she gets only to answer the questions asked by the lawyers on both sides and her ability to qualify and/or elaborate on her answers may be restricted by the court. Needless to say, she does not get to tell her story as if she were giving a lecture or writing a scholarly article.

   Defenders of historians serving as expert witnesses believe that these difficulties are manageable, that they are no different than the ones faced by experts in other disciplines—medicine, for example—and that any potential compromising of professional standards and values is overridden by the overall positive contribution of historians to legal proceedings. Conscience aside, the temptation to simply give the lawyers what they want is countered by the fact that the other side may cross examine the historian on her evidence and conclusions. Testifying in an implausible manner and contrary to one's convictions may backfire, producing

---

Disclosure: co-author William Stueck has served as an expert witness in litigation involving smokers and the tobacco industry.

personal and professional embarrassment and the loss of a case. Since any testimony is a matter of public record, it may be examined and evaluated by other historians. If deemed flawed by the standards of the profession, testimony may seriously undermine a historian's reputation before her peers. That outcome, in turn, may undermine her standing within her profession as well as her value as an expert witness (the latter is to a considerable extent dependent on the former). The second difficulty described in the above paragraph is to a degree beyond expert witnesses' power to control. Nonetheless, a skilled expert witness generally is able to get into her testimony both the essence of her conclusions and the key evidence on which they are based. Defenders of historians as expert witnesses claim that, precisely because lawyers are trained to be partisan, the legal process is enhanced by the participation of professionals who are trained to gather and arrange evidence without bias.

Now that you are familiar with some of the arguments for and against expert witnessing by historians, we ask you to decide which side is more persuasive. In doing so you are encouraged to think of arguments that have not been presented here. Once you have made up your mind, **write at least one paragraph on a separate sheet of paper supporting your position.** Be prepared to articulate your position in class.

Exercise 2: Evaluating Expert Witness Testimony

As mentioned earlier, tobacco litigation is one of the most controversial areas in which historians have served as expert witnesses. Such litigation began in the 1950s, when a large number of scientific studies appeared linking cigarette smoking to lung cancer and other fatal diseases. Plaintiffs (meaning those seeking relief in civil cases) claimed—and still do today–that the cigarette manufacturers were responsible for the smoking-related illnesses that smokers contracted and sought compensatory and/or punitive damages. The defendants (the cigarette manufacturers), on the other hand, contested the claim—as they do today–and often use as a key part of their defense the assertion that smokers knew that their behavior was risky. That being so, the defense argues, the cigarette manufacturers were/are relieved of any liability. During the mid 1980s the defendants began employing historians as expert witnesses to assist in their cause, and by the late 1990s plaintiffs had followed suit.

Historians for the defense in tobacco litigation have sometimes faced harsh criticism for their testimony, in part because they often began to study the topic of public awareness of the health risks and addictive nature of cigarette smoking only after being hired by defense lawyers. These historians are usually hired to collect information on the topic extending back to the late nineteenth century. The research involves examination of mass circulation newspapers and magazines, educational materials such as public school textbooks and course offerings on health issues, public opinion polls and surveys, movies, radio and television programs, the teachings and activities of churches and other voluntary organizations, and advertisements. The historians generally testify that at least from the mid 1950s forward there existed a high level of awareness among adult Americans that cigarette smoking could be difficult to quit, that it could be harmful to health, and that, over the long term, it increased the risk of contracting a fatal disease. Historians testifying for the plaintiffs, in contrast, downplay evidence on public awareness and focus mostly on tobacco company behavior, which until the late 1990s included denials to the public that scientists had <u>proven</u> a causal link between cigarette smoking and fatal diseases or that it was addictive. They also emphasize the distinction between public <u>awareness</u> of <u>claims</u> that cigarette smoking was potentially fatal, which public opinion polls indicate was quite high by June 1954, and the <u>belief</u> that those claims were true, which similar polls indicate was significantly lower until the late 1980s:

In this exercise, we present you with criticism of testimony by a historian that was reported in the <u>Wall Street Journal</u> in 1998.[5] The criticism pertains to the historian's characterization of a Gallup Poll of June 1954. We then provide two versions of the poll itself. After asking you to answer some comparative questions about the versions and their meaning, we provide the record in a later trial of two lawyers' questions on the 1954 poll and another expert witness's responses. The exercise concludes with some questions about that exchange and about the controversy in general.

Entitled "Gallup Accuses Big Tobacco of Misusing Poll in Court," the <u>Wall Street Journal</u> article began by reciting one of the questions in the poll: "Have you heard or read anything recently that cigarette smoking may be a cause of cancer of the lung?" Ninety percent of the respondents answered "yes." This figure, the article noted, had "become a key statistic for the tobacco industry" in its claim that "the risk of contracting lung cancer from smoking has been common knowledge for years." At two recent trials in Florida, the article reported, a historian had "pointed to the 90% figure as evidence that smokers understood the health risks of smoking in the early 1950s but chose to smoke anyway." Now, though, the Gallup organization claimed that this use of the poll was "misleading." Rather than being evidence of common knowledge among Americans that cigarette smoking was a cause of lung cancer, it was merely evidence of broad awareness of a controversy on the issue. In fact, the article continued, "Gallup contends . . . [that] responding to another question in the poll, only 5% said they thought smoking causes cancer." " 'Presenting selective data or distorting the meaning of individual Gallup poll questions out of context violates the purpose and the spirit in which these surveys were originally written,'" the Editor in Chief asserted in a letter to the historian.

We present below a graph that was published alongside the <u>Wall Street Journal</u> article (it does not appear in the on-line version of the article, but does appear in the microfilm version).

What is your opinion—do you think smoking is one of the causes of lung cancer?		In what way do you think cigarette smoking is harmful?		Why did you stop smoking cigarettes?*	
Yes	41%	Bad for lungs	31%	Didn't mention cancer	97%
No	31%	Causes lung cancer	5	Mentioned cancer	2
Not sure	28%	Other	64	Weren't sure	71

*Only former smokers were asked.

Now we offer more detailed figures from the poll that are available from a polling archive.[6] In addition to the numbers below, this record of the poll indicates that a representative sample of 1435 people from around the country were questioned and that pollsters did the questioning in person with people in their homes rather than over the phone. You will notice that the raw numbers provided are not percentages as in the graph above, so you will have to do your own math to check for accuracy.

Q. Have you ever smoked cigarettes regularly?
754 Yes
678 No
3 No Code or No Data

Q. Do you happen to smoke cigarettes now?
623 Yes
148 No

664	No Answer, Inapplicable
Q.	Why did you stop smoking cigarettes?
4	Any mention of cancer
122	No mention of cancer
6	No answer
1303	Inapplicable
Q.	Have you heard or read anything recently to the effect that cigarette smoking may be a cause of cancer of the lung?
1290	Yes
144	No
1	No Code or No Data
Q.	What is your own opinion—do you think cigarette smoking is one of the causes of cancer of the lung or not?
556	Yes
405	No
394	No Opinion
49	Qualified Yes
10	Qualified No
21	No Code or No Data

1. Does the percentage offered by the <u>Wall Street Journal</u> graph jibe with the number provided in the article regarding Americans who said they believed smoking was a cause of lung cancer? _____ What do you think is the significance of the disparity?

   _____

2. In the graph, should respondents who answered "Not sure" to the question of whether or not smoking is a cause of lung cancer be considered aware or unaware of a health risk in smoking? _____ Explain your answer. _____

   _____

   _____

3. Do the percentages in the <u>Wall Street Journal</u> graph jibe with the relevant numbers in the more detailed data on responses that follows? _____ If there are any differences, are they significant? _____ Explain your answer. _____

4. If you were a juror in a smoking trial, what additional evidence would you like to see regarding this poll? _____
   Why? _____

5. Are there any questions in the poll that might have revealed more valuable or accurate information regarding the awareness and/or beliefs of Americans on the smoking issue had they been worded differently? _____ If so, rewrite the question(s) as you would have preferred it (them).

   _____

   _____

The excerpts below provide you with a historian's testimony in a recent trial on the poll discussed above. The first excerpt relates to the awareness part of the poll and the belief part of another poll and is in response to questions by a lawyer for the defense in direct examination.

Q . . . let's start a little bit about the background on Gallup Polls itself [sic] and what this particular Gallup Poll is showing to you as a historian.

A Can I put this in context of other evidence as well?

Q Yes, you may.

A Okay. . . . the question is, Have you heard or read anything recently to the effect that cigarette smoking may be a cause of cancer of the lung. And 90 percent who were questioned responded yes. 10 percent responded, no. Now, Gallup was generally considered to be . . . the most prominent pollster of the time. When I saw this poll—I actually came across this poll fairly early in my research many years ago, and I frankly was rather dubious about it initially. So I didn't accept it on its face.

I went back several months, in fact, to late 1953, and as I collected evidence on that period, 1953 to June of 1954, I was constantly asking myself, okay, is this poll reasonable, given what I can establish is being circulated in the mass media at the time.

. . . I think one of the problems with polls is they suggest perhaps greater precision than you can actually prove because you've got an actual number there and there is a margin of error. I think in this poll maybe four or five percent.

After doing that research, I concluded, yes, it was not an unreasonable figure, even though it was very, very high. . . .

Q . . . in talking about polling discussing the area of public awareness, is there such a thing as belief polls?

A Yes, there is.

Q . . . can you explain to the jury what a belief poll is?

A Well, instead of asking people what they are aware of and [sic] ask them what they believe. . . .

Q . . . can you explain to the jury what this slide is showing . . . ? [A slide showing figures from a Gallup poll is put on the screen in the courtroom.]

A This poll is from January of 1954 . . . Do you think cigarette smoking is harmful or not?

And the response is 70 percent yes; 23 percent no; 6 percent no opinion.

Q How . . . do you incorporate this poll into your analysis of the issues in this case as part of your research?

A . . . Well, it's indicative that at this time . . . a lot of people—most people believed that cigarette smoking was harmful.

The next excerpt is from the same historian's testimony in the same trial, but is a response to a question by a lawyer for the plaintiff in cross examination. The lawyer has placed the Wall Street Journal article, without the accompanying graph, on the screen in the courtroom.

Q Isn't it true, sir, that the Gallup organization contends that the 90 percent figure that you used reflected knowledge of the controversy, not a widely-held belief that smoking causes cancer; and, meanwhile, it says, Responding to another question in the poll, only 5 percent thought that smoking causes lung cancer . . . ?

A That's what it says in the article.

In light of the testimony you have been given above as well as the additional information about the June 1954 Gallup poll, we ask you to respond to the following questions.

1. Does the historian give an adequate explanation of his methodology in concluding that the 90 percent figure regarding awareness is reasonably accurate? _____ As a juror, is there more information you would have been liked to see as part of the explanation? _____ If so, what? _____

2. Assuming that the plaintiff's lawyer declined on cross examination to ask the historian further questions about the accuracy of the 90 percent figure, what would you tend to conclude about it if you were a juror? (That is, was it a reliable figure or not?)

   _____

3. Given the information you have been given for this exercise, is there anything you think the historian should have added to his answer above to the plaintiff's characterization of the Wall Street Journal article? _____ If so, what? _____

   _____

4. Do the questions asked by the lawyers on the two sides represent advocacy on their parts? (Hint: why did the defense lawyer ask the historian about the January 1954 poll regarding belief rather than the June 1954 poll? Why did the plaintiff's lawyer put the Wall Street Journal article on the screen for the jury to see but not the accompanying graph?) _____ Explain.

   _____

5. Within the limits created by the legal process, do you think the historian gave reasonable answers (that is, answers consistent with the rules of evidence of the historical profession as discussed in this book) to the questions asked him? _____ Explain.

   _____

6. Does the evidence you have encountered in this exercise alter your answer to the question in Exercise 1 at to whether or not historians should serve as expert witnesses? _____ Explain your answer. _____

   _____

   _____

Faked History

While American historians engaged in debates over the National History Standards, the Enola Gay, and impeachment, and historians aided law firms as expert witnesses, a historian of the Jewish holocaust came under attack from abroad. A British Holocaust denier named David Irving, himself an admiring chronicler of Adolph Hitler, was called out by Emory University's Deborah Lipstadt. Her <u>Denying the Holocaust: The Growing Assault on Truth and Memory</u> (1994), reported that Irving claimed that "Jews are not victims but victimizers' and that '[t]hey 'stole' billions in reparations, destroyed Germany's good name by spreading the 'myth' of the Holocaust, and won international sympathy because of what they claimed had been done to them." This was standard fare for the troop of Holocaust deniers. Lipstadt regarded Irving and his many books as dangerous, for he seemed, at least to some of his readers, to be a legitimate historian. He certainly offered documentary materials and primary sources to back up his claims. When closely examined, however, they turned out to be bogus. Irving sued Lipstadt for libel and the trial took place in England because copies of her book were sold there.

In depositions and at the trial, a parade of leading twentieth-century European historians demolished Irving's use of evidence, establishing that what he wrote was not history, and hence that Lipstadt was not libeling him by calling him an apologist for Hitler. Justice Charles Gray issued a strongly worded decision. Irving was and had been for thirty years "an active Holocaust denier, anti-Semitic, and racist, and associated with right-wing extremists who promoted neo Nazism." Irving had "persistently and deliberately manipulated historical evidence" to portray Hitler and his movement in a favorable light, and to deny the horrors of the concentration camps. What Lipstadt had said of Irving was true, a defense to Irving's suit for libel. Irving appealed, unsuccessfully, and faced over 1.5 million pounds in legal fees. Lipstadt herself was elated, exhausted, and vindicated, but her victory was more than hers. Irving started it–bringing a suit that denied both the immorality of history and the amorality of some historians. Lipstadt's motivation also lay beyond mere defense of her writing. It lay in the defense of the moral power of history. But historians who want their story to come out a certain way, regardless of the evidence, still publish, fitting bits and pieces of fact into a fabric of deceit.[7]

Exercise 3: Faking It

Faked history, history written contrary to fact, or with fabricated facts, is more common than historians will admit. Only a few cases like Irving's ever surface. In the following exercise, each passage from an entirely reputable secondary source on the 1990s and 2000s has a key piece of evidence that has been faked by the authors of <u>Reading and Writing American History</u>. Your job is to spot the fake. (We apologize to the fine scholars we have quoted for adding a poison pill to their words!) You can use your textbook, the Web, an encyclopedia, or any other published source you trust to help. After you have found what you believe to be the faked history, explain why it might be there–what did the faked history add to the account?

President George W. Bush's decision to open hostilities against Iraq in 2003, called "Operation Iraqi Freedom" is one of the most controversial presidential decisions of modern times. Evidence for the decision and evidence about President Bush himself was also controversial. In this context, faking a key piece of evidence might change the entire scope of the inquiry. Much, thus, was at stake.

> **A.** What can be noted about the legacy of a president who conducts a war of choice? To exemplify such a situation let us assume that a president has, at one time or another, stated various reasons for the conduct of such a war. So much so that average citizens find it difficult to ascertain the fundamental and real reasons for such an action. Furthermore, the president has cloaked the language justifying the war in the language of necessity (national defense) not choice. The president plays fast and loose with the facts to convince the public by using worst case analysis to bolster the need for war. In the case of the Iraq War of 2003 and after, the facts were clear, however, because the evidence that dictator Saddam Hussein had weapons of mass destruction was confirmed by many independent sources.[8]

> What is the faked history? _____
> What did it do to the rest of the passage? _____
> _____

> **B.** But how did a man who was born in Connecticut, attended elite institutions of learning, such as Andover, Yale, and Harvard, and whose father was accused of being a "blue-blood" persuade a nation to associate him with foundational cowboy characters like John

Wayne, Wyatt Earp, and Buffalo Bill? His east coast elite education would seem to disqualify him from ever achieving the working class role of the heroic cowboy. But George W. Bush himself bought into the cowboy image, riding horses, learning to rope cattle, and spending his vacation time hunting and fishing in Western nature reserves.[9]

What's the fake? _____

How does it change the account? _____

_____

C. Why did President George W. Bush, following advice from his cabinet, the top military command, and the express views of Congress and the public, refuse to withdraw from Iraq in late 2006 and instead announce that significant additional forces would be sent? The 'new way forward,' as the White House called it, or the 'surge,' as it was immediately branded in the public consciousness, was at its core a gamble—against long odds—that extra troops and a new way of using them could quell the violence and provide a window of opportunity for lasting progress. [10]

What is the faked evidence? _____

What impact does it have on the passage? _____

_____

Plagiarism

Plagiarism has reached epidemic proportions on college campuses, as cutting and pasting from internet sources has made it too easy for students to borrow the words of others without correct attribution. As one of the authors of this worktext defined the offense, "Plagiarism is commonly defined as the appropriation of another's work as one's own." Some definitions add the purposive element of gaining an advantage of some kind. Others include the codicil, "with the intent to deceive." The American Historical Association – the overarching organization for the historical profession – has adopted a broad and stern definition of plagiarism, based upon ethical rather than purely legal conceptions. Its definition of plagiarism is the "expropriation of another author's text, and the presentation of it as one's own." It does not require that the act be intentional, nor that the offender gain some advantage from it. Nor for historians is the ultimate sanction against the offense a legal one, but instead the public infamy that accompanies egregious misconduct."[11] Punishment for plagiarism on a college paper or examination vary from school to school, but it is never acceptable.

Imagine the surprise when two of America's most honored and loved historians were discovered to have engaged in plagiarism. Stephen Ambrose was a serial plagiarist going back to his dissertation and occurring throughout his many popular histories of the West, World II, and his biographies of the presidents. Doris Kearns Goodwin's offenses were less common and less serious, but she, unlike Ambrose, admitted error and accepted admonition for it. Ambrose passed away still protesting his innocence. Goodwin has gone on to write more books free of plagiarism and once more become a highly honored and easily recognized media personality.[12]

Plagiarism, if hard to precisely define and even harder to detect when practiced by skilled plagiarists, is not without its telltale signs. In a piece for the American Historical Association, then University of Wisconsin graduate student Michael Rawson, aided by Professor William Cronon, developed a set of indicators of plagiarism along with some practice exercises. With permission, we have reproduced them here:

1. Be sensitive to changes in writing style. An abrupt shift from poorly written to masterfully crafted prose might signal the start of a passage that the student cut and pasted

from somewhere else. A paper that contains excellent prose but lurches from paragraph to paragraph might be a compilation of passages taken from elsewhere.

2. Note any sophisticated or jargon-laden language that reflects knowledge or expertise beyond what you expect from the student.

3. Keep an eye out for references to works that are either very old or unavailable in your campus library, and for sudden changes in reference style (from MLA to Chicago, for example).

4. Make note of papers that do not directly address the assignment. Its author might originally have written it for a different class.

5. Watch for unusual changes in format (font, point size, margins), which sometimes result when a student cuts and pastes a passage into a paper.

6. Note phrases that refer to something in the paper that is not there (but might have been in the original from which the student took it).[13]

Exercise 4: Spotting Plagiarism

In the following pairs of passages on the 1990s, one of the authors has plagiarized from the other. Acting as a plagiarism detective, underline the language that raised your suspicions of plagiarism. In the write-on lines below each pair, **suggest** which of the passages was the original, and which the copyist's work. What led you to your conclusion? Remember that a clever plagiarist will always change a few words from the original to avoid detection. (Hint: in fact, one of each pair is taken from a major textbook. The other is a student plagiarism.)[14]

The first pair concerns President Bill Clinton and his wife, Hillary Clinton.

A. In 1993, William Jefferson Clinton became the first baby boomer to enter the White House. His wife, Hillary Rodham Clinton, would be the most politically involved presidential wife since Eleanor Roosevelt. Like many couples of their generation, the Clintons were a two-career family. Both trained as lawyer at Yale University during the tumultuous 1960s.

B. William Jefferson Clinton became president in 1993. He was a baby boomer and so was his wife, Hillary Rodham Clinton, who would be the most political president's wife since Eleanor Roosevelt. They both had careers as lawyers, attending Yale University during the troubled 1960s.

_____

_____

The second pair concerns the increased visibility of African-American celebrities.

A. In the 1990s the highest-paid celebrity in the world was an African-American—Michael Jordan. Oprah Winfrey, also an African-American, was the highest-paid woman in American. Although the situation of African-Americans had improved vastly compared with their position in the 1950s, race still mattered—as the case of Rodney King, a black motorist, showed.

B. Despite highly paid stars like basketball player Michael Jordan and television personality Oprah Winfield, African-Americans still faced racial discrimination. Their situation was a lot better than in the 1950s, but the case of Rodney King, a black car driver, showed that not everything had improved.

_____

_____

Exercise 5: Avoiding Plagiarism

When students use secondary sources, they need not plagiarize. Permissible alternatives include **paraphrasing**, **summarizing**, and **quoting from** the secondary source. In a paraphrase, the student uses his or her own words entirely to report what the secondary source said. The student may repeat technical terms, names, dates, places, and events in the source, but may not use the source's language beyond that. In summarizing, the student offers a more concise report on what he or she has read, again entirely in his or her own words, save for technical terms, names, dates, places, and events. If the student thinks that some of the language in the secondary source is so elegant, so unique, or so essential that it must reappear in the student's paper or exam, the smallest possible sample of that language can be quoted, with quotation marks, in the student's paper. In all cases, the student must cite to the secondary source, including the exact page numbers from which the source material came.

The following passages are taken from actual works of historians describing events in the 1990s. On the write-on lines following each of them, **paraphrase** what they say in your own words; **summarize** what they say in your own words, and construct an alternative passage using **quotations from** them along with your own words.

> **A.** Reports from the U.S. Census Bureau confirmed the explosive growth of the suburban South and the parallels with booming areas in the suburban West, as the top four states for total population increase in the 1990s were California, Texas, Florida, and Georgia. During the same decade, seventy-six of the eighty-six fastest-growing counties in the nation were located in the South and West, with Atlanta second only to Phoenix among large metropolitan areas for the highest percentage increase in population.[15]

Paraphrase:_____
_____
_____
_____

Summarize _____
_____
_____

Quote from _____
_____
_____
_____
_____
_____

> **B.** Contemporary congressional leaders use polls to set policy agendas and to build legislative coalitions. House Speaker Newt Gingrich (R-GA) and Republican leaders famously used polls and focus groups to defeat President Clinton's health care reform legislation . . ., to construct the 'Contract with America' . . ., and to 'craft their talk' on Medicare proposals . . . Not only do leaders use polls to monitor public opinion; they also use poll information in efforts to craft their talk on specific legislative proposals in order to change public opinion. Rejecting the view that polls are used primarily to monitor and then respond to, public opinion, a Republican leadership aide asserted, 'Polls did not drive what we did. . . . Instead, as another staffer observed, leaders and communications staff 'sit

down [with pollsters] and go over 'How do you want to manage this? . . . to tell the out-side?' And, yet another claimed that the dominant use of polls was . . . to discern the most helpful 'language pattern' and to 'find the right way to phrase' public statements on impending legislation. Gingrich's 'view . . . was . . . [not] to advertise an unpopular issue if he didn't have to.'[16]

Paraphrase: _____

_____

_____

_____

_____

_____

_____

_____

_____

_____

_____

_____

Summarize _____

_____

_____

_____

Quote from _____

_____

_____

_____

_____

_____

_____

_____

_____

_____

_____

Historians hold themselves to high standards, but in the tumultuous political contests and vituperative culture wars of the 1990s and 2000s, liberals and conservatives in and out of academe scrutinized the words of their intellectual opponents. Perhaps this led to more careful research and more precise writing of history. It also led historians to lament their new found celebrity. Greater visibility for historians came at great cost. The professional ethics of the historical profession came under a microscope as did academia in general. While some demanded accountability for "student learning outcomes," others called for more rigorous policies concerning academic integrity. As the universities became battlegrounds, both students and their instructors struggled with this newly challenging environment. Some concluded that history itself was in jeopardy from the push for accountability, the demands for a more practical education, and the perceived increasing irrelevance of academic history. We cannot determine the long term impact of these trends. As Chinese Foreign Minister Zhou Enlai remarked when asked about the effects of the French Revolution some two hundred years before, "It is too soon to tell."

Notes

[1] James D. Hunter, *Culture Wars* (New York: Basic, 1992), 34; Pat Buchanan, Speech at Republican National Convention, July 18, 1992, in Roger Chapman, ed. *Encyclopedia of the Culture Wars* (Armonk, N.Y.: M.E. Sharpe, 2010), 56.

[2] American Historical Association, *Statement on Standards of Professional Conduct* Approved by Professional Division, December 9, 2004 and adopted by Council, January 6, 2005; historians.org/pubs/Free/ProfessionalStandards.cfm.

[3] Honor Code, University of Georgia, 2010, www.uga.edu/honesty/ahpd/definitions.html#honesty.

[4] The quotation from Kousser on expert witnessing and the accompanying text is from Peter Charles Hoffer, *Past Imperfect* (New York: PublicAffairs, 2004), 124–127; the Kelly and Rothman quotations are from Ann Curthoys, Ann Genovese, and Alex Reilly, *Rights and Redemption: History, Law, and Indigenous People* (Seattle: University of Washington Press, 2008), 19, 16.

[5] *Wall Street Journal*, June 26, 1998, B1.

[6] Gallup Poll #532, June 12–17, 1954, The Roper Center for Public Opinion Research, Williams College, Williamstown, Mass.

[7] Deborah Lipstadt, *History on Trial: My Day in Court with David Irving* (New York: Harper Collins, 2005), 289–290; David Pallister, "The judgment Judge condemns deliberate falsification of historical record" *The Guardian* (London), April 12, 2000, 6.

[8] Adapted from Anthony P. Eksterowicz and Glenn P. Hastedt, "Wars of Choice: James Madison, George W. Bush, and the Presidential Legacy Question" *White House Studies*, 9 (2009), 111.

[9] Adapted from Ryan Malphurs, "The Media's Frontier Construction of President George W. Bush" *Journal of American Culture*, 31 (June 2008), 186.

[10] Adapted from Stephen Benedict Dyson, "George W. Bush, The Surge, and Presidential Leadership" *Political Science Quarterly*, 125 (Winter2010/2011), 557.

[11] Peter Charles Hoffer, "Reflections on Plagiarism, Part I," *American Historical Association Perspectives in History* February 2004, 17.

[12] See Hoffer, *Past Imperfect.* (New York: PublicAffairs, 2004).

[13] Michael Rawson, "Plagiarism: Curricular Materials for History Instructors" 2007, AHA website www.historians.org/governance/pd/curriculum/plagiarism_detecting.htm.

[14] Text taken from 907 and 915 of James West Davidson, Brian Delay, Christine Leigh Heyrman, Mark H. Lytle, and Michael B. Stoff, *Experience History: Interpreting America's Past* (New York: McGraw Hill, 2011).

[15] Matthew D. Lassiter, and Kevin M. Kruse, "The Bulldozer Revolution: Suburbs and Southern History since World War II," *Journal of Southern History*, 75 (2009), 693.

[16] Douglas B. Harris, "House Majority Party Leaders' Uses of Public Opinion Information," *Congress and the Presidency* 32 (2005), 133, 143.

Conclusion: America at a Crossroads

The history of the United States in the years since the Civil War is one of great change. From a largely rural nation whose staple crop agriculture was its most productive economic sector, we have become a largely urban, industrial (and most recently post-industrial) nation. Where racial and gender discrimination was once the rule, we have embraced gender equality and racial diversity. From a minor player on the world stage, we have become a major power in global politics. But the country is now at a crossroads. As the previous chapters have documented, our role in the world and our fate at home is very uncertain.

War, recession, internal dissent, and growing dismay with our government has revealed the cracks and hot spots in our society. In the period between 1865 and the present, strife between labor and capital, the rise and fall of Jim Crow, and growing disparity between the rich and the poor have come at a time of rising standards of living and life expectancy. Even the most dutiful study of history cannot reveal the ending places of these developments.

Nonetheless, the study of history enables all of us to understand how far we have come; to evaluate where we are; and to devise strategies—for ourselves, our nation, and our fellow inhabitants on earth—for coping with the challenges ahead. Whether we are choosing a career, raising a family, or determining how we will contribute to the life of our community, we ignore history at our peril. Our best goes to you and yours as continue this journey. We hope the preceding proves of value to you along the way.